The Web of Friendship

The Web of Friendship

Marianne Moore and Wallace Stevens

Robin G. Schulze

Ann Arbor

THE UNIVERSITY OF MICHIGAN PRESS

Copyright © by the University of Michigan 1995
All rights reserved
Published in the United States of America by
The University of Michigan Press
Manufactured in the United States of America
⊗Printed on acid-free paper

1998   1997   1996   1995   4   3   2   1

A CIP catalogue record for this book is available from the British Library.

Library of Congress Cataloging-in-Publication Data

Schulze, Robin G., 1961–
    The web of friendship : Marianne Moore and Wallace Stevens /
Robin G. Schulze.
        p.   cm.
    Includes bibliographical references and index.
    ISBN 0-472-10578-7 (hardcover : alk. paper)
    1. Moore, Marianne, 1887–1972—Criticism and interpretation.
2. Stevens, Wallace, 1879–1955—Criticism and interpretation.
3. Moore, Marianne, 1887–1972—Friends and associates. 4. Stevens,
Wallace, 1879–1955—Friends and associates. 5. American
poetry—20th century—History and criticism. 6. Modernism
(Literature)—United States. 7. Influence (Literary, artistic,
etc.)   I. Title.
PS3525.05616Z826   1995
811'.5209—dc20   95-12188
                                                         CIP

041596-3740XII

For Mom, Dad, and Dan

Acknowledgments

I have been fortunate throughout the development of this study to be surrounded by those whose council I trust and whose advice I value. I am deeply indebted to George Bornstein for his wisdom, humor, and acute suggestions. His guidance has been indispensable to this project, and my work owes much to his patience and profound humanity. I thank him for helping me to hear the keener sounds in my ghostlier demarcations.

Thanks are due as well to the University of Kansas for providing me with the time and money crucial to the completion of this project. I would like to thank the University of Kansas for awarding me a much-needed Development Semester and the Hall Center for the Humanities for supplying me with an all-important travel grant so that I could pursue archival work at the Henry E. Huntington Library in San Marino, California, and the Rosenbach Museum and Library in Philadelphia, Pennsylvania. I also want to thank the University of Kansas New Faculty General Research Program for generous support during the final stages of this study.

Those of us who spend our time in research libraries and archives know how critical the people who tend such places are to our work. I owe thanks to the staff of the Rosenbach Museum and Library, in particular Evelyn Feldman and Elizabeth Fuller, who kindly put up with my frequent visits and numerous requests for aid. Leslie Morris's humor, energy, and knowledge of the Marianne Moore Collection made working at the Rosenbach a true pleasure. I also want to thank the staff of the Henry E. Huntington Library and Sara Hodson, curator of manuscripts for the Wallace Stevens Collection, for her crucial detective work on my behalf.

Friends and colleagues have contributed much to this effort. My graduate school cohorts at the University of Michigan, Karen DeVinney, Lloyd Hemingway, David Holdeman, Mary Lacey, Patricia Plunkett, and Matthew Martin, all helped in the early stages of this project by offering their suggestions and support. I reserve my most profound thanks for two very special people. My husband and loving friend, Adam Rome, read this book many times and cast the keen eye of both historian and editor on its contents. Much that lies between these covers I owe to his encouragement. I also owe a debt beyond measure to my wonderful mother, who so graciously and competently served as my research assistant during my trips to the Rosenbach. Without her, neither I nor this book would exist.

Grateful acknowledgment is made to the following publishers and individuals for permission to reprint material from copyrighted materials.

From *Collected Poems* by Wallace Stevens. Copyright © 1954 by Wallace Stevens. Reprinted by permission of Alfred A. Knopf Incorporated and Faber and Faber Limited.

From *Letters of Wallace Stevens* by Wallace Stevens, edited by Holly Stevens. Copyright © 1966 by Holly Stevens. Reprinted by permission of Alfred A. Knopf Incorporated and Faber and Faber Limited.

From *The Necessary Angel* by Wallace Stevens. Copyright © 1951 by Wallace Stevens. Reprinted by permission of Alfred A. Knopf Incorporated and Faber and Faber Limited.

From *Opus Posthumous* by Wallace Stevens, edited by S. F. Morse. Copyright © 1957 by Elsie Stevens and Holly Stevens. Reprinted by permission of Alfred A. Knopf Incorporated and Faber and Faber Limited.

From *The Complete Prose of Marianne Moore* by Patricia C. Willis, Editor. Copyright © 1986 by Patricia C. Willis. Used by permission of Viking Penguin, a division of Penguin Books USA Incorporated.

"The Web One Weaves of Italy," copyright © 1956 by Marianne Moore, renewed 1984 by Lawrence E. Brinn and Louise Crane, Literary Executors of the Estate of Marianne C. Moore, from *The Complete Poems of Marianne Moore* by Marianne Moore. Used by permission of Viking Penguin, a division of Penguin Books USA Incorporated. Used by permission of Faber and Faber Limited.

From *Selected Poems* by Marianne Moore, copyright © 1935 by Marianne Moore; renewed 1963 by Marianne Moore and T. S. Eliot. Reprinted with permission of Simon & Schuster, Incorporated and Faber and Faber Limited.

From *What Are Years?* by Marianne Moore, copyright © 1941, and renewed 1969, by Marianne Moore. Reprinted with permission of Simon & Schuster, Incorporated and Faber and Faber Limited.

Mr. Peter Hanchak for previously unpublished letters by Wallace Stevens. All rights reserved.

Unpublished letters and other unpublished material by Wallace Stevens reproduced by permission of The Henry E. Huntington Library, San Marino, California.

Permission for quotations from Marianne Moore's unpublished work granted by Marianne Craig Moore, Literary Executor for the Estate of Marianne Moore. All rights reserved.

Unpublished letters and other unpublished material by Marianne Moore reproduced by permission of the Rosenbach Museum and Library, Philadelphia, Pennsylvania.

Previously unpublished material by Ezra Pound Copyright © 1995 by the Trustees of Ezra Pound Literary Property Trust; used by permission of New Directions Publishing Corporation, agents.

Contents

Introduction

> The web of friendship between poets is the most delicate thing in the world—and the most precious.

So wrote Wallace Stevens to Marianne Moore two years before his death in 1955. Stevens's kind words to his fellow poet, words from which this book draws its title, stand testament to a long-lived and little-known literary friendship between two American modernists. Over the course of forty years and across five decades, Moore and Stevens engaged in a complex and compelling poetic conversation, and it is the work of this book to bring their exchange and its significance to light. My book confirms that Stevens's metaphor for his relationship with Moore is an apt one. The "web" of friendship between Moore and Stevens consists not of a single tie, but of many intricately interlocking threads, numerous personal and artistic intersections between one poet's creative warp and the other's woof. Like the spider's careful lattice or the weaver's fabric on the loom, the web of Stevens and Moore's conversation is dynamic rather than static, changing over time in response to a variety of forces. Perhaps most importantly, however, Stevens's metaphor emphasizes the creative value of his connection with Moore. Stevens implies that without the support of Moore's crossing threads—without a precious friendship between poets—his own attempts at artistry, the very fabric of his life and work, would be incomplete. Together, the threads of the two poets intersect to form a different and, in Stevens's view, more valuable weave than either individual strand.

Given Stevens's resonant image of interconnectedness, it seems strange to think of reading either Moore's or Stevens's work without the company of the other's productions. Certainly, the many published intersections between Moore and Stevens throughout their writing lives would seem to suggest the merit of studying the two poets together. Moore found Stevens's work important enough to review all but one of his volumes at length—a body of critical prose that, I will argue, augurs important shifts in Moore's poetic development. Stevens in turn published two extensive essays about Moore's work—rare acts of attention on Stevens's part that reveal Moore's influential role in his poetic progress. Both Stevens and Moore also carried their conversation into their verse and printed poems directly addressed to one another. Add to these published exchanges the existing unpublished archival record of Moore's interactions with Stevens—letters, postcards, diaries, marginalia, and manuscripts—and the web between the two poets expands exponentially.

Yet, despite all of these connections, the personal and poetic relationship between Moore and Stevens has, with the notable exceptions of Bonnie Costello and Celeste Goodridge, not drawn much critical attention—an oversight due in part, I think, to the limitations of current paradigms of poetic influence.[1] In the critical discourse on American modernist poetry, the very words "poetic influence" have become synonymous with the word "anxiety," the defining term of Harold Bloom's theory of generational conflict between poets laid out in several books starting with his pivotal revisionist work of 1973, *The Anxiety of Influence*. Bloom's now well-known paradigm pictures the process of poetic influence in terms of family romance. The poet ephebe, gendered male, engages in an Oedipal struggle with his literary "father," a strong and domineering poet precursor whose work the ephebe must reject if he is to gain his own phallic creative power. Bloom posits a series of revisionary ratios by which the ephebe misreads his father's poems and, through various acts of "misprison," obscures and denies his debt to the precursor's texts. Where "weaker" talents idealize their precursors, Bloom insists that "major figures" attack them and "wrestle with their strong precursors, even to the death."[2] Bloom grudgingly admits that it may happen that "one poet influences another, or more precisely, that one poet's poems influence the poems of the other, through a generosity of the spirit, even a shared generosity," but he dismisses such a view as evidence of our all too "easy idealism." "Where generosity is involved," Bloom concludes, "the poets influenced are minor or weaker; the more generosity, and the more mutual it is, the poorer the poets involved" (30). In Bloom's paradigm, concord is clearly for the weak.

Countering the arguments of those critics naive enough to believe in supportive or collaborative effort, Bloom categorizes poets who share as minor figures unworthy of note because they remain weakly unconcerned with their own originality. Yet, Bloom's brief comments on the nature of poetic generosity, rather than disarm his opposition, instead point to an omission in his model. In Bloom's world, a poet-son pursues an isolated quest for originality, battling heroically and singly against received and established parent texts that prove the son's belatedness. But how can a belated son have a "mutual" or "shared" relationship, a reciprocal dialogue, with a predecessor? In his terse dismissal of poetic generosity Bloom strays from his strict generational model and implies that the poets involved in more generous influence relationships are most likely those who actively produce texts during each other's writing lives. The poet/parent who does the influencing here, if indeed he is a poet/parent at all in Bloom's terms, is living rather than deceased, reactive rather than static, one who shares in the other poet's development and who learns from his peer/pupil in turn. Bloom thus introduces the possibility of mutual influence between poetic contemporaries into his discussion—a form of influence he avoids for the most part in his model, perhaps because, as Bloom himself seems to suggest in his comments on poetic generosity, such relationships are more likely to contradict the purely combative metaphors of his paradigm.

Indeed, in those rare moments in *The Anxiety of Influence* when Bloom does pause to consider influence between peers, the "sons" in the family romance, he maintains his notion of poetry as anxious agon. Sons not only fight their fathers, they fight among themselves as well, and Bloom makes it clear that his concepts of misprison and swerving apply to son-son as well as son-father relationships. The poem of a strong sibling "rival" for the attention of the father's muse must also, as the scheme of family romance dictates, be the subject of the ephebe's anxious misinterpretation and hostile rejection. As Bloom explains in his interchapter "A Manifesto for Antithetical Criticism," the meaning of an ephebe's poem can only be another poem. Yet, rather than limit the meaning of the ephebe's poem/misinterpretation to the parent poem, Bloom states that the meaning of the ephebe's poem/misinterpretation may also be "a rival poem, son or grandson of the same precursor" (96). The sons of the parent poet produce "rival conceptualizations," or competing misreadings of the precursor's text that struggle against each other, as well as against the father. "More than ever," Bloom writes in *A Map of Misreading* of those authors who deny any share in the anxiety of influence, "contemporary poets insist that they are telling the truth in their work, and more than ever they tell continuous lies, particularly about their relations to one another, and most consistently about their relations to their precursors."[3] In the ephebe's quest for perfect solipsism, poetic peers prove as threatening as precursors.

Committed to the concept of poetic family romance and all of its Oedipal storms and stresses, Bloom's model of anxiety-ridden poetic influence leaves no room for cooperative relationships between strong poets, be they of different generations or contemporaries—an omission that, in recent years, has earned the reproof of many scholars of modernist poetry. George Bornstein, Christopher Beach, and Reed Way Dasenbrock have all taken Bloom to task for his refusal to warrant the more congenial model of poetic influence expressed in the poetry of Ezra Pound.[4] In his essay "Pound's Parleyings with Robert Browning," Bornstein argues that Pound's relation to his acknowledged precursor reflects his "continuing insistence on literary influence as a positive process of remaking tradition."[5] Pound's allegiance to Browning may "wobble" from time to time, but his periodic squabbles with his valued predecessor never display the vehemence or perverse distortion dictated by Bloom's notion of anxiety. Recognizing that Pound does not fit his paradigm, Bloom solves the problem of Pound's sins against solipsism by simply labeling him a weak poet and excluding him from the poetic canon.[6] In Bloom's terms, only the modernist Oedipal sons of the Romantic poets merit mention—a canon that many modernist critics find far too restrictive.

Yet another set of important challenges to Bloom's theory have come from feminist critics, who have found Bloom's patriarchal Oedipal

notions of poetic interrelations less than satisfying. Configuring the pro-
cess of poetic influence as essentially and oppressively male, a matter only
for fathers and sons, Bloom ostensibly excludes female poets from his
paradigm. In their book *The Madwoman in the Attic,* Sandra Gilbert and
Susan Gubar paved the way for subsequent feminist critiques of Bloom
by extending his model to examine the process of poetic influence among
the members of his all-but-forgotten sex. Considering the fate of women
authors in the nineteenth century, Gilbert and Gubar argue that the fe-
male poet does not experience the anxiety of influence in the same way as
her male counterpart because she "must confront precursors who are
almost exclusively male, and therefore significantly different from her."[7]
Faced with an oppressive array of male predecessors, all of whom repre-
sent the domineering presence of patriarchal literary authority, the female
poet, Gilbert and Gubar suggest, experiences not so much an anxiety of
influence as an "'anxiety of authorship,'—the radical fear that she cannot
create, that because she can never become a 'precursor' the act of writing
will isolate or destroy her" (49). The female poet ultimately fights, not
against her male precursor's view of the world, but against the male
precursor's view of the female poet—against the oppressive metaphors
and stereotypes that define female identity in male-authored texts. In
Gilbert and Gubar's model, the battle for self-creation leads women poets
to actively seek out the work of a female precursor who, "far from
representing a threatening force to be denied or killed, proves by example
that a revolt against patriarchal literary authority is possible" (49). Assert-
ing that female-to-foremother poetic influence results in a mutually sup-
portive and legitimizing model of shared endeavor, Gilbert and Gubar
recoup a pre-Bloomian male model of cooperative influence for feminist
purposes. In Gilbert and Gubar's paradigm, male poets battle each other,
but female poets band together to battle male hegemony.

Changing the locus of conflict from the power of the precursor to
the overwhelming power of patriarchy, Gilbert and Gubar's influence
model opened the door in the 1980s to a number of important anti-
Bloomian recuperations of women's literary history that stressed the
communal nurturance and shared generosity of sister poets.[8] As in
Bloom's case, however, critics have begun more recently to interrogate
the narrowness of Gilbert and Gubar's model. Like Bloom's paradigm,

Gilbert and Gubar's remains wedded to gender-essentialist notions of male and female behavior and, in its insistence on a common bond among literary sisters, elides or ignores important differences between authors, particularly those of race, class, ethnicity, and sexuality. In her recent book *The Wicked Sisters,* Betsy Erkkila draws on Marianne Moore's friendship with fellow poet Elizabeth Bishop to challenge the simple notions of identification, communality, and nurturing as the primary modes of female literary influence. Charting Bishop's relationship with Moore over the course of many years, Erkkila points out that the interaction between the two poets, often figured as a mother/daughter bond by Bishop herself, betrays evidence of struggle as well as mutual succor and support. Female literary friendships, Erkkila insists, are not free of conflict by some special fiat of gender. Jeredith Merrin, too, argues the limitations of Gilbert and Gubar's "us against them" mentality in her sensitive account of Moore's profound appreciation of, and debt to, George Herbert.[9] In a similar vein, Daniel Mark Fogel critiques both Bloom's and Gilbert and Gubar's models of influence in his study of James Joyce's and Virginia Woolf's responses to the work of their common precursor, Henry James.[10] Tracing Joyce's and Woolf's strikingly similar anxieties toward James—an author they both learned to emulate, yet developed similar strategies to usurp—Fogel suggests that both Bloom's and Gilbert and Gubar's gender-essentialist influence paradigms need revision. "Given the consensus that has emerged in much of feminist discourse that gender makes a radical difference in one's response to tradition and authority," Fogel asks, "what are we to make of the similarities in the responses of James Joyce and Virginia Woolf to Henry James?"[11] In Fogel's view both the male father/son model based solely on Oedipal struggle and the female mother/daughter model based solely on a rejection of patriarchy prove far too narrow and deterministic. "Literary traditions are not families," Fogel reminds us and, while maintaining a notion of influence as conflict, he ends his study with a plea for the creation of a more gender-neutral metaphor to define the struggle to deny influence and establish originality.[12]

While I am sympathetic to the revisionary efforts of critics opposed to Bloom's and Gilbert and Gubar's deterministic and gender-essentialist visions of influence, I would like to suggest that Marianne Moore's relationship with Wallace Stevens points to one significant revision yet to be offered. For all of the arguments made against the gender-essentialist tendencies of both Bloom's and Gilbert and Gubar's models, critics have rarely gone so far as to address the possibility of a supportive cross-gender relationship between poets. By Bloom's own admission, neither Moore nor Stevens can be considered a "weak" poet, yet their relationship reveals none of the consistently intense anxiety of influence or sibling rivalry that Bloom's model predicts. By Gilbert and Gubar's admission, Marianne Moore pens her lines in a "male-dominated" culture, yet her relationship with Stevens does not express the radical "anxiety of authorship"—the female poet's determination that "threatening male precursors and contemporaries must be annihilated"—that their influence model envisions.[13] Moore's relationship with Stevens reveals both mutual influence and, often, Bloom's dreaded "shared generosity"—an ongoing exchange not only of ideas and techniques, but of practical aid in the business of publishing poems. Through an examination of Moore's poetic and personal conversation with Stevens, I hope to offer a fresh picture of cross-gender poetic influence that will further question the gender-essentialist tendencies of the models that still dominate our current critical apparatus.

The possibility of a supportive influence relationship, regardless of gender, is one that Moore herself acknowledged. In a set of notes for a public lecture she tentatively entitled "The Creative Use of Influence," Moore defined the process of poetic influence as a broad and, in her own case, cooperative affair:

> When one is attracted to a thing one is subject to its influence. The influences, however, should be assimilated. The personality and mannerisms must not be copied, for when one imitates, the writer's self is not involved except in parody. . . . In my own case, I seem to import (incorporate bodily) it seems to me what is too unbearably valuable to let alone (dominates my imagination or ear) (haunting and takes charge of me). . . . Indeed, my thoughts are my reading—what I read and what friends say—apparently contradictory my emphatic advice is "Be Yourself." I would answer I suppose I am myself in the way I (take things) employ what I find.[14]

As Moore understood, influence could be wide ranging, subtle, and muta-
ble. It could come not simply from the received texts of acknowledged
masters, but from anything the poet happened to read—the newspaper,
the mail, the back of a cereal box—or hear in conversation with friends.
Moore states that what she hears or reads can "dominate," "take charge
of," and "haunt" her mind, all terms that seem to imply just the sort of
demonic possession that authors in quest of originality in Bloom's scenario
fear the most. Yet, rather than picture herself in anxious rebellion against
such forces and sources, Moore simply and frankly admits their power and
their utility. Alongside her vocabulary of possession in her unfinished
lecture notes, Moore invokes a much less mystical vocabulary of business.
Moore "imports" her materials, "incorporates" them, and "employs"
what she "takes" in. Moore pictures the play of poetic influence in practical
and unanxious terms of productive mercantile trade—each poet imports
from another the valuables that he or she does not have on hand and
integrates them into his or her own poetic economy. Yet, the way in which
each poet transforms or "incorporates" the valuable materials remains
unique. For Moore, the idea of "original" poetry pure of influence—like
the idea of an original culture pure of contact with cultural exporters—was
a fiction, pure and simple.

Certainly, however, to suggest merely that Marianne Moore and
Wallace Stevens had a supportive poetic exchange—that they often im-
ported and employed each other's goods—says very little about their
complex and varied relationship. Indeed, what makes the process of
poetic influence so difficult to model in the first place are the endless
numbers of variables that effect any two poetic careers—variables that
current influence paradigms patently ignore. As critics have noted,
Bloom's model remains strangely abstracted from the biographical and
historical details of the influence relationships he cites. Influence, for
Bloom, occurs in what George Bornstein terms "a social vacuum," a
never-never land where a poet's culture consists only of poetry and psy-
chology.[15] Gilbert and Gubar restore the social and biographical circum-
stance of gender to the process of poetic influence, but they, too, insis-
tently generalize the response of all twentieth-century women poets to a
totalized vision of "patriarchal literary culture" without examining the
particular historical and biographical circumstances of the female poets

they address. Both Bloom and Gilbert and Gubar body forth images of poets as fixed entities with determined responses—the poet (ephebe/female poet) at any given point in his or her career will respond to the same fixed text (rival text/patriarchy) in the same way.

Like any dialogue, however, Moore's poetic conversation with Stevens was far from static. Both poets changed over the years as they matured, and, as one might expect, the ways in which they read each other's work changed as well—partly to suit the separate paths of their own poetic projects. At certain points in their conversation, Moore and Stevens did, in fact, "misread" or project upon each other's work in a variety of ways. Yet, their moments of "misprison" do not display the rigid and anxious quest for ongoing destruction and denial that Bloom's model suggests. "What is closer to the truth," as Moore would say, is that Moore and Stevens often found themselves in need of artistic allies and projected upon each other in an effort to find support—searching for similarities rather than creating differences. Each frequently saw in the other's work the kind of poet they wished themselves to be. Moore's and Stevens's readings of each other's verse also changed in direct response to social and historical forces—the Great Depression, the rise of leftist poets in the 1920s and 1930s, the weight of the Second World War, and the death of Marianne Moore's mother all left their marks on Moore and Stevens's conversation.

In addition to exploring the historical and biographical circumstances of Moore's and Stevens's textual production, my study also makes extensive use of manuscript material to trace the process of poetic influence. As George Bornstein notes, the authors of a number of important studies of literary influence, including Bloom and Gilbert and Gubar, use terms like *revision* and *origins* figuratively rather than literally, making no reference to the concrete production of the texts they confront. "The high road of literary theory and the low road of textual scholarship," Bornstein laments, "never seem to meet."[16] At the risk of getting my shoes muddy, this book spends quite a bit of time in the lowland of concrete textuality—the difficult bogs of textual details that make literary influence hard to generalize. Tracing Moore's poems back to their textual origins in diaries and manuscripts, as well as through multiple published versions and presentations, often directly demonstrates the influence of

Stevens's poetry on Moore's literary production. Stevens's letters and marginal comments on Moore's work, in turn, point concretely to Moore's influence on his creations.

Restoring a number of contexts to Moore and Stevens's dialogue, this study ultimately seeks to expand the notion of poetic influence generally, moving away from dry acts of source hunting or anxious prescripted confrontations with indomitable literary pantheons toward a more shifting and unstable sense of personal and poetic exchange—one that acknowledges that poets and contexts change over time. Rather than a synchronic "model" of poetic influence, I would prefer, rather, to suggest a diachronic metaphor (one that I have gestured toward several times in this introduction)—poetic influence as extended conversation. Lively talk implies a constantly changing relationship between two parties. Each statement in a good conversation between friends responds to one that came before and may revise or reflect on a comment made long ago. Like good conversationalists, poets change their minds in response to one another as their exchange builds and deepens. Like good conversationalists, poets alter the subject of their talk and the substance of their ideas in response to a host of events that affect their lives. Such a metaphor speaks to the value of studying poets in the context of their important conversations. Without the company of the answering voice or poem, we hear only one participant in a dialogue, and, like an eavesdropper who listens to one side of a telephone conversation, we are apt to misread the content of the fleeting, isolated remarks we overhear.

In keeping with the notion that poets and their concerns change over time in response to a variety of vital contexts, I have arranged this study chronologically. The story of influence between Moore and Stevens begins from Moore's perspective. Moore was deeply attracted to Stevens's verse from the earliest days of her career, and I have devoted the first three chapters of this study to tracing Moore's changing response to Stevens's poetry from the final years of the First World War on into the early 1930s. Chapter 1 explores the two poets' mutual involvement with Alfred Kreymborg's little modernist magazine *Others* and considers Moore's earliest sense of the pleasures and pitfalls of Stevens's verse. In chapter 2, I examine Moore's complex response to *Harmonium,* "Well Moused, Lion," a review that, in my view, signals a distinct shift in

Moore's reading of Stevens's verse in the 1920s. Chapter 3 focuses on Moore's further rethinking of Stevens's poetic importance in the years of the depression as expressed in her major poems of the period: "The Plumet Basilisk," "The Jerboa," and "The Frigate Pelican." In the 1930s, Stevens enters the poetic conversation in earnest with the publication of his review of Moore's *Selected Poems,* "A Poet That Matters." Chapter 4 addresses Moore's significant influence on Stevens's artistic philosophy of the "new romantic," and chapter 5 examines Moore and Stevens's pivotal and mutually influential exchange on the subject of social poetry in the mid-1930s. In 1943, after years of exchanging letters, Moore and Stevens finally met face to face, and their artistic conversation, by virtue of their introduction, became more personal. In chapter 6, I move to the years after the Second World War to explore Stevens's second major review of Moore's verse, "About One of Marianne Moore's Poems," and the direct role that Moore plays in the formulation of Stevens's postwar poetic. I conclude this study with a consideration of the numerous poetic and personal exchanges between the two poets in the 1950s, their final years of close friendship before Stevens's death in 1955.

Chapter 1

Marianne Moore, Wallace Stevens, and the Search for Proper Poetic Surroundings

In November of 1960, Donald Hall conducted an extensive interview with his fellow poet Marianne Moore, then seventy-two years old. Weaving through a host of topics, Hall at one point fastened on the issue of Moore's association with *Others,* the little avant-garde magazine edited by Alfred Kreymborg and funded by Walter Arensberg that published many of Moore's early poems from 1915 to 1919. "Someone called Alfred Kreymborg your American discoverer," Hall remarked to Moore. "Do you suppose this is true?" "It could be said, perhaps," she replied; "he did all he could to promote me. . . . Alfred Kreymborg was not inhibited. I was a little different from the others. He thought I might pass as a novelty, I guess." Asked by Hall to expound on her memories of the magazine and its contributors, Moore paused to recall the poets she deemed central to the *Others* crowd:

> *Others* was Alfred Kreymborg and Skipwith Cannéll, Wallace Stevens, William Carlos Williams. Wallace Stevens—odd; I nearly met him about a dozen times before I did meet him in 1941 [*sic*] at Mount Holyoke, at the college's *Entretiens de Pontigny* of which Professor Gustav Cohen was chairman. Wallace Stevens was Henry Church's favorite American poet.[1]

"Odd," Moore reflects when she remembers just how long she knew Stevens and his work before she met him personally. Odd, indeed. Moore's comment seems to indicate her quiet bemusement that it took her so long to meet someone who, from the earliest days of her career, formed a significant part of her writing life. As Moore recalls, both she and Stevens were active members of the *Others* milieu—a group of New York poets and artists (Mina Loy, Lola Ridge, Marsden Hartley, and Alfred Stieglitz also participated) that played a key role in establishing both Moore's and Stevens's poetic careers. Indeed, Moore was not the only member of the group who, in retrospect, found her lack of personal association with Stevens in these early years hard to believe. In his memoir of the *Others* experience, *Troubadour,* entrepreneur and editor Arthur Kreymborg mistakenly recalled the two together at *Others* meetings:

> Reading aloud was soon in order. Even Stevens was inspired to try something, but Wallace waited for conversation to reach a fairly confused height before he drew forth a paper that looked like a poem but sounded like a tête-à-tête with himself. Orrick Johns, Krimmie, Williams and the rest took their turn and finally Marianne Moore joined them. About two in the morning, she read something one could barely hear about "England with its baby rivers and little towns," "Italy with its equal shores," "Greece with its goats and its gourds," "the far East with its snails, its emotional shorthand and jade cockroaches," "and America . . . where there are no proof-readers, no silkworms, no digressions; the wild man's land . . . in which letters are written . . . in plain American which cats and dogs can read!"[2]

In Kreymborg's faulty memory, Moore and Stevens not only attended the same *Others* meetings but were equally reluctant to read their work aloud in front of the group. "Even" retiring Stevens shared his poems under the safe cover of frantic conversation, and "finally" Marianne Moore was induced to try her voice. The two not only knew each other in the *Others* years, they were both, in Kreymborg's memory, equally shy. William Carlos Williams makes a similar mistake in regard to Moore and Stevens's early relationship in comments he made about Stevens and *Others* to William Van O'Connor:

Stevens kept up his acquaintance with the entire New York group—
Kreymborg, Arensberg, Marianne Moore, Lola Ridge, myself, even
Cummings, coming to New York on several occasions to parties,
meetings—but always in a distant manner, shyly, unwilling to be
active or vocal. Everybody knew him, knew him well—but he
never said much. He was always the well-dressed one, diffident
about letting down his hair, precise when we were sloppy. . . . But
we all knew, liked, and admired him. He really was felt to be part of
the gang.[3]

Williams, too, thinks back to the *Others* group and remembers Moore and
Stevens as well-acquainted members of a tightly knit group who "kept up"
with each other over the years. Even though Moore and Stevens did not
actually meet until 1943, those, like Williams and Kreymborg, who knew
them both looked back to the *Others* years and assumed that, in 1915, they
already knew each other well.

Kreymborg's and Williams's less than perfect memories and Moore's
own sense of the oddity of her not meeting Stevens sooner speak, in part,
to the close current of Stevens's and Moore's careers from their earliest
verses. Indeed, even though Moore and Stevens did not cross paths person-
ally in the *Others* years, they crossed paths in print many times. Both
Stevens and Moore began their national careers as poets during the First
World War, primarily in response to what each saw as the prevalent abuses
of war rhetoric and the hopeless inability of old imaginative systems to
confront the conflict adequately. In April of 1915, Moore published her
first professional lyrics, "To a Man Working His Way Through a Crowd,"
and "To the Soul of 'Progress,'" in Harriet Shaw Weaver's London-based
magazine, the *Egoist,* for which poets Ezra Pound, Richard Aldington, and
Hilda Doolittle (H.D.) all worked, on and off, as literary editors. Moore
subsequently began personal correspondences with both Pound and H.D.
and associated herself briefly with the expatriate imagist movement. In
May of 1915, Moore also made her first professional appearance in print on
native shores in Harriet Monroe's Chicago-based magazine, *Poetry.* The
fall of the same year marked Moore's important first foray into the literary
scene in New York City, a well-documented trip that featured her initial
meeting with Kreymborg. Kreymborg was greatly impressed with

Moore and her work and she soon became a frequent contributor to *Others* and an active member of the crowd. In 1918, lured by New York's irresistible "accessibility to experience," Moore and her mother moved to Greenwich Village.

Stevens began to generate similar literary connections during the years of the war—many of them in New York City, Stevens's wartime home until his move to Hartford in 1916. While in New York, Stevens kept up with his Harvard friends Pitts Sanborn, an editor of *Trend* magazine who printed Stevens's first nationally published poems, Carl Van Vechten, head of a postdecadent literary circle dubbed the Patagonians, and Walter Arensberg, wealthy patron of the arts who supplied the financial backing for *Others* magazine and who conducted a literary salon where Stevens was a frequent guest. Stevens developed a close association with Harriet Monroe and *Poetry* magazine, where he published, at Monroe's request, a truncated version of "Sunday Morning" (sections 1, 8, 4, 5, 7) in 1915.[4] In August 1915, Stevens also published "Peter Quince at the Clavier" and "The Silver Plough-Boy" in Kreymborg's *Others,* and he, like Moore, became a frequent contributor to the magazine and a member of the *Others* gang.[5]

Moore's and Stevens's poetry often appeared side by side in the regular issues of *Others* and again in each of Kreymborg's yearly *Others* anthologies. From 1916 until the magazine folded in 1919, Stevens published twenty-eight poems in the *Others* anthologies, and Moore twenty-two—a significant portion of each of their poetic outputs for the period. The *Others* anthology for 1916, for example, contained Moore's "Blake," "George Moore," "The Past Is the Present," "To a Friend in the Making," and "To Statecraft Embalmed," and Stevens's "Peter Quince at the Clavier," "The Silver Plough-Boy," "Six Significant Landscapes," "The Florist Wears Knee-Breeches," "Tattoo," "Song," "Inscription for a Monument," "Bowl," and "Domination of Black."

Placed regularly together in print in the *Others* years, Moore and Stevens had numerous opportunities to study each other's early work, and Moore was quick to acknowledge Stevens's talents. With some two dozen professionally published poems under her belt, Moore felt artistically secure enough in 1916 to step back from her verse and survey her intellectual milieu in a major piece of analytical prose. In October 1916,

"The Accented Syllable"—Moore's first major essay and her first published mention of Wallace Stevens—appeared in Harriet Shaw Weaver's *The Egoist.*[6] A personal exploration of an aesthetic paradox, Moore's essay sets the tone for her pre-*Harmonium* readings of Stevens's verse.

A precursor of Moore's long line of eclectic reviews, "The Accented Syllable" begins with a disarmingly simple proposition: "For the most part, in what we read, it is the meaning rather than the tone of voice which gives us pleasure." Moore, however, declares herself most interested in the exceptions to the rule. "In the case of the following groups of words," she qualifies, "I am inclined to think that the meaning has little to do with the pleasure the words give us" (*CPrMM*, 31). Moore follows her statement with a quirky potpourri of quotes that fascinate her ear—passages gleaned from sources as diverse as Fielding's *Tom Jones, Life Magazine,* Strindberg's *Easter and Other Plays,* the *Boston Evening Transcript,* and an Augier drama, from which she cites the footnote: "Three chops well peppered." Examining her array of pleasing phrases, Moore concludes that certain groups of words attract her, not because of their sense, but because of their sound. The author's tone of voice has the power to "repel" or "compel" the reader quite apart from the trend of the author's ideas. The same, she claims, holds true for verse. Turning to her own milieu, Moore offers what she deems "rare" examples of poets who manage to achieve natural and distinctive tones of voice in rhyme. Moore's three-person list of compelling poets includes Hamilton Sorley, D. F. Dalston, and, in her first published reference to his work, Wallace Stevens. To illustrate Stevens's unique cadence, Moore quotes from his verse play *Three Travelers Watch a Sunrise,* first published in Harriet Monroe's *Poetry* in 1916.

> He will be thinking in strange countries
> Of the white stones near her door;
> But it is me he will see
> At the window, as before.
>
> (*CPrMM,* 34)

Simply put, Moore delights in Stevens's music.

Of all the authors Moore cites in her first major critical essay, Stevens is the only one of her modernist poet peers who Moore deems worthy of mention. As "The Accented Syllable" shows, drawn to Stevens's harmonies, Moore particularly admired his ability to create a natural tone of voice without abandoning the formal constraints of his art. Using Stevens's work as a proper example of careful rhyme, Moore concludes "The Accented Syllable" with a complaint against those poets content to work in lesser forms:

> So far as free verse is concerned, it is the easiest thing in the world to create one intonation in the image of another until finally one has assembled a bouquet of vocal exclamation points. I can read the following advertisement with a great deal of pleasure but I am not sure that it would give me pleasure to read this identical advertisement every day in the week. An intonation must have meaning behind it to support it, or it is not worth much:
>
> > Venus pencils are made in seventeen black and two copying degrees, each degree guaranteed never to vary: softest and blackest, very very soft and very black, very soft and very black, very soft and black, soft and black, soft, soft medium, firm, medium hard, hard, very hard, extra hard, very very hard and firm, extra extra hard and firm, extra extra hard and extra firm, hardest and firmest. (*CPrMM*, 34–35)

Gaudy bouquets of unstructured verbal exclamation points may seem pretty, but, Moore argues, without the substance of a satisfying idea such poems, like arrangements of cut flowers, quickly fade and die. Even while Moore dismisses "pleasurable" free verse poems as the vacuous equivalent of advertising, however, she cannot avoid her obvious attraction to the sound of the catchy copy she recites. Moore ends her essay by implying that the tone of certain words may be dangerously seductive. The sound of a poem may draw us, like a good advertisement, toward trivial or dangerous ideas not our own and compel us to revel in meaningless music.

Moore's simultaneous delight and dissatisfaction with the words of the Venus pencil advertisement parallel, in many ways, Moore's earliest sense of Wallace Stevens's poems. Throughout the early years of her career, the sound and technique of Stevens's verse fascinated and excited Moore, but, as her various responses to Stevens in the *Others* years suggest, she was not always equally pleased with his content. Following her publication of "The Accented Syllable" in the *Egoist,* Moore sent her friend H.D., then a literary editor of the magazine, a list of topics she wished to pursue in future essays. Like her juxtaposition of Stevens's lyrical lines and the words of the Venus pencil advertisement, Moore's list expresses both her interest in Stevens's poems and her doubts about his work:

> I should like to try a comparison of George Moore and Fielding; also one of Knut Hamsun and Carlyle and one of Wallace Stevens and Compton Mackenzie. I am interested also in William Carlos Williams's work, but I am a little afraid to undertake a criticism of it. I feel that I have not seen enough of it to justify my writing one.[7]

Moore never found the time to complete any of her eclectic comparisons, but her note speaks to her abiding fascination with Stevens's work and her confident knowledge of his early poems. Where in 1916 Moore reserves her judgment of Williams on the grounds of unfamiliarity, she readily embraces Stevens as an important subject alongside George Moore and Carlyle, two literary figures that stirred her to direct address in her verse. Yet, while Moore's letter acknowledges the value of Stevens's poems, her connection between Stevens and the popular British novelist Compton Mackenzie points to her conflicted sense of Stevens's verse in the early years of her own career. In October 1913, Moore began to collect and record reviews of Compton Mackenzie's racy work, most notably his notorious novel *Sinister Street,* which Moore, like many of her modernist peers, read with attention. *Sinister Street* charts the decline and fall of Michael Fane, a young Englishman handicapped by a public-school and Oxford education who adopts the pose of a decadent dandy and moves from Oxford to the seedy streets of bohemian London in quest of "experience." A master of detail, Mackenzie peppers his novel with lush, graphic descriptions of London low life clearly intended to shock a prudish public. Despite, or perhaps because of, its questionable

moral character, Mackenzie's book was immensely popular. The reviews
of *Sinister Street* that Moore records in her reading diaries, however,
maintain a distinctly skeptical attitude toward Mackenzie's literary abili-
ties.. The critics Moore cites find Mackenzie's work fascinating, colorful,
and lively, but they also criticize his novel as the indecorous product of an
overeager adolescent whose imagination simply runs away with his bet-
ter judgment. In her reading diary dated 1913 to 1916, Moore notes a
critique of the first volume of *Sinister Street* by Martin Secker of the
English Review. While Secker approves of Mackenzie's vivid descriptions
and wicked satire of the British school system, he concludes that

> Mr. Mackenzie . . . errs . . . in the emphasis he gives to certain excep-
> tional influences in the life of his hero. . . . Many clever schoolboys
> are in danger of becoming aesthetes, whether it be of the George
> Moore or the Oscar Wilde type; but Michael outdoes them all. . . .
> We think that he [Mackenzie] has, considering his whole scheme,
> attempted a task which is rather too large for his philosophy.[8]

In her reading diary dated 1907 to 1915, Moore records a similar com-
plaint lodged by an anonymous reviewer in the *New York Post*.

> Compton Mackenzie: "the main trouble w Mr. M seems to have
> been one of arrested development. All of his books have revealed
> undeniable talent but it is the talent of the undergraduate. The curios-
> ity felt by well brought up young men of 25 or there abouts in the
> class of women politely known as 'unfortunate' is a commonplace of
> youth. . . . But this is their stuff out of which to make a book."[9]

In all of Moore's cited reviews, Mackenzie appears as one who, drawn to
sordid subjects, courts decadent profusion at the expense of higher pur-
pose. Eschewing noble or profound visions and lacking a clear philoso-
phy, Mackenzie squanders his "undeniable talent" in novels meant
merely to shock.

Against the backdrop of her recorded reviews, Moore's association
between Compton Mackenzie and Wallace Stevens seems to imply both
an endorsement and a critique of Stevens's early poems. Stevens's vivid

and riotous imagination, like Mackenzie's, attracted Moore, but she remained doubtful about the sometimes aggressive and indecorous nature of Stevens's verses. Enamored of his sound, Moore felt that Stevens, like Mackenzie, at times assaulted his audience in his attempts to escape the restrictions of artistic decorum and reveled in pure sensation at the expense of higher moral purpose. As Moore commented of another of her favorite aesthetes, George Moore, whose words she borrowed to make her point, "'We must not ask more of paganism than it can give; its gift is beauty'" (*CPrMM,* 73).

In the period following the First World War, however, Moore continued to ask more of Stevens's art than mere beauty, and, throughout the *Others* years, her response to Stevens's verse formed an important part of her own wider debate about the moral responsibility and the ultimate utility of verse in general—a debate tied in part to the artistic venue she and Stevens shared most frequently, *Others* magazine. Wrapped between covers of *Yellow Book* yellow and backed by Arensberg and his flamboyant coterie, *Others,* as Milton Bates points out, carried with it certain "post-decadent" associations—art for art's sake—that Moore herself well understood and, for the sake of seeing her work in print, rather uncomfortably accepted.[10] Moore's account of her first meeting with editor Kreymborg indicates that she was trepidatious about both his, and the magazine's, supposed bohemian bias and much relieved to find Kreymborg a pleasant and down-to-earth dinner companion in spite of his reputation as an aesthete. As Moore's postwar poems suggest, however, Moore found her close association with the somewhat hedonistic bent of *Others* magazine itself a bit more difficult to resolve. Indeed, Moore's poems of the *Others* years are haunted by difficult questions of aesthetic responsibility and value. Can beauty and sophistication, without particular moral purpose or a sense of human connectedness, ever be the sole ingredient of satisfying art? Can poetry ever be more than the sealed, self-indulgent revery of the individual artist? Such queries radiate through Moore's work and reflect directly on her association with the *Others* milieu. In "Critics and Connoisseurs," first printed in *Others* in 1916, Moore critiques those poets and critics who value the "conscious fastidiousness" and sophisticated "coach / wheel yellow" complexity of merely decorative art at the expense of spontaneous, compassionate, and less perfect productions.[11] Moore's "In the

Days of Prismatic Color" states that poetic "complexity is not a crime,"
but then argues that complexity taken too far results in meaningless and
damaging obscurity. "Sophistication is as it al- // ways has been—," she
complains, "at the antipodes from the init- / ial great truths."[12] In "Those
Various Scalpels," Moore examines the aesthetic perfections and decora-
tive magnificence of a fellow female artist and condemns her poems as
works "Whetted // to / brilliance by the hard majesty of that sophistication
which is su- / perior to opportunity."[13] Committed to its own beautiful
complex constructions, such a mind abhors, for the sake of its own solip-
sistic entertainment, all simple, natural, or genuine expressions of human
experience. Moore's poem "England," printed in the *Others* anthology for
1919, criticizes the decadent symbolist poems of France as those in which
the "mystery of construction diverts one from what was originally one's /
object—substance at the core."[14] In the midst of her complaints about the
abuses of sophisticated art, Moore transcribed into her reading diary Ar-
thur Symons's comments on the decadent artist Aubrey Beardsley—art
editor of the *Yellow Book* from which *Others* took its flavor and its color:

> His world is a world of phantoms in which the desire of the perfect-
> ing of mortal sensations, a desire of infinity, has overpassed mortal
> limits, and poised them, so faint, so quavering, so passionate for
> flight, in a hopeless and strenuous immobility. They have put off the
> common burdens of humanity, and put on that loneliness which is
> the rest of the Saints and the unrest of those who have sinned with
> the intellect.[15]

Turning his back on human burdens and imperfections for the sake of his
own perfect visions, Beardsley strives artistically toward a prideful ideal
he, a mere mortal, can never achieve. Symons claims that Beardsley, in
his search for the perfect and the eternal, becomes a reflection of the
phantoms he creates and retreats from life's flux into an immobile world
of his own making. Like the sophisticated thinkers Moore critiques
throughout her poems of the *Others* years, Beardsley revels in his own
intellectual quest at the expense of all human connection.

    Ringing changes on the problem of haughty artistic complexity,

Moore's postwar verse consistently argues against poetry that offers a beautiful sophistication at the expense of useful and understandable substance. Again and again, Moore equates the artistic satisfactions of the clever mind with a prideful and hostile solipsism; content in their beautiful and artificial imaginative involutions, poets, Moore contends, often care little for the natural, imperfect human world that lies outside their creations. Moore's insistent critique of poetic sophistication, however, often seems as much directed at her own work as at any of her subjects.

As Moore herself understood, her poetry contained its fair share of complexity—a fact rather harshly brought to Moore's attention by the first critical symposium on her work in the pages of Harriet Monroe's *Poetry* in January 1922.[16] Monroe's symposium was prompted by the appearance of Moore's first book of verse, a small pamphlet simply entitled *Poems* issued in England from the Egoist Press and collected and published without Moore's knowledge or consent by fellow poet H.D. and historical novelist Bryher (Winifred Ellerman).[17] The act clearly upset Moore, who responded angrily to being forced into print. She wrote to Bryher, "You say I am stubborn. I agree and if you knew how much more than stubborn I am, you would blame yourself more than you do, on having put a thing through over my head."[18] Moore's anger at the personal betrayal, however, was surpassed by her genuine fear of public response to her verse. As Moore put it to H.D., "And when Bryher says: I don't like your work but I like you, what will the public's sentiments be, who don't even like ME?"[19] *Poetry*'s critical symposium supplied the unhappy answer to Moore's anxious question. Monroe opened a discussion of Moore's work by quoting the only two poets inclined to see value in Moore's verse, H.D. and Yvor Winters:

H.D., surely a critic of authority, calls Miss Moore a poet, and a number of young radicals are eager to pronounce her "a very great poet," as Yvor Winters did in a recent letter. "With the exception of Wallace Stevens," he wrote, "she is about the only person since Rimbaud who has had any very profound or intricate knowledge and command of sound; and I am not sure but I think her about the best poet in this country except for Mr. Stevens."[20]

Monroe, however, was less than appreciative of Moore's poetic command. To counter Winters's approval and to separate Moore's verse from that of Monroe's adored Stevens, Monroe mustered a series of critiques of her poetry that must have stung Moore in light of her own consistent railings against sophisticated and impenetrable artistic surfaces. Winifred Bryher claimed that Moore's verse was "but a play with the outside of substances and the inside of thoughts too tired to feel emotion." Admitting Moore's technical triumphs, Bryher found her poems to be "perfect but static studies of a highly evolved intellect."[21] Marion Strobel, in turn, damned Moore's poems as the "contortions" of a too well-developed intelligence. "Because we are conscious that she has brains, that she is exceedingly well-informed," Strobel complained, "we are the more irritated that she has not learned to write with simplicity."[22] To such comments Monroe added her own assessment of Moore's poems as a "deliberately patterned crust" of "stiffly geometrical" and haughty intellectuality.

Moore thus found herself accused of the very abuses she consistently condemned in the work of other artists throughout her postwar poems. Casting Moore's verse as a collection of static and sophisticated surfaces, the critics of Monroe's symposium marveled at Moore's technique but questioned her philosophy and her essential humanity. "Brilliant to the point of gaudiness," Moore's verse seemed, to Monroe in particular, an expression of prideful egotism. Even Winters's commendation, given Moore's lurking reservations about the moral philosophy of Stevens's aestheticism, must have seemed a bit disturbing. Winters applauded Moore's poems for precisely the same reason that Moore, in her early years, praised Stevens's—for their music. However, in placing Moore alongside Stevens and Rimbaud as a poet of beautiful sound, Winters mentioned nothing of the quality of Moore's content. While Moore must have appreciated Winters's compliment, he problematically likened her verse to both that of the French symbolists—poets Moore critiqued as those "in / whose products, mystery of construction diverts one from what was originally one's / object—substance at the core"—and Wallace Stevens, her gaudy compatriot whose gorgeous singing often eclipsed his better moral judgment. In both its blame and praise, *Poetry* pictured Moore as an intellectual sinner of the first order at the furthest antipodes from initial truths.

Such a portrait hurt Moore deeply, and, at the height of her personal debate about the responsibility and utility of verse, she produced a major poem questioning the relationship of her art to the poetic approaches of her contemporaries: "People's Surroundings." Printed in June 1922 in the *Dial*, "People's Surroundings" constitutes a survey of Moore's poetic environment of the *Others* years, and the poem includes, as John Slatin notes, her first extended published response to the work of Wallace Stevens.[23] Within "People's Surroundings," Moore presents a series of habitats, each of which reflects a particular poetic style or mental approach that Moore deemed an important part of her artistic milieu. Moore's examination of poetic technique ranges from a minimal room that resembles the compressions of William Carlos Williams's verse, to an overstuffed palace of French curios, to a stripped-down "necropolis" of separable units suited to unimaginative minds obsessed with modern efficiency, to sculpted gardens "twisted into permanence" that reflect the work of poets wedded to traditional forms, to the empty desert distances of the American Southwest that suit minds that move inexorably in straight lines and prefer common sense to poetic utterance. Behind each of Moore's visits lies the question of her own potentially sinful intellect. Condemned as static, sophisticated, complex, gaudy, and detached, Moore set out to judge her own reprobate verse alongside the work of her peers. In part, I believe, in response to Winters's close association between Stevens and herself in Monroe's *Poetry* symposium, Moore devoted the largest segment of her poem to the exploration of an exotic tropical locale that reflected her sense of Stevens's poetry. Stevens emerges again in 1922 as an important, if problematic, part of Moore's poetic surroundings.

Moore's reading diaries once again provide the context for her renewed conversation with Stevens's work. In October 1921, Stevens published a set of twelve poems entitled "Sur Ma Guzzla Gracile" in Harriet Monroe's *Poetry:* "Palace of the Babies," "From the Misery of Don Joost," "The Doctor of Geneva," "Gubbinal," "The Snow Man," "Tea at the Palaz of Hoon," "The Cuban Doctor," "Another Weeping Woman," "On the Manner of Addressing Clouds," "Of Heaven Considered as a Tomb," "The Load of Sugar Cane," and "Hibiscus on the Sleeping Shores."[24] Stevens's buffo title, "From Out of My Slender Gullet," marks the cycle as an exercise in ventriloquism. All the lyrics issue from the throat of a single poet who, in his punning brashness, resembles Stevens's foppish alter ego, Peter Parasol. Stevens's set consists primarily of paired characterizations—the Cuban doctor and the Genevese doctor, the speaker who addresses the clouds and the speaker who considers heaven a tomb, the red-turbaned boatman of "The Load of Sugar Cane" and the impoverished auditor of "Gubbinal," Hoon and the snow man. Each pair of poems explores the relationship of mind and world and asks which to prefer, the imagination's fancy or the realm of bare facts. The speaker of "On the Manner of Addressing Clouds," for example, longs for divine presences in the "drifting waste" of the sky and peoples the heavens accordingly, making the clouds into "Gloomy grammarians in golden gowns" who elicit poetic "pomps of speech." The speaker of Stevens's counterlyric, "Of Heaven Considered as a Tomb," offers an opposing view of the same sky. Stripping the heavens clean of poetic images, the speaker of "A Tomb" replaces the anthropomorphized clouds with an empty and icy "nothingness." The same opposition holds true for Stevens's well-known pair of poems "The Snow Man" and "Tea at the Palaz of Hoon." The snow poet in search of the "real" longs to extinguish his thoughts and become "nothing himself," nothing more than a part of the cold tropeless landscape. Hoon, on the other hand, revels in an opulent interior world of his own making and triumphantly proclaims his creative mastery: "I was the world in which I walked, and what I saw / Or heard or felt came not but from myself." Each pair of poems in Stevens's set constitutes an imaginative cycle. Linking oppositional lyrics, Stevens implies that no one mental state can satisfy for long. Hoon, for all his fiery fancy, will tire of his palace, cast off his protective images, and become the snow poet. The snow man in turn will yield to the warming sun of the imagination until he shines like Hoon. Stevens's set portrays the act of imaginative creation as an endless cartwheeling motion—the mind makes, the creations become old, stale, abstract, and the mind tears them apart only to start the cycle again.

Moore encountered Stevens's "Sur Ma Guzzla Gracile" set during her production of "People's Surroundings," and, taking a special interest in his poems, she preserved them for further study. In Moore's reading diary for 1921, underneath the large bold heading "Wallace Stevens *Poetry* October," appear her transcriptions of passages from Stevens's lyrics

"The Doctor of Geneva," "The Cuban Doctor," "The Snow Man," "On the Manner of Addressing Clouds," and "Hibiscus on the Sleeping Shores."[25] Alongside her copied-out lines, Moore supplies brief commentaries that indicate that she detected several different poetic personalities within Stevens's set. The stripped-down simplicity of Stevens's "Gubbinal"—"That strange flower, the sun, / Is just what you say"— reminds Moore of William Carlos Williams's crisply compressed poetic utterances. "Cf. WCW ms," she jots next to Stevens's concise statement of disgust, "Have it your way." Beside the final stanza of "The Snow Man" Moore writes "cf T. S. Eliot." Stevens's snow poet who becomes "nothing himself" in a quest for tropeless vision brings Eliot's antiromantic insistence on impersonal reason and control of the imagination to Moore's mind. Yet, while Moore sees glints of a less riotous, more imaginatively restrained Stevens in "Sur Ma Guzzla Gracile," she pays the most attention to, and copies the most lines from, the final poem of his set, "Hibiscus on the Sleeping Shores."

In "Hibiscus," Stevens creates a tropical landscape that, as in many of his Florida poems, represents the warm lush realm of the poet's active imagination. A dramatic monologue on the subject of the imagination's relation to the actual, Stevens's poem constitutes an early draft of his 1935 lyric "The Idea of Order at Key West." The speaker stands on the shore with his friend Fernando, a precursor of Ramon Fernandez, and recounts, in a simile, a peculiar mental journey—the day his mind "roamed as a moth roams" among the hibiscus blooms "beyond the open sand." Moore recorded the bulk of the speaker's recollection in her diary:

Then it was that that monstered moth
Which had lain folded against the blue
And the colored purple of the lazy sea,

And which had drowsed along the bony shores,
Shut to the blather that the water made,
Rose up besprent and sought the flaming red

Dabbled with yellow pollen—red as red
As the flag above the old café—
And roamed there all the stupid afternoon.

(CPWS, 22–23)

As in "The Idea of Order at Key West," Stevens pictures the sea as a place of inhuman verities that cannot form to mind or voice. The dark speech of the actual amounts to noise and "blather"—nonsensical sounds that remain meaningless without the organizing activity of the mind. From such a dead desolate and "bony" shore stripped of the imagination, however, the speaker's fancy takes flight. Shut to the rasps of the veritable ocean, the speaker's mind rises up in solitary splendor like the woman's spirit in "The Idea of Order at Key West." Wandering through hibiscus blooms rich with yellow pollen—an image of the imagination's sensual fecundity—the moth of the mind moves "beyond" the empty sea into a flaming red flurry of creation.

Yet, while Stevens describes the beauty of the moth's journey, he also, in keeping with the rest of the "Sur Ma Guzzla Gracile" set, indicates that its sublime flight cannot satisfy for long. Separated from any sense of the actual, the imagination becomes grotesquely distorted and unnatural—"monstered" in its excesses. The speaker's burst of red rage quickly lapses into torpor as the tropes of his detached vision become as old and worn as the familiar "flag above the old café." Meandering from bloom to bloom, the moth of the imagination loses all vitality. The realm of the imagination's monstrous delights becomes as dull and senseless as the empty shore without the mind.

Despite the more restrained poetic personalities that Moore discerned in Stevens's "Sur Ma Guzzla Gracile," her reading diary indicates that Moore found "Hibiscus on the Sleeping Shores" the most intriguing and the most typically—and disturbingly—Stevensian poem of the set. Indeed, the tropical setting that Moore presents as an example of Stevens's poetic milieu in her subsequent poem, "People's Surroundings," springs directly from her reading of "Hibiscus" and reveals her ongoing internal debate over the value of Stevens's verse. Taking her cue in "People's Surroundings" from the speaker of "Hibiscus on the Sleeping Shores," Moore continues to read Stevens's poems as verbally beautiful, yet potentially monstrous and morally purposeless, fictions—the products of an imagination grown too grotesquely, violently, and self-indulgently assertive. In "People's Surroundings" Moore casts Stevens as that favored subject of the French symbolists, the exotic and disfigured Bluebeard who marries and murders his wives in turn:

and Bluebeard's tower above the coral reefs,
the magic mousetrap closing on all points of the compass,
capping like petrified surf, the furious azure of the bay
where there is no dust and life is like a lemon-leaf,
a green piece of tough translucent parchment,
where the crimson, the copper, and the Chinese vermilion of the
      poincianas
set fire to the masonry and turquoise blues refute the clock;
this dungeon with odd notions of hospitality,
with its "chessmen carved out of moonstones,"
its mocking-birds, fringed lilies, and hibiscus,
its black butterflies with blue half circles on their wings,
tan goats with onyx ears, its lizards glittering and without thickness
like splashes of fire and silver on the pierced turquoise of the lattices
and the acacia-like lady shivering at the touch of a hand,
lost in a small collision of the orchids—
dyed quicksilver let fall
to disappear like an obedient chameleon in fifty shades of mauve and
      amethyst:
here where the mind of this establishment has come to the conclusion
that it would be impossible to revolve about one's self too much,
sophistication has, like an escalator, cut the nerve of progress.[26]

Filled with monstrous black butterflies and flaming red hibiscus and
poincianas, Moore's tropical seascape repeats the latitude and tropes of
"Hibiscus on the Sleeping Shores." Moore envisions the splendid excess
of the Stevensian imagination as a beautiful, but harmful trap. A lime-
stone spire atop a maze of hidden coral reefs, Bluebeard's tower bounds
the bay and turns the protected water a "furious azure." The blue, Ste-
vens's hue of transcendent imagination, is both vivid and lovely, but
Moore implies that such a color can only result from a detached and
decadent imaginative stasis. Shut from the blather and confusion of the
actual sea beyond the bay, the poet's escapist thoughts ossify into a glossy
and perfect permanence that denies all change. Where there is no dust,
there is no decay—the mind of the tower lays egocentric claim to an
eternal ideal vision that "refutes the clock." Moore ultimately pictures
Stevens's/Bluebeard's tower as an unchanging palaz of Hoon. "I was
myself the compass of that sea," Hoon announces in Stevens's lyric: "I
was the world in which I walked, and what I saw / Or heard or felt came

not but from myself." Like Hoon, the mind of Bluebeard's tower expands, godlike, to create and control all compass points of the sea. "It is human nature to stand in the middle of a thing," Moore admits of the imagination in her sea poem "A Grave," "but you cannot stand in the middle of this: / the sea has nothing to give but a well excavated grave." Bluebeard/Stevens stands as a pinnacle in the midst of the ocean. Presuming to order the sea's confusion with his vibrant turquoise mind, he gazes only at a narcissistic reflection that denies his own mortality. As Moore concludes of Bluebeard's tower, "here where the mind of this establishment has come to the conclusion / that it would be impossible to revolve about one's self too much, / sophistication has like an escalator, cut the nerve of progress." Scornful complexity and sophistication replace sincerity, and Stevens's verse becomes an "escalator"—a mechanically created upward motion devoid of feeling. As Moore argues in "Picking and Choosing," "Words are constructive / when they are true; the opaque allusion—the simulated flight // upward—accomplishes nothing." The poet of the escalator seems to move up and out into sublimity but, in fact, goes nowhere in a static projection of the ego that does not permit growth, change, or genuine vision.

Moore thus pictures Stevens as a violent and successful aesthete who, spurning the disorder of the actual world, sacrifices all life—and love—to his furious craving for his own perfect visions. Enraptured by the ideal, Bluebeard seeks a mate but can admire only himself. Moore pictures Bluebeard's bride as an "acacia-like" lady who, once touched by the artistry of the proprietor, loses her identity in a collision of color and disappears "like an obedient chameleon in fifty shades of mauve and amethyst." Equating Bluebeard's lady with an acacia, Moore invokes the tree that in America and England is popularly known as the common locust or "false acacia," a slender tree with large, fragile white blossoms suited to cool climates. Preferring, like Shelley's Alastor youth, the "many-coloured woof and shifting hues" of his own soul to the company of a pale maiden, Bluebeard cannot rest content with his fragile white mate and dyes her to match his tropical vision, extinguishing the actual lady beneath his projected image of perfection. Moore implies that Stevens violently transplants his "acacia-like" poetic subjects, dragging them into a static imaginative tropics where anything pale, imperfect, or mutable cannot possibly survive.

Yet, while Moore critiques what she deems Stevens's detached and solipsistic revery, she also reveals her tremendous attraction to his vibrant creations. Moore endows Bluebeard's tower with an eerie and opulent beauty that, in its color and careful alliteration, dominates the poem. As John Slatin notes, Moore invokes the legend of Bluebeard the cannibal husband in part to explore her fate as a poet who, drawn to Stevens's verse, might well be seduced into marrying her work to his at the expense of her own artistic life. Slatin, however, wrongly interprets Moore's fascination with Stevens as a mere matter of "style."[27] Moore does not, as Slatin suggests, fear the adulteration of her verse by Stevens's tone. What Moore detects in Stevens is the tendency for his imagination to claim too much—to create, like Beardsley, a gorgeous, complex, but potentially static world of its own that, in its "monstered" beauty, offers a false and too-easy haven from the shifting disorder of the actual world. Slatin also does not explore the possibility that Moore emphasizes one part of Stevens's poetic as a way of criticizing the potentially oppressive tendencies that critics pointed to in her own poetry. As Moore's comments on Stevens's "Sur Ma Guzzla Gracile" in her reading diary make clear, she well understood that the flaming red tropic of "Hibiscus on the Sleeping Shores" marked only one extreme of Stevens's complex poetic. In her reading diary, alongside the excesses of the monstered moth in "Hibiscus on the Sleeping Shores," Moore makes note of poetic moments in Stevens's set that, in her view, undercut his wilder reveries: the stripped-down minimalism of his Williams-like "Gubbinal" and the antiromantic restraint of his T. S. Eliot-like "The Snow Man." Moore thus acknowledges the provisionalizing tendencies of Stevens's set even while she chooses to cast him as a dangerously idealizing Bluebeard—a reflection of her anxieties about the potential complexity and detachment of her own verse. Praised alongside Wallace Stevens for her symbolist music by Yvor Winters and condemned as static, complex, and haughty in her "protective coloration" by Harriet Monroe's *Poetry* symposium, Moore transfers both Winters's praise and Monroe's critique of her poetry and person directly onto her image of Stevens and his work. Moore's depiction of Stevens as Hoon rather than the snow man serves as a projection of her fear that any sophisticated imaginative order, including her own, might easily degenerate into a static and prideful solipsism. Like Stevens, Moore valued the imagination, but, as her postwar poems attest, she also understood and acknowledged the tendency of any powerful and sophisticated mind to dangerously overstep its bounds—to revel in gaudy color and music at the expense of life itself. Indeed, Moore's image of the "acacia-like" lady in "People's Surroundings" seems engineered to suggest not only a condemnation of Stevens's potentially imposing vision, but of her own poetic bent as well. Where the popularly known North American acacia—the "false acacia"—is a trembling tree with white flowers, the acacia in its true form is a much different plant. In strict botanical terms, which Moore knew well, the true acacia is a tropical plant with bright fragrant flowers well suited to Bluebeard's milieu. If her lady is a "true" acacia rather than a false one—a point Moore leaves purposely unresolved—Moore's image of the "acacia-like" lady implies that, regardless of Bluebeard's/Stevens's influence, Moore sees herself as having tropical tendencies that she finds potentially dangerous.

Moore thus focuses on a single extreme of Stevens's poetic in her Bluebeard's tower episode as a means of expressing her doubts about the potentially prideful nature of the powerful poetic imagination—doubts not occasioned only by Stevens's poems. Indeed, throughout "People's Surroundings," Moore creates multiple settings that question whether the desire for the poetic imagination can ever lead to anything but static egotism, whether the mind of any imaginative establishment can ever keep from revolving around itself too much. Along with Bluebeard's tower, Moore presents two other ornate settings that speak critically of the imaginations that make them—a French palace stuffed full of elaborate porcelain figurines and modish furniture, and a manor house filled with old velvet and crystal, locked behind hand-forged gates and surrounded by landscape gardening "twisted into permanence." Like Bluebeard's tower, each of Moore's decorative settings shows the effect of tropes that have become static and oppressive. Wedded to outmoded fashions, the proprietor of the palace lives among a pile of old and useless imaginative knickknacks—merely frivolous images that satisfy a vain desire for decoration. Rooted in old ideas, the owner of the manor creates an aesthetic retreat of cultured beauty that, like Bluebeard's tower, resembles a dungeon with odd notions of hospitality. The rhododendrons of the manor have grown so deep that they prohibit any vision of what lies beyond the house—an image of the proprietor's inability to see beyond his long cultivated and static tropes. Under the touch of such an oppressive intelligence, the shadows of the cedars become as "iron" and immobile as the forged gates. Contentedly locked in a comfortable world of its own making, the mind of the manor twists all living things into a reflection of its rooted traditional artistry.

Yet, while Moore seems dissatisfied with each of her presentations of the world with imagination, she seems equally dissatisfied in "People's Surroundings" with her presentations of the world without imagination. Moore balances each ornate setting in her poem with a stripped-down or minimal setting meant to challenge the work of the more decorative or idealizing mind. Moore begins "People's Surroundings" with an image of functional simplicity—a compressed "deal table compact with the wall." The mind that values such a "dried bone of arrangement," however, proves too skeletal for Moore, and she moves to the palace stuffed with French curios. Rejecting the mind devoted to pretty but useless knickknacks, Moore presents an opposing law in her next setting—the habitat of a mind devoted to utter efficiency and utility. Unwilling to waste time on anything so frivolous as beauty, the efficient mind prefers to inhabit a "vast necropolis" of stripped-down "separable units" of steel, oak, and glass—a bare setting fit for a rigid, compartmentalized, and utterly unimaginative intelligence. The mind of this establishment prefers almanacs to poetry and values nothing but practical advice. Moore's image of devotion to utility, however, appears as stifling and unappealing as the mind crammed full of useless decorations, and the utilitarian necropolis of facts gives way to the more decorative diversions of the manor house. The manor, in turn, becomes an ornate prison of detached tropes and Moore escapes down the highway to the empty plains of the American Southwest:

> straight lines over such great distances as one finds in Utah or in Texas
> where people do not have to be told
> that "a good brake is as important as a good motor,"
> where by means of extra sense cells in the skin,
> they can like trout, smell what is coming—
> those cool sirs with the explicit sensory apparatus of common sense,
> who know the exact distance between two points as the crow flies;
> there is something attractive about a mind that moves in a straight line—
> the municipal bat-roost of mosquito warfare, concrete statuary,
> medicaments for "instant beauty" in the hands of all,
> and that live wire, the American string quartette. . .

The proprietor of this bare setting despises poetic or imaginative detours and responds quickly and coolly to the dictates of "common sense." Moore admits that "there is something attractive about a mind that moves in a straight line," but she insists that the mind that chooses such a path inhabits a mental desert, gaining clarity at the expense of all imaginative pleasure. The painstaking beauty of sculpture gives way to the "instant" slapdash erection of "concrete statuary"—the practical and democratically conceived municipal bat roost that passes for art. To the mind of such a setting "the American string quartette" is not a piece of music for two violins, viola, and cello, but a set of four wires that conduct electricity hung by the side of the highway—the only artistry fit for the quick synapses of such an austere and impatient intelligence. Once again, Moore finds such a vacant setting lacking in the necessary music, and she moves from the desert to the vibrant tropical reveries of Bluebeard's tower. While the world with the imagination seems oppressively full of static and detached tropes in "People's Surroundings," the world without the imagination seems oppressively common and empty of pleasure.

In its turns from setting to oppositional setting, Moore's poem reveals her perpetual dissatisfaction with both the actual world unadorned and the world of the mind unconstrained. Moore thus shows her deep affinity with Stevens at the same time that she registers her protest against the more domineeringly sublime moments in his verse. While Moore's Bluebeard tower episode of "People's Surroundings" critiques the Hoon-like, tropical extremes of Stevens's poetic, the larger formal arrangement of her poem reflects both the pattern and the spirit of Stevens's "Sur Ma Guzzla Gracile" set. Within "People's Surroundings," Moore creates a series of oppositional settings that explore poles of bare simplicity and heightened artistry in turn—a pattern that resembles Stevens's oscillations in "Sur Ma Guzzla Gracile" between the white landscape of the snow man and the reveries of Hoon, between the austere reserve of the doctor of Geneva and the dreamy excesses of the Cuban doctor, between the mind that sees heaven as a tomb and the mind that addresses the clouds. Moore's series of surroundings displays a cartwheeling search for a poem that will suffice, and she, like Stevens, implies that no one mental state can satisfy for long. The poetic imagination craves more than an oppressive bareness of separable units and creates an imaginative palace of order; the palace becomes a dungeon of false and stale tropes, and the mind tears it apart only to start the cycle again.

Thus, the larger form of "People's Surroundings," like Moore's notes on Stevens's "Sur Ma Guzzla Gracile" set in her reading diary, imply that Moore saw a far more multifaceted and skeptical poet than Bluebeard at work in Stevens's verse—one who, like herself, both actively acknowledged and resisted his tropical tendencies. The question remains, then, given Moore's seeming double response to Stevens's work, just what sort of poetic influence does Moore's poem display? In the light of the historical facts of the critical reception of Moore's *Poems,* her reading diary comments on Stevens's "Sur Ma Guzzla Gracile" set, and her use of Stevens's "Hibiscus on the Sleeping Shores" as a source for her poem, the issues of Moore's response and Stevens's influence clearly become complicated. Certainly in "People's Surroundings" Moore foregrounds the connection between herself and the Stevens that, in 1922, she feared the most. Reading Stevens as a creator of beautiful, complex, but heartless music, Moore projected onto Stevens's verse the flaws she feared in her own work— flaws that critics frequently cited—and attacked them accordingly. Moore rejected the Bluebeard/Stevens she envisioned, not because she feared for her poetic priority or originality, as Bloom would argue, but because her "misprison" depicted the sort of solipsistic verse that Moore could not morally defend, despite her attraction to the color and the sound. Moore's personal exorcism, then, would seem to indicate, in Gilbert and Gubar's view, an anxious response to a domineering transcendental male poetic that the female poet takes pains to reject. Yet, at the same time that Moore sees in Stevens's verse the sort of poetry she does not wish to write, she also seems to find, in Stevens's larger set, a way out of her dilemma. Adopting the form of "Sur Ma Guzzla Gracile"—the alternation between simple and complex settings—Moore echoes in "People's Surroundings" the strategy of skeptical imaginative motion that she discerned in Stevens's set, even while she critiques one of his poetic poles. Rather than wholly rejecting Stevens's poetic, Moore imports what she now finds valuable—the potential solution to the perceived threat of her own poetic stasis.

Thus, where Slatin reads Moore's critique of Bluebeard's tower as the end of her poetic conversation with Stevens, I read it as only the barest beginning of their exchange. As Moore's comments on "Sur Ma

Guzzla Gracile" and her considerations in "People's Surroundings" indicate, Moore saw a more contingent poet in Stevens's work than she initially envisioned—a poet not of intellectual stasis, but of change, dissatisfied, like Moore, with both bare and opulent surroundings. Even as Moore portrayed Stevens as Bluebeard, she discerned a more varied voice in his poetry than her own portrait of detached sophistication would allow. Moore's view of Stevens and his verse in 1922 was neither simple nor static. Indeed, by 1923 and *Harmonium,* Moore's comments show that she had again changed her mind about Stevens's poems, in part due to the introduction of yet another context, her growing sense of Stevens the man.

The View from the Romantic Mountaintop: Marianne Moore's Response to *Harmonium*

Around 1920, like a private detective, Marianne Moore began to record bits of conversation among her modernist friends and acquaintances into her notebooks. Some such snippets find their way into Moore's poetry as memorable testimony to the daily epiphanies of life. Other transcriptions, however, amount to juicy literary gossip that offers a fascinating glimpse into the New York modernist milieu. Throughout Moore's conversation notebooks, William Carlos Williams, Ezra Pound, H.D., Bryher, T. S. Eliot, Alfred Stieglitz, Alfred Kreymborg, Yvor Winters, Scofield Thayer, James Sibley Watson, Richard Aldington, and Archibald Mac-Leish all reveal their passing thoughts and take their lumps in turn. Pound comes across as a garrulous eccentric who does not quite know when to give his audience a rest. "He is like a dead frog that keeps on striking out for hours," says Thayer, editor of the *Dial*.[1] A further anonymous comment in Moore's notebook confirms Pound's desperate need to communicate his thoughts: "If he can talk to a suitable confidant he will, if he can't do that then he'll tell it to a butler. If he can't tell it to a butler he will babble to a pillar, and that robs him of all formidableness."[2] In contrast "Billy" Williams, as the gang calls him, appears to be a playful prankster, "like a chow dog rolling over and over on the floor that won't come when he's called."[3] Stieglitz the photographer comes to light in a conversation with Moore as a thoughtful intellectual fascinated with the Greeks. Kreymborg, the entrepreneurial editor of *Others,* finds H.D. an appealing presence, remarking

that she is "the sweetest thing in the world." Bryher, the historical novelist
and H.D.'s wealthy lover and patron, subsequently types Kreymborg as
"a traveling salesman."⁴ Clearly, in a group with so many egos at stake, not
everyone could get along.

Such a thought proves particularly relevant in the case of Wallace
Stevens. In 1921 Moore began to record numerous comments about
Stevens that mark her growing interest in his poetry and his elusive
person, a generous curiosity shared by few of her artistic peers. On the
whole, Moore's diaries reveal the uneasy attitude of the modernist set
toward Stevens, whom Moore's peers viewed with a mixture of profes-
sional respect and personal distaste. In the spring of 1921 Moore tran-
scribed a conversation between H.D., then newly arrived in the United
States for a visit after the First World War, and Alfred Kreymborg:

> HILDA: This is my first introduction to the world of poets in Amer-
>   ica.
>
> ALFRED: We have them by the gross.
>
> ALFRED: Was Wallace Stevens at the party the other night?
>
> HILDA: No, but I saw him. He was *more* than ever a terrible snob.⁵

The tendency to find Stevens personally abrasive was certainly not lim-
ited to H.D. Moore's notebooks indicate that even those who appreciated
Stevens's poetry had difficulty reconciling the work with the man. Poet
and critic Yvor Winters, a fan of both Moore and Stevens, had a hard
time keeping his patience in the face of Stevens's apparent rudeness.
Winters reported to Moore a comment he heard from fellow poet
Glenway Wescott about Stevens's epistolary manner. As Moore recorded
Winters's report, Wescott said that Stevens

> wrote as if he were the Czar of Russia, made the 4th person of the
> Trinity. [Stevens] said about my poems—"It is asking too much of
> such sophisticated poems that they should fly but at least they trem-
> ble and shake."⁶

The picture of Stevens that emerges in Moore's transcriptions is that of a haughty and reticent man unable or unwilling to accommodate his artistic acquaintances with the proper courtesies.

Despite Stevens's tendency to aggravate his peers, however, Moore's diaries reveal her own sense that Stevens's rudeness might issue, not from arrogance, but from insecurity. Damned for her own haughty and emotionless verse, for her "psychological uneasiness" and "scornful intellect," Moore perceived that she and Stevens were, perhaps, misinterpreted as heartless or snobby for much the same reasons. Moore recorded a conversation she had with Archibald MacLeish on the subject of Stevens following the publication of *Harmonium* that speaks to her more generous assessment of Stevens's standoffishness:

MR. MACLEISH: I know somebody that's very anxious to meet you—that is Wallace Stevens. I went to see him and at first he was very shy. He thought I wanted to interview him but afterward he talked a great deal about his work. I asked him if he were going to get another book out. His wife seems to be not much interested, a good deal of a millstone. They've been married 15 years and now they are going to have their first baby and he said he thought the baby would have to be his next book of poems. He is financially hampered I think, worried I think about expenses; a baby's quite an undertaking you know. He makes a good deal of money, that is what he does is well paid, but he has to keep at [his insurance] work rather closely and I think he finds that trying. You know something seems wrong to me about a person's refusing to talk about his work. That affected indifference seems insincere.

MYSELF: Well, I think it is the result of a really acute and intensely concentrated interest in the work and a sense of deprivation perhaps in not being able to get at writing things which one is very eager to do. . . .

> I think I understand his aloofness, although I've
> never met him.[7]

Where MacLeish interprets Stevens's unwillingness to talk about his verse as a matter of snobbish affectation, Moore attributes Stevens's reticence to both profound creative passion and intense artistic frustration. His inability to write what and how he wishes, his "sense of deprivation," causes his feigned indifference. Trapped in the demands of everyday life yet yearning for poetry, Stevens adopts his apparent "aloofness" in artistic matters to protect himself from a painful sense of thwarted effort—he pretends not to care about his verse simply because he cares so deeply. Moore reads Stevens as a compulsive poet who, disappointed in his artistic quest, would rather keep his troubles to himself.

Moore's interpretation of Stevens's aloofness rings once more of a goodly amount of self-projection. Moore often equated deep feeling with restraint—the more at stake, the more difficult the speech. Moore too felt the pull of everyday necessities and suffered pangs in her career at the thought of sharing work or ideas she felt less than fully developed. As she wrote to Yvor Winters, her one champion, after the disastrous 1922 *Poetry* symposium on her unauthorized *Poems*: "Speaking of the harassing circumstances under which you labor reminds me of certain difficulties under which I have labored—from arty contemporaries. I feel, however, that being thwarted in one's preferences is not an insuperable disadvantage so long as one has occasional space to breathe, and quiet."[8] Intuiting that she and Stevens might share certain difficulties—that their poetic aloofness and reserve might be similarly misconstrued—Moore's image of Stevens as a static and rapacious Bluebeard started to fade in the mid-1920s under her growing sense of Stevens's artistic insecurities and struggles with imaginative deprivation. Where Moore envisioned Bluebeard as permanently and decadently ensconced in his turquoise tower, she pictured Stevens the man as struggling passionately against obstacles to achieve visions that inevitably left him dissatisfied. Yvor Winters himself noted a pertinent similarity between Moore's and Stevens's attitudes toward their poetry in a letter to Moore dated June 6, 1921. After complimenting Moore's latest verse, Winters, then a brash young man of twenty, offered her some friendly, if somewhat presumptuous, advice:

It would be a kindly act on your part, I think, to publish a book—I know many people who want your poems, and want them badly, and it is very difficult to gather them up from magazines, especially if one lives in the desert as I do. Why won't you? I hope you don't have Mr. Stevens' unwashed aversion to book-publication. It *is* untidy, you know. People who leave poems littered around in the magazines are so very much like people who leave papers around in the parks. But that, I suppose, is their own affair.[9]

Winters accused both Moore and Stevens of being shy, self-deprecating perfectionists for whom all previous poems, never good enough in retrospect, become trash. Stevens himself made no bones about his distaste for collecting his own verse. During his struggle to put *Harmonium* together Stevens wrote to Harriet Monroe that producing a book was a painful project because "to pick a crisp salad from the garbage of the past" was "no snap."[10] As Winters sensed, Moore shared Stevens's "unwashed aversion" to formal literary events, a fact confirmed by the drastic measures Bryher and H.D. took on her behalf. Book publication marked Moore's poetry as a finished product rather than a process and preserved poems the poet already felt as old or inadequate. As their responses to the trial of publication confirm, both Moore and Stevens shared a horror of perceived totalizing moments. Neither felt comfortable enshrining their verses within the finalizing confines of a book. Both shunned a hardening of the poetic personality.

Ironically, Stevens's reticence proved as problematic as his apparent arrogance. When Stevens finally did produce a volume in September 1923, Moore's conversation diaries reveal a sense among his peers that perhaps he had waited too long to make his book and there was no "crisp salad" left to pick out of Stevens's self-acknowledged dump. Moore records snatches of a conversation she had with fellow poet Glenway Wescott in which Wescott's comments make Stevens's verse seem, at best, passé:

Glenway—Stevens—In these early things there are the seeds of his rhetoric, aren't there? Like him better without nightgowns. Its a nice tune. . . . Its a contraption. Sensationalisme. Its a thrust. He ought to have placated his admirers earlier. Its too late now.[11]

In Wescott's view, Stevens's volume offered little more than a retrospective, a look back to the verse of an earlier self that Stevens had already outgrown. *Harmonium* played a nice tune, but Stevens's instrument struck Wescott as little more than a passing French fad that could not sustain poetic interest. In the absence of an earlier collection, Wescott feared that Stevens's "fans," few as they were, had moved on.

Wescott's grim pronouncement about Stevens's career, "Its too late now," must have proved particularly ominous to Moore, who, as of 1923, still had not released a book of verse in her native country. The sense that she, like Stevens, could be forgotten or passed over in the absence of a volume made her all the more eager to pay attention to Stevens's work when *Harmonium* finally appeared. Moore received her first copy of *Harmonium* in mid-October of 1923 from Yvor Winters, who remained Stevens's advocate despite their differences. On October 30, 1923, Moore wrote to Winters, "I think you can hardly guess what a satisfaction it is to me to have these Stevens poems which I have been so wishing to see."[12] Soon after receiving Winters's gift, Moore met with Scofield Thayer, and the two decided that Moore should review the book for Thayer's *Dial*. Moore carefully records the date of her conversation with Thayer in her notebooks (November 3, 1923), enshrining alongside it a single comment of Thayer's about Stevens: "I like his poems. I rather wish I didn't, I dislike him so personally."[13] Despite Thayer's obvious distaste for Stevens the man, Moore forged ahead with her critique and completed her review of *Harmonium* in record time. Moore sent her finished piece, "Well Moused, Lion," to the *Dial* a scant nine days after she and Thayer met, an indication that her study of Stevens to date was cumulative and ongoing rather than a wholly new project requiring significant research.[14]

On the whole, "Well Moused, Lion," constitutes an important readjustment of Moore's reading of Stevens and his verse that surfaced in "People's Surroundings." In "Well Moused, Lion," Moore, once again, critiques Stevens's moments of imaginative savagery. Yet, rather than condemn such instances as the product of sheer poetic egotism—the creative will turned cannibal king—Moore draws on her dawning notion of Stevens's artistic struggles and begins to fashion an image of Stevens as a poet under psychological siege. Where in "People's Surroundings" Moore pictured Stevens as Bluebeard lodged in a perpetual palace of static and predatory ideals, in "Well Moused, Lion" Moore's dominant sense of Stevens's verse is that of constant, and often unnerving, change—the poet constantly, and desperately, in search of what will suffice.[15] "In his book," she remarks at the opening of her review, "he calls imagination 'the will of things,' 'the magnificent cause of being,' and demonstrates how imagination may evade 'the world without imagination'; effecting an escape which, in certain manifestations of bravura, is uneasy rather than bold" (*CPrMM*, 91). Stevens's poems, Moore implies, often do not reflect the confidence of his aesthetic assertions. He may claim that the imagination is "the magnificent cause of being," but many of his lyrics betray his doubts about the very imaginative structures he creates. Moore reads Stevens's poetic "bravura," his musical skill and agility, as nervous whistling in the dark—the anxious intonings of a poet who craves the ideal yet fears that no product of the mind can ever truly avail his escape from a difficult world. Frightened of being trapped in the mundane "world without imagination," Stevens insists on imaginative excess, and his tendency to overreach—to change and change and change—becomes a sign of his own persistent skeptical anxiety that no one creation can satisfy for long.

Taking the uneasy nature of Stevens's escapes as a starting point for her analysis, Moore ponders what she sees as the poet's two minds—his apparent belief in the noble and synthetic power of the imagination and his undeniable distrust of its power. On the one hand, Moore admires what seem to be Stevens's moments of lyric surety. "One feels," she writes of his volume, "an achieved remoteness as in Tu Muh's lyric criticism: 'Powerful is the painting . . . and high is it hung on the spotless wall in the lofty hall of your mansion'" (*CPrMM*, 91). In some of Stevens's poems Moore detects the calm assertive confidence of a strong and lofty intelligence able to rise above common concerns and find itself, like Crispin, "'free / and more than free, elate, intent, profound'" (*CPrMM*, 92). Moore appreciates the "resilience and certitude" of "Hymn from a Watermelon Pavilion" and discerns Stevens's "positiveness, aplomb, and verbal security"—his sage "mind and method of China"—in "Metaphors of a Magnifico." In the matter of diction, Moore favorably compares Stevens to Shakespeare and states that he shares the bard's "immunity to fear" and "is properly courageous" with his words. Like Shakespeare, Stevens takes "liberties" with his speech, but he does not give the effect of "presumptuous egotism" or "unavoided outlandishness" (CPrMM, 94). At many points in her review, Moore credits Stevens with the imaginative poise of an accomplished master who has complete control and confidence in his poetic power. "There is the love of magnificence and the effect of it in these sharp, solemn, rhapsodic, elegant pieces of eloquence," Moore writes admiringly of Stevens's proper, correct, and profound verses. Quoting some of her favorite lines from Harmonium, Moore envisions Stevens's imagination as "'The young emerald, evening star,' 'tranquilizing . . . the torments of confusion'" (CPrMM, 93). Bringing imaginative peace and order out of chaos, Stevens proves his faith in the controlled imagination as the "magnificent cause of being."

Yet, side by side with the calm, secure, and lofty Stevens, Moore detects the less certain workings of an apparently more troubled mind. His moments of tranquil assurance give way to a confusion of colors and sounds, an "infinitude of variation" that often produces, in Moore's view, a dizzying and uneasy imaginative excess. "The riot of gorgeousness in which Mr. Stevens's imagination takes refuge," Moore remarks, "recalls Balzac's reputed attitude to money, to which he was indifferent unless he could have it 'in heaps or by the ton'" (CPrMM, 92). In the extremity of his imaginative verve, Stevens's aplomb and certitude come to "riot" as his "rage for order" becomes more rage than arrangement. Craving imagination "in heaps or by the ton," Stevens, Moore suggests, often reaches a point in his wilder poems where he can no longer keep track of his riches. His images frequently lie in a mass, not sorted but heaped in a way that reflects confusion rather than noble order. "One is excited," Moore admits, "by the sense of proximity to Java peacocks, golden pheasants, South American macaw feather capes, Chilcat blankets, hair seal needlework, Singalese masks, and Rousseau's paintings of banana leaves and alligators," but the exotic profusion and tonal bravura of Stevens's poems also impress Moore as the high-pitched products of insecurity (CPrMM, 92). Doubting the balm of his visions and fearing the restrictions of the mundane, Stevens protests too much, offering excessive evidence of his fluency that, in Moore's view, betrays both his dislike of the bare realities of the actual world and his anxieties about finding a poem that will suffice for his escape. Stevens's verse, Moore remarks, "gives ultimately the effect of the mind disturbed by the intangible; of a mind oppressed by the properties of the world which it is expert in manipulating" (*CPrMM*, 93). Both "disturbed" by the world with imagination, and "oppressed" by the world without imagination, Stevens strikes Moore as a difficult skeptic who, while writing poems "suggestive of masterly equipoise," cannot, in truth, find his balance.

Indeed, Moore frequently finds Stevens's dissatisfaction at the root of his poetic agitation. Moore complains:

There is a certain bellicose sensitiveness in

> I do not know which to prefer . . .
> The blackbird whistling
> Or just after,

and in the characterization of the snow man who

> . . . nothing himself, beholds
> Nothing that is not there and the nothing that is.

(*CPrMM*, 94)

Moore casts Stevens's poetic indecision—his inability to choose between the natural sound of the blackbird (the actual) and the poet's reflection inspired by the song (the imagination)—as unnecessarily quarrelsome.[16] His consistent arguments against the sufficiency of his own creations reveal a mind in some ways too readily disturbed—a mind, like the snow man's, unwilling or unable to consistently assert its identity or create lofty, ordered thoughts. In Moore's view, Stevens's nervous and skeptical dissatisfaction leads ultimately to overt hostility against all forces that threaten his imaginative escape. Indeed, Moore finds his most violent efforts to prove the power of his mind downright insulting. "One resents the temper of certain of these poems," writes Moore:

Mr. Stevens is never inadvertently crude; one is conscious, however, of a deliberate bearishness—a shadow of acrimonious, unprovoked contumely. Despite the sweet-Clementine-will-you-be-mine non-chalance of the "Apostrophe to Vincentine," one feels oneself to be in danger of unearthing the ogre and in "Last Looks at the Lilacs," a pride in unserviceableness is suggested which makes it a microcosm of cannibalism. (*CPrMM*, 93)

Moore complains that, in certain poems, Stevens attempts to effect his escape at the expense of all poetic decorum, giving way to his rage against convention in a way that Moore judges uncontrolled and consciously unkind to his audience. Where, in his calmer moments, Stevens offers his readers beautiful and noble visions that tranquilize "the torments of confusion," Moore argues that Stevens disdains such propriety and utility in his less secure verses and, in his frantic attempt to shake his mind free of old thoughts, resorts to vulgar images meant merely to shock. Feeding on taboo subjects, Stevens the imaginative cannibal violates the deepest of social codes.

Moore thus discerns two different poets in the pages of *Harmonium*: one controlled, secure, solemn, and lofty; one angry, riotous, and, ultimately, rude. Yet, even while Moore chastises Stevens for his wilder moments of poetic impropriety and anxiety, throughout her review she is most apt to praise Stevens for what she claims to despise. Moore asserts that, in "its nimbleness con brio," "Nomad Exquisite" is a piece of that "ferocity" for which she "values Mr. Stevens most: 'As the immense dew of Florida / Brings forth / The big-finned palm / And green vine angering for life'" (*CPrMM*, 94–95). Moore revels in the intensity, opulence, and anger of Stevens's "flambeaued manner." "Imagination implies energy," she states approvingly of his poems, "and imagination of the finest type involves an energy which results in order 'as the motion of a snake's body goes through all parts at once, and its violation acts at the same instant in coils that go contrary ways'" (*CPrMM*, 96). Fascinated by the same contradictory and skeptical energy that she finds disturbing, Moore openly admires the exciting motion that results from Stevens's poetic "violations" as he creates and decreates in turn—slithering free, again and again, of any idea or image that threatens to become banal. Referring again to her reptilian image, Moore claims that Stevens's verse "recalls the snake in *Far Away and Long Ago,* 'moving like quicksilver in a rope-like stream' or the conflict at sea when after a storm, the wind shifts and waves are formed counter to those still running" (*CPrMM,* 97).

According to Celeste Goodridge, Moore's image of the quicksilver snake refers to Stevens's inaccessibility and unpredictability, a reflection of his tendency to disappear, uncontainable as mercury, behind an ever changing array of poetic disguises.[17] Although I agree with Goodridge's reading—certainly Stevens's changeability lies at the heart of Moore's interest—I see Moore's image as a further reference to her lurking if reluctant enthusiasm for Stevens's provisionalizing intelligence. Placed next to an image of deconstructive mental conflict—the waves after a violent poetic storm that undo or undercut the direction of those thoughts just penned—the quicksilver snake appears as an image of endless internal opposition. Like the sea, the snake moves in waves, pressing against itself and contradicting its own motions in a way that Moore sees as both fascinating and dangerous. Like quicksilver itself, the snake is beautiful and poisonous. Moore compliments Stevens for the flowing and ferocious nature of his poetic even while she fears that, in its violent attempts to escape the confinement of any one belief or common utterance, such tormented verse, raging beyond controlled poetic decorum, might coil and strike those who gaze on its brilliance.

Moore thus takes a kind of guilty pleasure in Stevens's gorgeousness and appreciates the riot that often seems at odds with her own sense of the imagination's loftier and more orderly missions. At the end of her review, Moore ultimately decides that the dangers implicit in Stevens's endless violent contradictions are worth the risk, but the tenor of her finish is hesitant. After listing several poems she would rather Stevens not have omitted from his collection, she concludes:

> However, in this collection one has eloquence. "The author's violence is for aggrandizement and not for stupor"; one consents therefore, to the suggestion that when the book of moonlight is written, we leave room for Crispin. In the event of moonlight and a veil to be made gory, he would, one feels, be appropriate in this legitimately sensational act of a ferocious jungle animal. (*CPrMM,* 98)

In her final lines of "Well Moused, Lion," Moore adopts a tone of judicial authority that bespeaks exoneration as much as praise. Having heard the evidence both for and against Stevens, she "consents" to the suggestion that Stevens's wilder poetic acts are "appropriate" and "legitimate" as if condoning his violent crimes. His poems increase our range of sensations rather than diminish them, so the lion's bloodier leaps, the judge decides, should be excused under the prevailing laws. Moore appreciates the power of Stevens's imaginative rage but feels compelled to place his verse in relation to what she sees as the authorized boundaries of poetic decorum.

"Well Moused, Lion" thus stands as a testament to Moore's changing opinions about Stevens's verse in the early 1920s. Like the snake in the stream or the lion on the loose, the violent and riotous manifestations of Stevens's imagination elicit Moore's admiration, but she also fears such utterances as the nervous, antisocial products of a mind that wanders too far in its attempt to escape old tropes and beliefs. Stevens's distrust of imagined constructs leads him to endless acts of poetic subversion—violations that Moore finds both exciting and unnerving in their denial of any stable and recognizable ideas of order.

Indeed, as Moore's conclusion indicates, the Stevens of *Harmonium* reminds her of none other than Shelley. In the months prior to her composition of "Well Moused, Lion" Moore embarked on something of a study of Shelley; as her reading diaries reveal, she collected articles about the poet and reread "A Defence of Poetry" with attention. Moore's image of Stevens's "veil to be made gory" recalls a familiar passage from Shelley's "Defence" that Moore copied into her notebook dated 1923:

> All things exist as they are perceived: at least in relation to the percipient. "The mind is its own place, and of itself can make a heaven of hell, a hell of heaven." But poetry defeats the curse which binds us to be subjected to the accident of surrounding impressions. And whether it spreads its own figured curtain or withdraws life's dark veil from before the scene of things, it equally creates for us a being within our being. It makes us the inhabitants of a world to which the familiar world is a chaos. It reproduces the common universe of which we are portions and percipients, and it purges from our inward sight the film of familiarity which obscures from us

the wonder of our being. It compels us to feel that which we perceive, and to imagine that which we know. It creates anew the universe after it has been annihilated in our minds by the recurrence of impressions blunted by reiteration.[18]

In Moore's view, Stevens, like Shelley, sees poetry as a means to remove from our minds the "dark veil" of habitual thoughts—the "film of familiarity"—that, as Shelley puts it, "obscures from us the wonder of our being." Moore's reference to Shelley's veil in "Well Moused, Lion" casts Stevens as a poet forever in search of new tropes. Each universe he creates grows old, "blunted by reiteration," and must be remade in turn, the veil of mental habit stripped again and again. "The mind in creation is as a fading coal," writes Shelley in "A Defence of Poetry," "which some invisible influence like an inconstant wind, awakens to transitory brightness: this power arises from within, like the colour of a flower which fades and changes as it is developed."[19] Like the veil, Shelley's image of the fading coal appears in Moore's reading diary of 1923 and offers her a further analogue to Stevens's poetic alternations.[20] Drawing on Shelley's representation of the creative mind as a colored flower that blooms brightly but dims with age, Moore describes Stevens's verse in "Well Moused, Lion" as "hypnotically incandescent like the rose tinged fringe of the night blooming cereus" (CPrMM, 95), a tropical plant that flowers in the dark and produces large garish blossoms that last only a few hours before they wilt. In Moore's view, Stevens's poetry takes Shelley's sense of the transitory brightness of the imagination to new extremes. In the verse of both poets, each thought, or flower, grows old and fades under the weight of blunted impressions. Moore's metaphor, however, transforms Shelley's generic flower into an exotic and gaudy expression of Stevens's imaginative ferocity that parallels her mention of his "veil to be made gory." Where Shelley's poetry merely removes the veil of worn ideas, Moore insists that Stevens's verse tears it to bloody pieces. In the violence of his frequent imaginative rendings, Stevens, to Moore's mind, proves a more savage and changeable Romantic than Shelley.

Glancing back to Shelley, then, Moore corrects her earlier projection of Stevens in "People's Surroundings" as the deadly proprietor of Bluebeard's tower—a self-absorbed poet who exists in a sealed and static world of his own making that petrifies his subjects and "refutes the clock." In "Well Moused, Lion," Moore reads Stevens, through Shelley, as a dissatisfied Romantic devoted to constant intellectual change, a poet both oppressed by the world without the imagination and disturbed by the world with the imagination. "Well Moused, Lion" still casts Stevens as in some ways a dangerous poet, but in her review Moore fears only the most extreme indiscretions of his temporary poetic violence rather than the consistently cannibalistic nature of his stasis. In Moore's view, the Stevens of *Harmonium* commits the occasional "microcosm of cannibalism," but, distrusting his own visions, he no longer, like Bluebeard, consumes his wives in turn. Moore replaces the furious Shelleyan "azure" of Stevens's imagination that she invokes as an image of petrified permanence in "People's Surroundings" with a series of images in "Well Moused, Lion" that picture Stevens's imagination as Shelley's fading coal—a force that both waxes and wanes.

In seems that in her rereading of Stevens, however, Moore trades one dissatisfaction for another. Recuperating Stevens from her earlier critique of detached decadence, Moore reconceives his poetic as one at war with itself, given to difficult and thwarted attempts at order. In Moore's view, both Stevens and Shelley struggle against worn visions in a way that defeats the threat of mental stasis but, in doing so, challenges the construction of all stable, comforting, or coherent ideals. As her image of the poisonous snake in the stream suggests, Moore senses that in their vibrant beauty such conflicted verses may prove a false temptation, like Eve's temptation in the garden, to the abandonment of all secure beliefs. In the violent turmoil of their poems, both Stevens and Shelley pose significant questions about a priori order and transcendent vision that Moore takes up on a cosmic scale in her great poem of the 1920s, "An Octopus."

"An Octopus" is in part the result of two trips Moore made to the Northwest, the first in July 1922 and the second the following summer of 1923, to visit her brother Warner, a chaplain in the navy stationed at a base near Seattle. During the first of her two stays, Moore traveled with her family up to Paradise Park, a large alpine meadow on Mount Rainier that overlooks the grand eight-pronged Nisqually glacier—"an octopus of ice." Moore began compiling notes and collecting materials for "An Octopus" between her two trips to Washington, but she did not begin to craft the poem in earnest until the late summer of 1923.[21] Moore's work on "An Octopus" thus coincides with both her review of *Harmonium*, begun and completed in November of 1923, and her study of Shelley, ongoing during both 1922 and 1923. Moore's thoughts on both Stevens and Shelley find their way into her poem. An address to a high, white, glaciered Mount Rainier "damned for its sacrosanct remoteness," "An Octopus" constitutes Moore's response to Shelley's romantic quest for ultimate knowledge in "Mont Blanc." Like Shelley, Moore approaches her mountain in search of the intelligence or "hidden power" that may or may not order the everlasting universe of things. Probing the mountain with her mind, Moore tries her best to understand its nature and discern its agency, only to find, like both Shelley and Stevens, that attempts at stable or unifying vision are, for the poet of particulars, inherently slippery.

"An Octopus" begins with a difficult view of the glacier that, as Patricia Willis puts it, combines "land and sea, rock and cephalopod."[22] As Moore's opening lines suggest, Mount Rainier, like Mont Blanc, does not easily give up its secrets:

An Octopus

Of ice. Deceptively reserved and flat,
it lies "in grandeur and in mass"
beneath a sea of shifting snow dunes;
dots of cyclamen red and maroon on its clearly defined pseudopodia
made of glass that will bend—a much needed invention—
comprising twenty-eight icefields from fifty to five hundred feet thick,
of unimagined delicacy.
"Picking periwinkles from the cracks"
or killing prey with the concentric crushing rigour of the python,
it hovers forward "spider fashion
on its arms" misleadingly like lace;
its "ghostly pallor changing
to the green metallic tinge of an anemone starred pool."[23]

Viewed from a distance and obscured by blowing snow, the glacier at first appears static and featureless—a "geographical blank," as Moore terms it in her notes, that supplies no ready evidence of a controlling intelligence or a connection to human concerns.²⁴ Yet, Moore states that the glacier's flatness and reserve are "deceptive"; the mass of ice may seem empty, but as her opening lines suggest, some hidden and mysterious force lurks within. Adopting the pose of a cartographer, Moore attempts to describe and delineate the glacier—to determine the nature of its power—in a way that consciously reveals the difficulty of her task. From the scientist's point of view, the tentacles of the octopus glacier seem "clearly defined," as transparent and potentially revealing as window glass. The whole of the massive formation may be charted and plotted and counted—"twenty-eight icefields from fifty to five hundred feet thick." Moore quickly implies, however, that such easy definitions are a delusion. Comprised of "glass that will bend," the glacier may, Moore suggests, constitute a kind of fun-house mirror that merely gives back distorted pictures of the human observer's thoughts and categories. The "clearly defined" feet of the glacier become, in Moore's paradoxical juxtaposition, (pseudo)podia—false forms that bear no genuine relation to the clear surface definitions they suggest. On the heels of her numerical calculations of the glacier, Moore states that, despite such attempted reductions, the mountain remains a place of "unimagined delicacy," a site of exquisite rarities and intricacies beyond the reach of the human mind. Turning her attention to the glacier's motion, Moore displays the strength of the ice even as she questions her ability to name or define its power. Unstoppable in its flow, Moore's glacier moves like an octopus, a spider, or a python; it hovers and crushes indiscriminately and instinctually, a brute inhuman force utterly alien to human intelligence and potentially hostile to human life itself. "Its 'ghostly pallor changing / to the green metallic tinge of an anemone starred pool,'" the glacier refutes its deadness but proves its strength in a way that gives little comfort. Moore's "geographical blank" becomes a place of stars, a small reflection of an even vaster universe that we can never truly know.

The ontological and epistemological questions Moore confronts in the opening of "An Octopus" thus resemble what Harold Bloom terms the subjects of "Mont Blanc": "the relation between individual mind and the universe, and also the problem of what rules the universe, and to what moral end."²⁵ Like Shelley, Moore pictures her mountain as a beautiful but potentially unknowable thing whose dangerous power may teach only an "awful doubt" of any benevolent design in nature. Moore's imputation of the mountain's inaccessibility, however, only makes her all the more eager to plumb its depths. Abandoning the role of the cartographer, Moore dons instead the hat of the naturalist and embarks on a quest for knowledge—an intellectual tour of the living particulars of the glacier that considers just how close the mind can come to sharing the mountain's secrets. As Patricia Willis notes, Moore guides the reader through two separate visual journeys in "An Octopus," each from the forest floor to the top of the surrounding peaks.[26] On her first trip up the mountain, Moore examines the glacier's fauna as her expedition moves from the property of the porcupine and the rat at the base, to the habitats of the beaver and the bear, to the goat who stands at the summit on "cliffs the colour of clouds." Returning to the forest floor, Moore climbs the mountain a second time to conduct a study of its flora that begins with the low-lying ferns and birch trees and ends with the Calypso orchid—"'the goat flower . . . fond of snow'"—that clings to the glacier's highest ledges. Rather than answer ontological questions, however, Moore's efforts to catalog the mountain consciously resist the quest for complete or ultimate knowledge.

Throughout both legs of her expedition, Moore encounters the glacier's rampant living diversity—a profusion that denies the all-too-human desire to find an order or a pattern to the universe of things. A place with "merits of equal importance / for bears, elk, deer, wolves, goats, and ducks," the ever-higher climes of the mountain constitute a complex environment full of agents and motions that humans cannot fully understand or, despite their best efforts, predict. The "'thoughtful beavers'" may fashion drains that "'seem the work of careful men with shovels,'" but Moore denies the appearance of discernable design in her following image of bears that make their way "unexpectedly" into the poem. Moore conducts the same sort of careful refusal in her description of the bears' den:

Composed of calcium gems and alabaster pillars,
topaz, tourmaline crystals, and amethyst quartz,
their den is somewhere else, concealed in the confusion

of "blue stone forests thrown together with marble and jasper and agate as if whole quarries had been dynamited."

"Concealed" and crystalline, the bears' den reflects the rich, beautiful interior of the mountain's deeper secrets that the mind can never truly know. Imagining the den as a gorgeous place artistically "composed" of gems and "pillars," Moore admits that such an ordered vision overstates her knowledge and belies her experience. Such an ideal image of design, however pleasant, cannot stand in the face of the visible violent "confusion" of rocks and trees "thrown together" by the mountain's haphazard and destructive forces. The den must remain forever "somewhere else," off the map and beyond the reach of human intelligence.

Moore thus undercuts her desire for stability and deconstructs the image of order that she presents, an act she repeats again for the sake of intellectual honesty on the mountain's highest peak. As the naturalist moves further up the mountain in her quest for knowledge, she enters icy and forbidding realms that, while less and less hospitable to human life, seem to offer access to a transcendent vision of the mountain's hidden truths:

> And farther up, in stag-at-bay position
> as a scintillating fragment of these terrible stalagmites,
> stands the goat,
> its eye fixed on the waterfall which never seems to fall—
> an endless skein swayed by the wind,
> immune to force of gravity in the perspective of the peaks.
> A special antelope
> acclimated to "grottoes from which issue penetrating draughts
> which make you wonder why you came,"
> it stands its ground
> on cliffs the colour of the clouds, of petrified white vapour—
> black feet, eyes, nose, and horns engraved on dazzling icefields,
> the ermine body on the crystal peak;
> the sun kindling its shoulders to maximum heat like acetylene,
> dyeing them white;
> upon this antique pedestal—
> "a mountain with those graceful lines which prove it a volcano,"
> its top a complete cone like Fujiyama's
> till an explosion blew it off.

On the highest ledges of the glacier, the naturalist's field of vision changes from one of physical particulars to the "perspective of the peaks," a scope that seems to promise the panoramic completeness of a better view. The farther up Moore's eye travels, however, the more rarified her vision of the universe of things becomes. In the poetic "perspective of the peaks" physical laws of gravity and entropy have no power. The waterfall does not fall, the goat becomes an idealized and ageless statue welded on an "antique pedestal," the borders between heaven and earth, cliffs and clouds, dissolve as the mountain becomes an image of eternal being. The glacier's "confusion" resolves into a beautifully composed order that Moore finds "scintillating" and "dazzling." Yet, as her verse connotes, she also finds such a sublime perspective inherently dangerous. Idealizing vision, in denying confusion and change, denies life itself. The goat on the summit stands frozen in "stag-at-bay" position, the very image of a creature trapped by hostile forces. Moore suggests that the poet who attempts to keep the world's confusion endlessly "at bay" is, like the proprietor of Bluebeard's tower, a hunter who kills his subjects by turning them into beautiful objects. Like Bluebeard, the poet on the peak "dyes" his subject to match his beliefs, a word that aurally suggests the deadly nature of his imposition.

Moore's journey to the top of the mountain thus results in an intriguing paradox. The "perspective of the peaks" that promises a better view of the mountain—that is, a knowledge of its hidden power—in fact destroys the poet's ability to see the mountain at all. By Moore's account, the poet who fashions the glacier into a symbol of eternal presence and claims to see more and more of its "true" meaning in fact sees less and less of the mountain's substance. Dyeing the goat, the clouds, and the cliffs a gleaming and empty white, the poet on the summit erases the very objects she meant to contemplate. Moore dismisses the poet's supposed vision of the mountain's higher truths as a vacant artistic fantasy. Choosing the confusion of the unknowable over the ordered stasis of false and blinding belief, Moore ultimately rejects the "perspective of the peaks" in another violent image of mutability and ends her vision of the goat with a volcanic explosion that destroys the imagination's petrifying abuses. The squirming facts of the mountain's disordered physical presence exceed the squamous mind, and Moore ends her ascent by falling back down to the mountain's base:

> Maintaining many minds, distinguished by a beauty
> of which "the visitor dare never fully speak at home
> for fear of being stoned as an impostor,"
> Big Snow Mountain is the home of a diversity of creatures . . .

"Distinguished," or made separate by an undefinable, unknowable, and unspeakable power, the mountain's mysteries remain hidden from the minds that perceive its surface. Moore fiercely deconstructs her own insufficient moment of fixed, singular, transcendent fiction and returns to a chaos of "many minds," a skeptical disorder of ideas that negates the notion that human knowledge can ever be complete.

Opting to dwell in an honest confusion of "nothing that is not there," the empty world that Stevens's snow poet finds after all imaginative imposition has been stripped away, Moore returns to an account of the particulars of the physical mountain and seems to reach a resting point in the welter of experience. Yet, no sooner does Moore complete one thwarted trip up the mountain in quest of an ultimate idea of order than she begins another. Turning her attention upward to the circling flight of "the eleven eagles of the west," the naturalist comments: "They make a nice appearance don't they, / happy seeing nothing?" The eagles' "nothing" rings of the "nothing" in the last line of Stevens's "The Snow Man"—"the nothing that is." Untroubled by the ontological questions that wrack the speaker, the eagles live at peace in a natural presence—an "isness"—that the human mind interprets as utter absence—a "nothing." The implication that the natural world, deprived of governing intelligence, is empty of human meaning drives the naturalist back up the mountain in search of answers.

Shifting her attention from the glacier's animals to its plants, Moore makes a second bid for the summit and constructs another catalog of the living mountain that attempts to tap its riches. Once again, Moore's journey reveals a struggle between the mountain's shifting diversity and the mind's desire for discernable design. At the start of her second journey, the naturalist perceives the fungi on the glacier as a "cavalcade of calico" whose color competes with the "original American 'menagerie of styles'" present in the flowers:

Larkspur, blue pincushions, blue peas, and lupin;
white flowers with white, and red with red;
the blue ones "growing close together
so that patches of them look like blue water in the distance":
this arrangement of colours
as in Persian designs of hard stones with enamel,
forms a pleasing equation—
a diamond outside; and inside, a white dot;
on the outside, a ruby; inside, a red dot;
black spots balanced with black
in the woodlands where fires have run over the ground . . .

The naturalist breaks off her scientific catalog of the different types of wildflowers and, intrigued or distracted by the thought of the glacier as a homespun quilt, begins to consider the "arrangement" of the colors rather than the particulars of the plants. The living flora suddenly become "patches" of red, white, and blue—a vision of domestic order that implies the controlling touch of a careful and caring hand. Seduced by her own image of beauty and comfort, the naturalist eventually transmutes the glacier's confusion into a hard-and-fast mosaic design, an idea of order that, like her vision of the goat-statue on the mountain's summit, changes living things into static works of art. Once more, however, Moore insists that the glacier cannot be contained by such a picture, no matter how "pleasing" the "equation" between mountain and mosaic and its implication of a guiding intelligence in nature. The black spots in the design are, in fact, the random products of rampaging forest fires that have run loose over the ground. Moore's reference to the destructive and chaotic power of nature undermines the all-too-easy notion of the glacier as carefully and benevolently composed.

Upon reaching the sublime "perspective of the peaks" a second time, Moore admits that the mind's search for the mountain's ultimate truths has been misguided. Atop the cold glacial ledges, Moore finds the Calypso orchid or "goat flower," the floral counterpart to the goat that inhabits the same peak. Named for the seductive sea nymph Calypso, who offers Ulysses refuge and immortality on her magnificent isle, the snowy orchid suggests that the "perspective of the peaks" offers merely a pleasing and potentially dangerous retreat rather than the honest end to a quest. Those who claim access to transcendental absolutes indulge in easy illusions that Moore deems solipsistic reveries. Glancing back to the opening of the poem, Moore makes a connection between the goat flower, the goat in "stag-at-bay" position, and the part of the glacier called "The Goat's Mirror— / that lady-fingerlike depression in the shape of the left human foot, / which prejudices you in favour of itself." Like the Goat's Mirror, each subsequent summit view of the goat image invites the naturalist to read some trace of human intelligence in the landscape. To interpret the mountain as a footprint of cosmic order, however, merely leaves us gazing, like Narcissus, at our own mirrored reflection.

Thoughts of Ulysses and Calypso inspire Moore to thoughts of the ancient Greeks, the founders of Western philosophy and the first in a long line of metaphysical questioners. Despite their obvious wisdom, Moore reads the Greeks as mirror gazers, hopelessly duped by the neat intellectual products of their own making. Assured of the power of the mind and disliking confusion, the Greeks chose to live on the transcendental mountaintop and adopted the static and prideful perspective of the peaks. "The Greeks liked smoothness," Moore explains,

> distrusting what was back
> of what could not be clearly seen,
> resolving with benevolent conclusiveness,
> "complexities which will remain complexities
> as long as the world lasts. . ."

A people of conclusions rather than curiosity, the Greeks closed themselves off from nature's chaos and mentally resolved the mysteries of existence that Moore insists are, for the truthful poet, unknowable quantities. Moore's critique of the Greeks leads her, through a reference to Milton, back to Shelley's "A Defence of Poetry." "All things exist as they are perceived: at least in relation to the percipient," writes Shelley in "A Defence," and he follows his claim with an exemplary quote from Satan in *Paradise Lost:* "'The mind is its own place, and of itself can make a heaven of hell, a hell of heaven.'"[27] Recalling Shelley's comment on perception, Moore casts the Greeks as "happy souls in Hell." Content to spin neat and static abstractions to explain the mountain's power, the Greeks remained blissfully ignorant of nature's unruly and unresolvable particulars. In Moore's view, the Greeks made a heaven of the hell more skeptical intelligences, alive to the pangs of doubt and committed to doing hard things, cannot escape.

Disgusted with the impudent knowingness of the Greeks, Moore turns upon them and the present-day public who also desire easy answers, with the violence she wields against her own creations throughout the poem. "Neatness of finish! Neatness of finish!" Moore exclaims in frustration, "Relentless accuracy is the nature of this octopus / with its capacity for fact." As Moore has proved to her own growing dissatisfaction throughout the poem, "neatness" and "accuracy" are antithetical terms. Moore's phrase "neatness of finish" implies that those who intellectually resolve the world's confusion merely apply a surface coating to experience that ignores the complexities beneath. While it is the nature of the glacier to be relentlessly accurate—that is to forever resist such errors of human vision—it is equally the nature of the mind to impose reductive designs on what it perceives. As if attempting to wipe all trace of "neatness" from her sight, Moore ends "An Octopus" with a final, terrifying vision of the mountain's chaotic and unfathomable power:

> "Creeping slowly as with meditated stealth,
> its arms seeming to approach from all directions,"
> it receives one under winds that "tear the snow to bits
> and hurl it like a sandblast,
> shearing off twigs and loose bark from the trees."
> Is tree the word for these strange things
> "flat on the ground like vines"?
> some "bent in a half circle with branches on one side
> suggesting dustbrushes, not trees. . ."

The mind here does not receive or take mental possession of the mountain but rather is "received" by the mountain on its own chaotic terms. Moore pictures the glacier's violent winds and snow as a "sandblast," an air-driven stream of sand specifically designed to remove an unwanted coating from an object and clean its surface. The poet who strips away all "neatness of finish" from the mountain, however, enters an alien landscape of disordered impressions that "approach from all directions" and threaten to bury the poet alive. Lost in the mountain's strange and mindless whiteness, the poet lacks the power to express what she sees. The mountain's true nature, Moore concludes, lies beyond language itself. Words become just one more "neatness of finish," an intelligible abstract surface of the mind's making that can never reach the truth beneath. Convinced of the ultimate folly of her attempt to plumb the mountain's secrets in a poem, Moore ends "An Octopus" with a final violent image that again denies the mind's desire to see the glacier as a product of design:

> the glassy octopus symmetrically pointed,
> its claw cut by the avalanche
> "with a sound like the crack of a rifle,
> in a curtain of powdered snow launched like a waterfall."

Moore's image of the glacier's ordered geometric symmetry ends in a chaotic avalanche. Ringing the curtain down on the poem itself, Moore violently unmakes her own fiction and leaves the mountain as she found it—a geographical blank that the mind must fill once again.

Moore thus joins both Stevens and Shelley in composing a great poem of romantic winter vision. Like Stevens's speaker in "The Snow Man," Moore's poet attempts to remove the imagination's neat finish from the world and confront nature in all its relentless accuracy. The quest to see "nothing that is not there," however, leads the poet to a cold, white space beyond human reason where all efforts to create meaning, including language, break down. Moore thus asks the same question of Mount Rainier at the end of "An Octopus" that Shelley poses to his peak at the end of "Mont Blanc": "And what were thou, and earth, and stars, and sea, / If to the human mind's imaginings / Silence and solitude were vacancy?" Moore's implied answer echoes Stevens's reply to Shelley's query in "The Snow Man": the mountain without the imagination is "nothing" since only the mind can assign value and transform the mountain into something more than an indifferent and destructive waste of confusion. "The deep truth," Shelley states, "is imageless," and Moore agrees.

The question that remains for Moore at the end of "An Octopus," then, is how do we live in such a world? Moore concludes that to see a benevolent pattern in nature, however attractive, is to indulge an unsupportable and impudent fantasy. Any claim of access to transcendent truth, an idea of order most Plantagenet and most fixed, remains a lie. By the same token, however, to approach the world without the imagination leaves the poet alone in a hostile and destructive "universe of things." Throughout the poem, Moore travels back and forth between these poles in search of what will suffice. Dissatisfied by the world without imagination, she climbs to the height of beautiful transcendent vision, only to blast such notions apart as all-too-easy fancies. Each violent moment of unmaking, however, leads to the growth of yet another idea of order. The poem as a whole presents a relentlessly skeptical imaginative cycle that demands humility and negates the prospect of ever knowing anything of the mountain's deeper mysteries. "Completing a circle," Moore writes of her travels on the glacier, "you have been deceived into thinking that you have progressed." The imagination can only wax and wane, it cannot discover absolute truth.

Moore thus betrays the same sort of skeptical contrary motion (creative/decreative) in "An Octopus" that she claims for Stevens in "Well Moused, Lion." Indeed, looking back to Moore's essay through the lens of "An Octopus," it seems that Moore's changing image of Stevens as a troubled skeptic reflects her own growing sense of creative impasse. Wedded to the notion of the imagination's balm and desiring lofty spiritual visions to "tranquilize the torments of confusion," Moore, like Stevens, recognizes the egotistical sterility of such comforting ideals. Moore's assessment of "Sunday Morning" as a poem that "gives ultimately the effect of the mind disturbed by the intangible; of a mind oppressed by the properties of the world which it is expert in manipulating" relates to the difficult motions of "An Octopus" as well. Like Stevens, Moore is "disturbed" by the potential stasis of the world with imagination and "oppressed" by the sheer disorder of the world without imagination. Each time Moore ascends to the heights in "An Octopus," her own transcendent escape becomes, as she says of Stevens's wilder moments, "uneasy rather than bold," a reflection of her own doubts about the imagination's potentially stifling powers. Moving from forest floor to visionary mountaintop and back again, Moore betrays that she too lacks the "masterly equipoise" that she finds missing in Stevens's verse. Unable and unwilling to rest content in images that "tranquilize the torments of confusion," Moore, like Stevens, writes a poetry of the snake's body that wriggles through an endless series of violations, its coils moving in contrary ways.

Chapter 3

Finding the Proper Way to Fly

In the summer of 1929, the *Dial* closed its doors for good, ending Marianne Moore's tenure as literary editor of one of America's most prestigious publications. Moore met the news of the magazine's demise with a mixture of disappointment and relief. She openly enjoyed the financial security and thoughtful community the job afforded, but the work in the *Dial*'s small, understaffed office could also prove crushing. During her years as editor (1925–29), Moore wrote over one hundred pieces for the "Comment" and "Briefer Mention" sections of the magazine and annotated and returned thousands of manuscripts to anxious authors. Engaged in the duties of her editorship, Moore had little time to devote to her verse. Following the publication of *Observations* in 1924, Moore did not publish a new poem until "Part of a Novel, Part of a Poem, Part of a Play" appeared in *Poetry* in June 1932. Her years at the office in the late 1920s were ones of poetic silence.

By an interesting coincidence, Stevens, too, was poetically mute during the late 1920s. After the release of *Harmonium* in 1923, Stevens turned his attention to his financial security, his insurance career, and his newborn daughter. As a result, for almost a half-dozen years (1924–30) Stevens, like Moore, published no poetry. While Stevens certainly had a number of professional and personal reasons for setting his verse aside, both A. Walton Litz and George Bornstein speculate that his silence resulted in part from the aesthetic impasse played out in his verse autobiography, "The Comedian as the Letter C."[1] "The way of all mind," Stevens wrote of Crispin's voyage, "is from romanticism to realism, to

fatalism and then to indifferentism, unless the cycle re-commences and
the thing goes from indifferentism back to romanticism all over again."[2]
As Bornstein points out, Stevens was unwilling to turn his mind back to
the same old romanticism that prompted his escape in the first place and
decided instead to lay down his pen.[3] Stevens's years of artistic with-
drawal thus corresponded with Moore's years of editorship, a coinci-
dence that kept her, not for want of trying, from publishing his work in
the *Dial*. Throughout his silence, Moore repeatedly wrote to Stevens
requesting verse and assuring him that the readers of the *Dial* would be
interested whenever he felt he had anything to say. Stevens appreciated
the attention and returned Moore's interest by requesting an inscribed
copy of her book *Observations*.[4]

Whatever the reasons for their years away from poetry, both Stevens
and Moore returned to their craft at roughly the same time, prompted, in
part, by the pressures of national turmoil. In October 1929, the bottom
fell out of the stock market, plunging America and Europe into the
desperation and want of the Great Depression. For Moore, the crash
seemed an inevitable comeuppance for years of profligacy, irresponsibil-
ity, and selfishness. Throughout her term as editor of the *Dial,* Moore
frequently used her "Comment" to critique America's growing obses-
sion with wealth and competition at the expense of generosity and co-
operation. "The brittle, brilliant character of life today," she complained
in 1926, "is varyingly exposited. Speed and sport are, it would seem,
indigenous to this country."[5] Moore found her concerns about America's
self-interested opulence confirmed in the 1926 cry for protective tariffs
against European countries struggling desperately to rebuild from the
First World War—a policy which ultimately contributed to the collapse
of the world economy.[6] "We are often reminded that the civilized world is
uncivilized," Moore wrote of such American isolationist practices, "The
malevolence of a protective tariff seems to be as great as that of the 'trust.'
We are begged to realize that among human beings, 'there should be no
power to exploit and no fear of being exploited.'"[7] Moore also saw the
avarice and competitive drive of American governmental policy reflected
in the country's more creative pursuits. "The world of art," she wrote,
"also is assailed by a spirit of domination, gainfulness, or expediency."
Looking about at a country obsessed with decoration and commodities,

Moore recalled Clement of Alexandria, who "with the averted eye of the jailer, deplored as it were prophetically, an admiration for green stones and for pearls and wished that 'our life might be anything rather than a pageant.'"[8]

Disgusted with American selfishness, Moore devoted one of her final "Comment"s penned on the eve of the 1929 crash and the *Dial*'s demise to a poignant consideration of the world's growing dangers and the potential costs of America's seemingly blind desire for self-satisfaction. Frankly questioning the wisdom of "complacently self-dependent" American isolationism in the face of aggression such as Mussolini's plunder of eastern Africa, Moore reminded her readers that "complacency is not, as we know, an element of peace." America, in other words, had obligations to less fortunate countries that, consumed by its own desire for comfort, it refused to fulfill. "True non-materialism," Moore wrote, "is . . . itself a war on self-interest." Quoting from architect Claude Bragdon's book *The New Image,* Moore concluded that, for the world to truly be at peace,

> "Each must pour out affection which is unrequited, for to be thrifty in love is to be vile; each must pay debts never in his life contracted, and redress wrongs he knows not of. To reconcile these conflicting and often opposite obligations—of the world and of the spirit—constitutes the real art of life, and to this each should address himself, paying all debts and spending only the surplus, be it of energy, money or time."[9]

Recasting America's beloved language of commerce as a language of moral obligation, Bragdon's words reflected Moore's sense of America's unwillingness to honor its moral debts. Content to spend all of its vast energy, money, and time upon itself, America in the late 1920s was a nation of brittle illusions of magnitude rather than ideals of magnanimity—in Moore's view, the poorest rather than the richest of nations.

America's desire to remain opulently isolated from world affairs, however, eventually led Moore from considerations of the nation's moral economy to further questions about the relationship between art and society at large. As Moore's quote from Bragdon attested, the questions of what each person owed and to whom could be dauntingly complex.

Each individual, Moore acknowledged through Bragdon, had obliga-
tions to both "the world" and "the spirit"—conflicting debts that proved
difficult to balance. For the artist in particular, the call to worldly obliga-
tions and the fulfillment of the imaginative spirit might remain forever at
odds.

   In October 1929, the question of the artist's debt to society came
even more sharply into focus for Moore as the bright pageant of Ameri-
can prosperity ground to a halt, confirming her sense of the shallow
nature of the charade. Isolation and contentment with selfish pleasure led,
as Moore predicted, to national collapse. Faced in the post-*Dial* years
with the growing weight of American misery, Moore began to wonder
as she returned to the task of writing verse if the poet could ever balance
the pull of worldly obligations with the potentially escapist call to spiri-
tual heights. Could poetry ever be more than selfish and opulent
detachment—an avoidance of moral obligation to the world on an indi-
vidual level equivalent to America's tragic isolationism? In a letter to her
former *Dial* colleague Kenneth Burke, penned in the worst days of the
depression, Moore complained that the artists of her time seemed deter-
mined to avoid civic duties even while supposedly concerned with the
state of the world. Ezra Pound, she charged, "disapproves so strongly of
Washington that he writes it a pamphlet of instructions but he has not
been voting and does not expect to vote," while Glenway Wescott "asks
the world to give him the necessary hours in which to write a book about
its troubles and when we have the book, it is about him and not about the
world." In Moore's view, American artists had a nasty habit of asking
parents "to eat their third baby, for to see so many hungry mouths about
us is agitating and a menace to art." Turning a critical eye to her own
behavior, Moore continued:

   I am not prepossessed by patriotism in absentia, but hypocrisy is
   equally abhorrent and at the risk of making myself look worse than I
   am, I confess to buying butter and potatoes at the A. & P. though my
   small grocer whom I occasionally patronize, goes out of business;
   and to writing a poem on a persimmon, let us say, instead of joining
   with our capitalist friends in handing out the local dole; and I should
   hate to see you interrupt your remarkable writing, for it is that, to

make speeches for Norman Thomas or organize such emergency unemployment for labor as you yourself approve.[10]

While chiding herself for taking an easy road around social problems, Moore equally regretted the sacrifice involved when artists abandoned their work to pursue social causes. Should Burke neglect his "remarkable writing" and devote himself to stumping for the Socialists, the world, Moore implied, might ultimately be a poorer place for his choice. Satisfying a debt to the world might leave the debt to the spirit unpaid. "We, most of us," Moore admitted to Burke with a sigh, "abhor public service."

Choosing to forgo "public service," Moore returned to writing verse in a time of national upheaval that nonetheless prompted her to pose disturbing questions about the potentially isolationist nature of poetic activity. In 1931, just as Moore began serious work on her major poems of the 1930s, Stevens, too, rejoined the poetic ranks in earnest and issued an expanded version of *Harmonium,* subtracting three poems from the original text ("The Silver Plough-Boy," "Exposition of the Contents of a Cab," and "Architecture") and adding fourteen more, eight that could have appeared in the 1923 text ("The Man Whose Pharynx Was Bad," "The Death of a Soldier," "Negation," "Lunar Paraphrase," "The Surprises of the Superhuman," "Sea Surface Full of Clouds," "New England Verses," and "The Revolutionists Stop for Orangeade"), and six that were written (but not published) between 1927 and 1930 ("Anatomy of Monotony," "The Public Square," "Sonatina to Hans Christian," "In the Clear Season of Grapes," "Two at Norfolk," and "Indian River"). Moore found Stevens's additions to *Harmonium* so intriguing that she offered to review the book for *Poetry,* only to find that Morton Zabel, the current editor of the magazine, already had a review of his own in process. As Moore graciously wrote to Stevens of the mix-up, "I daresay the younger reviewer is better. . . . the better the book, the more important it is that it should be a text for the young."[11]

While she did not have the opportunity to write her review, the reissued *Harmonium* gave Moore yet another chance to pore over Stevens's work, both old and new, at the very time she was struggling to resolve her own qualms about the relationship between the poet and a troubled society at large. Wondering if the artist could, or should, serve

two masters—the world and the spirit—Moore turned her attention back
to Stevens to reexamine the work of the most imaginatively ferocious
and potentially lofty of her peers. In the pages of "Well Moused, Lion,"
Moore pictured Stevens as a poet of endless and sometimes dangerous
change—one who, at times, seemed calmly secure in his visions, but
who proved willing to break all boundaries of poetic decorum in quest of
ideals that the actual world could never match and, by virtue of their
eventual banality, the mind could not maintain. Attracted in 1923 to
Stevens's violent, lionish rendings of the habitual veil of familiar percep-
tions, Moore's conclusion to "Well Moused, Lion" made clear that she
felt uncomfortable sanctioning the gorier moments of Stevens's verse.
Yet, as the world around the two poets grew worse, Moore returned to
Stevens's poetry to consider again the value of his imaginative power.
Given her admiration for Stevens's gorgeous riot of verbal fluency and
her appreciation of his spirit like Crispin's "free, elate, intent, profound,"
Moore set out to rethink the nature of his beautiful and sometimes bear-
ish evasions in the current social context. Were his flights of spirit desir-
able, or even excusable, given the problems of the day? Could poetry
based on a "love of magnificence"—poetry that desired imagination, as
Balzac desired money, "in heaps or by the ton"—be more than an opu-
lent, and ultimately selfish, verbal show? Like Clement of Alexandria
deploring an admiration for green stones and pearls, Moore reread Ste-
vens's verses and wished that they, like her own poems on a persimmon,
might be read "as anything rather than a pageant."

The question of the continued legitimacy of sensationally romantic acts
like those performed by her favorite jungle animal—Wallace Stevens—
ultimately prompted Moore to write some of her most complex and
rewarding verse. Throughout the years of the depression, Moore filled
her notebooks with images and phrases that she eventually shaped into
three closely related poems with animal subjects: "The Plumet Basilisk"
and "The Jerboa," both published in Hound and Horn in October 1932,
and "The Frigate Pelican," published in Eliot's Criterion in 1934. Notes
for all three poems are jumbled together in Moore's workbooks along-
side direct comments about Stevens and his verse. Read collectively,
Moore's three poems form an argument about art, isolation, and social

responsibility—an argument, in Moore's terms, about the proper way for a poet to fly.

In several key ways, "The Plumet Basilisk" sets the terms for Moore's reconsideration of Stevens's violent verse and romantic evasions in general. One of Moore's longest poems, "The Plumet Basilisk" occurs in four sections, each devoted in part to the habits of a particular reptile: "In Costa Rica," "The Malay Dragon," and "The Tuatera" followed by a reprise of "In Costa Rica." Although many critics read "The Plumet Basilisk" as a purely descriptive poem that revels in concrete particulars, Bonnie Costello is right to point out that the two principal subjects of Moore's piece are Wallace Stevens and the imagination.[12] Each lizard in Moore's poem represents through its behavior and environment a different sort of poetic intelligence whose artistic method holds both dangers and rewards.

Moore begins the poem with a portrait of her primary and perhaps best-loved subject, the plumet basilisk. Her opening stanzas reveal, however, that while she admires the basilisk's captivating demeanor, he may not be the proper poet for his time:

The Plumet Basilisk

In Costa Rica

In blazing driftwood
    the green keeps showing at the same place;
as, intermittently, the fire-opal shows blue and green.
    In Costa Rica the true Chinese lizard face
is found, of the amphibious falling dragon, the living firework.

He leaps and meets his
    likeness in the stream and, king with king,
helped by his three-part plume along the back, runs on two legs,
    tail dragging; faints upon the air; then with a spring
dives to the streambed, hiding as the chieftain with gold body hid in

Guatavita Lake.
    He runs, he flies, he swims, to get to
his basilica—"the ruler of Rivers, Lakes, and Seas,
    invisible or visible," with clouds to do
as bid—and can be "long or short, and also coarse or fine at pleasure."[13]

As both Celeste Goodridge and Costello note, Moore's description of the plumet basilisk and his home immediately suggest Stevens and his poetry as a subtext.[14] Moore's lizard inhabits a dense jungle that, in its exotic lushness, recalls Crispin's Caribbean amphitheater and Stevens's Florida of "big-finned" palms and green vines "angering for life." Behind such a "flourishing tropic" of imaginative plenty and intensity, Moore tells us, lies a supremely attractive and powerful poetic intelligence. Moore's first glimpse of the basilisk reflects her initial compliment to Stevens in the pages of "Well Moused, Lion": she admires the lizard's vibrant colors. Showing green among the driftwood, the basilisk poet, like Stevens, has the power to animate whatever seems pale, dead, and hollow in his surroundings with a burst of blazing color. The basilisk instantly captivates Moore, who forgets the rest of Costa Rica and fixes her attention on the "show," a word that reflects the lizard's artifice, that recurs in one small space in the jungle. Such a swift narrowing of vision from all of Costa Rica to a single pile of driftwood, to a flash of green "at the same place" among the logs, bespeaks the magnetic and hypnotic quality of the basilisk's creations. Drawn to the creature, Moore examines and admires his display with the minute eye of a jeweler, fascinated with his appearance as with the rarest of gems, the fire opal.

As in her comments on Stevens in "Well Moused, Lion," however, Moore appreciates not only the basilisk's beguiling beauty but also his aggressive and wild imaginative vigor. "Imagination implies energy," Moore writes in her review of *Harmonium,* and the basilisk exemplifies her decree. A "living firework," he explodes into the poem in the second stanza and, in a flurry of active verbs, refuses to stand still for an instant— the image of a ferociously active mind. Leaping with abandon into his own reflection, the basilisk enacts a romantic trope for immersion in the self that makes him the ruler of all he surveys. Basilisk and basilica, poet and place, become one as the lizard dives inward into an imagined world of his own creation. Within the liberating space of his art the basilisk poet acquires the powers of the mythical Chinese dragon and may order all of nature and change his persona at will—an image that recalls Stevens's multiple masks in "Sur Ma Guzzla Gracile." Ending her portrait with an image of complete creative mastery, Moore borrows a phrase from a discussion of the Chinese dragon in the *Illustrated London News* that once again echoes her sense of Stevens's poetry. In "Well Moused, Lion," Moore finds Stevens's oeuvre a mix of "deliberate bearishness" and "rhapsodic elegance," of fiery outbursts and cool remoteness. Like Stevens, the magical basilisk may be "coarse or fine at pleasure," performing rude or lofty transformations, depending on his mood.

While Moore's description of the Stevensian basilisk suggests her delighted admiration for the show he provides, her opening stanzas also present some potentially troubling questions about the basilisk's romantic nature. As Moore's portrait makes clear, escape and isolation are the bases of the basilisk's art. The poem begins with the lizard poet's hasty retreat to a solitary hiding place, where he chooses to revel in his own company rather than come into contact with the speaker—the very sort of isolationist aesthetic that Moore found problematic in her peers and chastised in herself during the depression. As Bonnie Costello points out in her book *Marianne Moore: Imaginary Possessions,* Moore's poetry workbooks for "The Plumet Basilisk" contain direct references to Wallace Stevens and his verse that reflect further on the elusive nature of his poetic.[15] Immediately above the discarded lines "Basilisk Basil the harmless / the dragon flying / diving not like a kite that dives + jerks / breaks itself to pieces on the ground," Moore writes in her worksheets:

> W. Stevens—a pride in unserviceableness
>   that is not synon. with the beauty of
>   aloofness self-sufficiency
> the fairy and the brute
> a big ogre stalking toward one w a knobbed club
> well moused, lion
> Leigh Hunt—rhyme
> Java peacocks argas pheasants toucan
>   palaces
> aurora borealis, ice floes & hair seal needlework
> Rousseau's paintings
> Stevens recoils from admitting the force of the basic emotions
> obliquely treats of it thru the interacting vibrations
> of allusive imagery[16]

In part, Moore's comments recap her remarks in "Well Moused, Lion." Looking back at Stevens's poetry during the days of the depression,

Moore still associates his work with the colorful plumage of exotic birds and the "banana leaves and alligators" of Rousseau's wild paintings—the basilisk's native habitat. Yet, where Costello claims that Moore's basilisk worksheets reflect her overall delight in Stevens's "aura of vagueness," Moore's manuscript comments are not without complaint, as Celeste Goodridge points out.[17] While still appreciative of his sensory and technical virtuosity, Moore continues to cast Stevens as a brute as well as a fairy. Dispensing with the qualifications she penned in "Well Moused, Lion," Moore now sees the ogre that lurked beneath the surface of *Harmonium* as a full-fledged threat wielding a "knobbed club." The beauty of Stevens's work, she concludes, is not "aloofness"—not that of one who simply and serenely pursues his own course, unconscious of his artistic exile. Stevens, instead, deliberately stalks his reader and takes "pride" in creating poetry so wild, extravagant, and impractical, so detached from common language or worldly concerns, that it purposefully drives people away. Stevens specifically cultivates his violent imaginative detachment and inutility, a position that, as Moore's letter to Kenneth Burke attests, she found hard to defend in difficult times.

Yet, seek to defend it, or at least to explain it, she does. In an effort to better understand her Stevensian lizard's aggressive imagination, Moore draws on the form of "The Comedian as the Letter C" and sends her poem traveling to far-flung locations, each the mental habitat of a distinctly different lizard intelligence. Moving from Costa Rica, to Malaysia, to New Zealand, Moore follows her description of the basilisk with studies in turn of the Malay dragon and the tuatera. With each supplemental and contrasting portrait, Moore redefines her sense of the costs and rewards of the basilisk's wildly sublime poetic escape. Moore begins "The Malay Dragon" with a definite statement of both allegiance and contrariety: "We have ours; and they / have theirs." Counting herself as a resident of the plumet basilisk's American jungle, Moore goes on to describe the demeanor of his less decorative and ultimately less interesting cousin:

> Ours has a skin feather crest;
> theirs has wings out from the waist, which is snuff-brown or sallow.

Ours falls from trees on water; theirs is the smallest
dragon that knows how to dive head-first from a treetop to something
   dry.

Floating on spread ribs,
     the boatlike body settles on the
clamshell-tinted spray sprung from the nutmeg-tree—minute legs
     trailing half akimbo—the true divinity
of Malay. Among unfragrant orchids, on the unnutritious nut

tree, *myristica*
     fragrans, the harmless god spreads ribs that
do not raise a hood. This is the serpent-dove peculiar
     to the east; that lives as the butterfly or bat
can, in a brood, conferring wings on what it grasps, as the airplant does.

As if contemplating her manuscript comments about Stevens's poetic "unserviceableness," Moore presents a contrasting lizard portrait of a creative intelligence both aloof and self-sufficient—a study in the sort of beauty she felt Stevens's imagination lacked. Unlike the basilisk, the Malay dragon does not "raise a hood," making no attempt to hide from the speaker's gaze. Rather than leaping and running wildly away, the dragon floats delicately into the poem and "settles," unconcerned, in full view, the image of an aloof intelligence that sees no need for violent and sensational evasions. Moore's image of the dragon's sailing "boatlike body" itself recalls the nautical origins of the word "aloof"—a term meaning to steer a ship into the wind in order to avoid the shore, the land the lizard shuns. More bird than reptile, a peaceful fairy poet rather than a brute, the Malay dragon spends most of its time in the air calmly detached from worldly concerns. Less imposing than the plumet basilisk, the "harmless" Malay dragon gracefully ennobles the poetic subjects that it "grasps" with no intent to shock or disturb. Independent like the air plant, this mind barely touches the material world and derives no sustenance from its minimal contact.

Yet, when compared to Moore's vision of the basilisk's unserviceableness, the Malay dragon's aloof poetic self-sufficiency seems far from "beautiful." Where the basilisk and his habitat flicker with blazing color, the Malay dragon wears sickly snuff-brown and sallow, dull shades

suited to his strangely pigmentless backdrop. At home in the clamshell-
tinted spray of the nutmeg tree, the Malay dragon rests in a realm of
deadly pale opal surfaces unrelieved by the basilisk fire opal's blues and
greens. Detached from the material world and aloof from worldly con-
cerns, the Malay dragon creates a poetic environment that reflects his
sterile sensory deprivation. The orchids have no fragrance, the nutmeg
tree offers no nourishment, the plants have no hue.[18] Where the basilisk's
powerful legs are the image of poetic energy, the Malay dragon, who
never touches ground, trails his "minute" and atrophied limbs behind
him "half akimbo." The Malay dragon's imagination, while neither brut-
ish nor violent, lacks all color, life, and excitement, a sorry trade for the
Stevensian basilisk's poetry of wild ferns.

Having concluded that the attraction of Stevens's verse outweighs
the appeal of poetic aloofness, Moore turns her eye to a more grounded,
less remote lizard mind—the tuatera—to assess again the costs and bene-
fits of the basilisk's wild romantic behavior:

> Elsewhere, sea lizards—
>   congregated so there is not room
> to step, with tails laid crisscross, alligator-style, among
>   birds toddling in and out—are innocent of whom
> they neighbour. Bird-reptile social life is pleasing. The tuatera
>
> will tolerate a
>   petrel in its den, and lays ten eggs
> or nine—the number laid by dragons since "a true dragon
>   has nine sons."

Unlike the leaping basilisk or the floating Malay dragon, the tuatera
seems utterly content on the ground and in the world, making no effort
to escape, or even to move, when the speaker trips over their tangled
mass. Where the basilisk prefers "unserviceable" isolation, the tuatera has
a social life that Moore frankly tells us "is pleasing." Members of a
congregation, the tuateras are "laid criss cross," literally woven together
in a posture that reflects their sense of interconnected social responsibil-
ity. Where the imagination of the Stevensian basilisk is always divisive
and threatening, stalking toward one with a knobbed club, the tuatera

mind is harmless and guileless, accepting its neighbors without question even when they are potential prey. Rooted in the material realm of social and economic concerns, the tuateras embody a mentality that embraces, rather than evades, worldly responsibilities.

Once again, however, while Moore finds some aspects of tuatera life "pleasing," the picture she paints pales in comparison with her portrait of the plumet basilisk. If the Stevensian lizard "demonstrates how imagination may evade 'the world without imagination,'" then the tuateras happily settle in the space without artifice that Stevens tries so hard to avoid. Members of an indistinguishable mass, the tuateras embody unthinking conformity—minds that go along with the crowd and find safety in numbers, taking no pleasure in individual flights of fancy. Unmoving and uncurious, these lizards form an image of complete mental sluggishness—what Coleridge called in *Biographia Literaria* "the lethargy of custom." The basilisk, powerful in his uniqueness, leaps and "runs on two legs" covering vast mental distances; the tuateras, in contrast, prefer to bask where "there is not room to step." As Moore's notes to her poem point out, the tuatera, while it resembles a lizard, has characteristics of the tortoise—the fabled antipode of agility.

Stevens's imaginative escapades, then, despite their potential for ogreish insult and troubling evasion, remain far more interesting to Moore than the mental habits and habitats of his lizard peers. Indeed, the failings of Moore's supplemental lizards seem to reflect the moral difficulties of paying personal debts in bad times that Moore had considered in her 1929 *Dial* comments on Claude Bragdon. As Moore quoted from Bragdon: "To reconcile these conflicting and often opposite obligations—of the world and of the spirit—constitutes the real art of life." The Malay dragon's intelligence satisfies its debt to the spirit, but knows and gives nothing to the world. The tuatera's mind, rooted solely in the world, pays no debt to the spirit. Both approaches, in Moore's view, are destitute.

Leaving her other lizards behind, Moore travels back to the American jungle in an effort to better explain to herself and her reader why Stevens's verse, by comparison, seems so satisfying and necessary. Moore resumes her portrait of the basilisk as if returning from an unfruitful digression:

                                                           Now,
                         In Costa Rica
            where sapotans drop
                their nuts out on the stream, there is, as
        I have said, one of the quickest lizards in the world—the
                basilisk . . .

Placing the lizard once again above the water, Moore repeats the basilisk's opening posture, seeming to start the poem again. On second look at her lizard, however, Moore emphasizes not the basilisk's wild poetic power, but its vulnerability:

                                                           If
            best, he lets go, smites the water, and runs on it—a thing
                difficult for fingered feet. But when captured—stiff
        and somewhat heavy, like fresh putty on the hand—he is no longer

            the slight lizard that
                can stand in a receding flattened
        S . . .

For the first time in her poem, Moore considers the threat of the lizard's entrapment. No matter how aggressive or agile his unique intelligence, the basilisk, Moore implies, lives in constant danger of losing his identity to the mind of the mass. If caught by the pressures of conformity and worldly concerns, unable to recede into the free space that letters provide, the basilisk becomes as "stiff," colorless, and earthy as the tuatera. Imprisonment turns the once creative basilisk into a mere medium, so much putty to be shaped by the will of others.

Rejecting the unsatisfactory artistic alternatives posed by the Malay dragon and the tuatera, Moore thus returns to her favorite lizard and freely admits that the Stevensian basilisk is at his best when he "lets go," abandoning himself to his imaginative impulses, however wild, strange, or indecorous. She further insists that such violent poetic leaps and smites, rather than mere prideful displays of "unserviceableness," are necessary to the basilisk's survival. In constant fear of losing his identity in mundane concerns and old habits of thought, the basilisk jumps not because he wishes, but because he must, enacting an escape that, as Moore noticed in "Well Moused, Lion," "is uneasy rather than bold." The dynamic of the basilisk's violent poetic response echoes comments that Moore copied from Isabel Cooper's article "Wild Animal Painting in the Jungle":

> There is a blazing green wood-lizard who becomes ashen in captivity and remains so except when he is particularly enraged. When he flares up again into brilliant green you can watch the waves of color flowing rapidly like a revolving spotlight.[19]

Like Cooper's wood lizard, Moore's blazing green basilisk creates beauty out of rage. When harassed by "the world without imagination," Stevens responds with a volley of angry and acrimonious colors that Moore now reads as a justifiable and, indeed, necessary form of self-preservation.

Throughout the final section of her poem, Moore does all she can to pardon the basilisk's poetic violence by emphasizing his state of constant risk. Comparing the stripes of his banded tail to the keys of a piano, Moore claims

> This octave of faulty
> decorum, hides the extraordinary lizard
> till night-fall, which is for man the basilisk whose look will kill; but is
>
> for lizards men can
> kill, the welcome dark— . . .

The basilisk's outrageous poetic creations keep it safe from men who fear the night—Moore's image for those afraid to venture beyond the visible sunlit realm of ordinary life into the invisible world of imagination. Such spiritless and worldly men, Moore tells us, kill what is extraordinary as a matter of course. Reexamining her lizard in a threatening context, Moore concludes that the basilisk's "look of whetted fierceness" results from "what is merely / breathing and recoiling from the hand." In Moore's metaphor, the basilisk's romantic evasions become acts as natural and necessary as respiration—functions performed as a matter of course to stay alive.

Moore thus excuses Stevens's poetic improprieties on the grounds of self-protection—a revision of her earlier, grudging comments in "Well

Moused, Lion," where she found his ogreish behavior "unprovoked." In
1933, however, Moore looks back at Stevens's "contumely" and con-
cludes that, given the increasingly hostile and fatalistic nature of the age,
Stevens was well within his rights to fight back against its appropriating
and conformist notions in whatever way he could. In part, then, Moore
projects onto Stevens her own growing sense that the world was becom-
ing an increasingly difficult place in which to remain imaginatively
alive—a possible reflection of her own recent experience of more practi-
cal activity. Throughout the late 1920s, both Stevens and Moore aban-
doned their art for a time in favor of the worldly pursuits of the office—
Stevens at the Hartford and Moore at the *Dial*. Unable to devote her time
to writing poetry while on staff at the *Dial,* Moore perhaps felt more
intensely than Stevens the ongoing threat that such a life in business,
however tied to arts and letters, posed to her poetry.

Such a revised understanding of Stevens's need for imaginative vio-
lence, however, does not in itself explain Moore's tremendous attraction
to Stevens's poetry in the early 1930s. As the last section of "The Plumet
Basilisk" attests, Moore also was drawn to Stevens because she saw his
work as an important, and specifically American, recasting of a romantic
tradition—a revision, as it turns out, vitally important to her questions at
the time about art and social responsibility. In the final section of her poem,
Moore becomes a fellow introspective voyager and, in order to listen
closely to his music, ventures with her basilisk into the darkness that most
men fear. Pursuing the basilisk downward and inward, Moore compresses
her conversational syllabic stanzas into short stanzas with closing couplets
that gig with dactyls—a formal reflection of the basilisk's visionary space.
The images Moore constructs of the basilisk's art in her musical stanzas
question the relationship between Stevens's verse and the worn romantic
tropes of his, and Moore's, inheritance. Moore claims that with

> wide water-bug strokes,
> in jerks which express
> a regal and excellent awkwardness,
>   the plumet portrays
> mythology's wish
> to be interchangeably man and fish—

traveling rapidly upward, as
spiderclawed fingers can twang the
bass strings of the harp, and with steps
as articulate, make their way
back to retirement, on strings that
vibrate till the claws·are spread flat.

   Among tightened wires
  minute noises swell
  and change as in the woods' acoustic shell
   they will . . .

In a bold sweep, Moore transforms the whole of the basilisk's jungle into a giant harp—tightened wires of vines strung in the woods' acoustic shell. The image of the basilisk's harp, in which "noises swell / and change as . . . / they will," readily recalls what Harold Bloom dubs "the most prevalent of Romantic symbols," the aeolian harp.[20] An emblem of mediation between nature and man, between inarticulate inspiration and organized music, the aeolian harp recurs throughout the poetry of Wordsworth, Shelley, and Coleridge as an analogue of the poetic mind that, subject to outer impressions, rises to visionary song. Through her lizard's harp, Moore invites an examination of the Stevensian basilisk's imaginative flights in light of the much-copied, lingering tropes of his romantic predecessors. Invoking the ancient lute of the British Romantics, Moore prompts a direct comparison between the basilisk's brand of romanticism and the outmoded vestiges of the British romantic tradition that, collapsed to mere convention, persisted ad nauseam in the popular poetry of the day. Moore's poem makes it clear, however, that the noises that swell in the basilisk's jungle sound nothing like the stock dreamy intonings of derivative romantic verse. The Stevensian harp produces:

         the galloped
ground-bass of the military drum, the squeak of bag-pipes
  and of bats. Hollow whistled monkey-notes disrupt
the castanets. Taps from the back of the bow sound odd, on last year's
  gourd,

or when they touch the
  kettledrums . . .

Here, then, is the sound of American poetic "faulty decorum." Discarding the stock tropes of derivative romanticism, Moore's basilisk revels in aggressive and percussive noises, creating a poetry of harsh drones and rhythms specifically opposed to seductive elfin melodies. Endowed with relentless primal drive, the basilisk's martial tones replace a stale sense of the romantic imagination's floating witchery with a vision of violent energy. To emphasize the irreverence and unconventionality of the lizard's imagination, Moore pictures his musical score as one that does not use instruments in traditional ways. The violinists in the basilisk's ensemble make "odd" sounds by tapping the backs of their bows on gourds and kettle drums and, using their traditionally obbligato instruments as percussion, make even the familiar fiddle unrecognizable to the ear. "No anonymous / nightingale," Moore concludes approvingly, "sings in a swamp." Stevens's barbarous American romantic poetic eschews such niggling images that, now so overused, have no individuality or personality.

Thus, Moore suggests that the basilisk's violent poetry springs not only from a need for self-protection, but out of a desire to strip the world free of conventional fictive coverings. Like the chieftain with gold body who hides in Guatavita Lake to evade the Spaniards, the New World basilisk escapes the pressures of the Old World by diving inward and ridding himself of old tropes. Perhaps most importantly, however, Moore sees in Stevens's romantic aesthetic a continued and difficult wish to be refreshed by the soil. As Stevens wrote: "The imagination loses vitality as it ceases to adhere to what is real. When it adheres to the unreal and intensifies what is unreal, while its first effect may be extraordinary, that effect is the maximum effect that it will ever have."[21] The music of Moore's basilisk reflects Stevens's provisionalizing revision of romanticism. Moore pictures the basilisk's grating song as a mixture of natural and man-made sounds, a wild medley of bagpipes and bats that draws directly on the jungle for its substance rather than drifting wholly into abstract or refined forms. The basilisk also plays nothing but bass notes—his spider-clawed fingers twang the "bass strings" of the harp, sounding a "loud-low chromatic listened for down-scale" of a continuo bass line. His military drum plays a "ground-bass," a musical term for a repeating set of unchanging bass notes that underlie a work's shifting melody and harmony. The word "bass" supplies Moore with an evident pun. The basilisk's music may be base, as in crude or indecorous, but it is also a base, something fundamental and close to origins. A "ground bass," the basilisk's music, Moore implies, draws its lushness and drive from the ground itself, the jungle upon which the lizard feeds.

A "ground bass," however, also repeats itself. Moore's image argues that Stevens's poetic freshening occurs, not once, but again and again, a point supported by the lizard's frenetic movement in her poem. Throughout "The Plumet Basilisk," Moore's lizard travels back and forth between the realm of the actual and the realm of the imagination, between the sunlit world of man and the dark inward water world of the creating mind. "Interchangeably man and fish," the basilisk makes neither land nor water his permanent home. The poetic of Moore's Stevensian lizard depends on change, a condition that recalls Crispin's quest in "The Comedian as the Letter C":

> Thus he conceived his voyaging to be
> An up and down between two elements,
> A fluctuating between sun and moon,
> A sally into gold and crimson forms,
> As on this voyage, out of goblinry,
> And then retirement like a turning back
> And sinking down to the indulgences
> That in the moonlight have their habitude.
> But let these backward lapses, if they would,
> Grind their seductions on him, Crispin knew
> It was a flourishing tropic he required
> For his refreshment, an abundant zone,
> Prickly and obdurate, dense, harmonious,
> Yet with a harmony not rarefied
> Nor fined for the inhibited instruments
> Of over-civil stops.
>
> (*CPWS*, 35)

Echoing Stevens's diction, Moore pictures her lizard poet as one who "travels rapidly upward" only to make his way "back to retirement." Like Crispin, Moore's basilisk "sinks down" into the indulgences of watery moonlight, grows bored with the stale detachment of his own creations—the unreal intensified—and longs again for the refreshment of the flourishing tropic. Once landed, however, the basilisk, dissatisfied with and threatened by the world without imagination, leaps again. Moore portrays the Stevensian imagination as a cyclic process—a voyage between regions forever in search of a perfect balance between matter and mind. What Moore admires most about her basilisk is not his underwater state, where he becomes "regal" but "awkward," or his landed state, where he remains panting and vulnerable, but his magic moments of transition between the two states in his furious and divine dives.

Paying homage to Stevens, Moore herself creates a cyclic poem and ends "The Plumet Basilisk" where it began—with yet another of the lizard's leaps. In her final image of the basilisk, Moore insists that his plunge into the imagination remains an instant of both loss and gain: "his quicksilver ferocity / quenched in the rustle of his fall into the sheath / which is the shattering sudden splash that marks his temporary loss." Moore implies in the word "quench" that the lizard's fierce leap both satisfies his need to fly and extinguishes his fire. The instant the basilisk's imagination ceases to adhere to what is real, it loses vitality. The quicksilver sword drops into a restrictive sheath, a cover that instantly inhibits its movement—the metaphorical equivalent of an empty trope. Like Stevens, Moore grants that the "first effect" of such a loss of contact "may be extraordinary," a "shattering sudden splash," but she agrees with Stevens that "that effect is the maximum effect that it will ever have." The key to the basilisk's beauty is the "temporary" nature of his escape. His moonlight mind will be refreshed again by the world of living green in a continuous cycle of advance and retreat that Moore identifies with Stevens's American romanticism.

Moore's poem, then, ends on a note of admiration and understanding that marks an important revision of her earlier views of Stevens's verse. In "People's Surroundings," Moore envisions the watery zone of Stevens's "quicksilver" imagination (she uses the word in both poems) as Bluebeard's tower—a sealed and isolated place of petrified beauty that constitutes the poet's permanent residence. In "The Plumet Basilisk," Moore pictures Stevens's water world as only a transitory retreat for a mind that craves contact with the actual. In "People's Surroundings," Moore paints Stevens as a menacing intelligence who kills one subject after another by casting them in a static and death-dealing poetic glaze. In "The Plumet Basilisk," Moore pictures Stevens himself as the one threatened by outside forces bent on squelching his brilliant individuality. Moore's distinct change of heart reflects her own changing assessment of the term *romantic* in the days of the depression. Making Stevens a test case for her own anxieties about romantic poetry, Moore concludes that it is possible to write verse without sacrificing either personal vision or worldly connections. Paying its debts to both the world and the spirit in turn, Stevens's poetry, as Moore reads it, escapes without becoming escapist, preserving the author's individuality without succumbing to isolation and detachment. Through Stevens, Moore justifies her own apparent evasions—her poems about persimmons or basilisks in times of economic collapse—as the temporary leaps into allusive imagery of a poet whose wish to adhere to the world clashes with a nervous naked need to preserve the unique vision of the sensitive self.

In process at the same time as "The Plumet Basilisk," "The Jerboa" proves a companion piece to Moore's reassessment of romantic verse that again argues the necessity of potent, yet grounded, personal vision. Where the basilisk reflects Moore's impressions of Stevens and his work, the jerboa, as critics recognize, reflects Moore's sense of her own poetic project. A small brown jumping rat, the jerboa embodies Moore's family nickname of "Rat" (her brother and mother were "Badger" and "Mole" respectively), taken originally from *The Wind in the Willows*. Making use of her own private mask, Moore writes another long poem that seeks to save her own poetry from charges of social irresponsibility and prideful escapism. Like "The Plumet Basilisk," "The Jerboa" is a multi-section travelogue—a journey from Rome, to Egypt, to the African desert—in which each country represents a habit of mind. The poem opens in Italy, the land of "Too Much," where the creative intelligence has become a menace to society:

> A Roman hired an
> artist, a freedman,
>   to make a cone—pine cone
>   or fir cone—with holes for a fountain. Placed on
>   the Prison of St. Angelo, this cone
>   of the Pompeys which is known

now as the Popes', passed
for art. A huge cast
    bronze, dwarfing the peacock
    statue in the garden of the Vatican,
        it looks like a work of art made to give
        to a Pompey, or native
of Thebes.[22]

"'The people,' you and I, and always the artist," Moore wrote to Kenneth Burke, "elude responsibility and the result is likely to be a dictatorship such as they have in Russia or in Spain or in Italy."[23] As the opening of "The Jerboa" implies, Moore sees Mussolini as only one in a long line of Italian dictators enabled and empowered by irresponsible creations that "pass for art." Imagination gone wrong on a cultural level, the art of the Pompeys has long since neglected to adhere to the real. Bloated beyond recognition and abstracted from its natural source, the great Roman cone, Moore tells us, could be either pine or fir—a fitting product of a culture that cares little for accurate observation or individual differences. Like the overused stock image of the nightingale in "The Plumet Basilisk," the cone has become an anonymous, empty, and lifeless cliché. A seed turned to cast bronze and placed atop a prison, the cone stands as a symbol of thwarted transformation in a realm of oppressive images that have ceased to grow or change and inhibit all free thinking. Worst of all, Moore implies, the artist participates freely in such degradation. A man for hire, the artist here sacrifices his personal vision to the lure of gold and chooses to support those in power rather than challenge existing tropes.

    Moving to the realm of a different artistic temperament, Moore claims that the Egyptians liked "small things," but their diminutive artifacts reflect the same oppressive cultural stasis as the Romans' huge ones. Like the Roman, the Egyptian mind has ceased to adhere to what is real. Distorting and destroying the particularities of living things, the Egyptians arrange all of nature into a static portrait and view life as "a picture with a fine distance." Lords and ladies of Egypt crush geese into body paint, grinding unique living animals into an indistinguishable artistic paste in a brutal trade of life for vain decoration. The royals then place their makeup in "round bone boxes with pivoting / lid incised with the duck-wing // or reverted duck- / head." Preferring artifacts to creatures, the Egyptians replace their living animals with dead, unchanging images. The duck becomes a duck-shaped box, a restrictive, hollow aesthetic container that has no real substance. Moore implies that, in Egypt as well as Rome, the irresponsible artist who unthinkingly reproduces worn and dead images helps to empower those "with, everywhere, // power over the poor." All the artists of Egypt, it seems, work for the king and his court and reinforce royal control with their creations—the garments, toys, gardens, and gems that litter the poem. The artists give the king totems of royal power, "basalt serpents and portraits of beetles," and Moore tells us that "the / king gave his name to them and he was named / for them." Like the Roman "freedman," the Egyptian artists carve symbols of change that prove ironically self-defeating. The Egyptian scarab beetle, revered as a symbol of transformative resurrection, becomes in the artist's hands a static intaglio with the king's name inscribed on its belly. Like the Roman seed turned to stone, the beetle that should be an image of rebirth becomes merely an unchanging reflection of the powerful and stultifying ego that orders its production. The artists of Egypt, like those of Rome, merely reproduce the detached, life-denying images that perpetuate the gross unreality of the status quo.

In both Rome and Egypt, then, life has become nothing more than a pageant. Like Bluebeard's deadly tower, both locations reflect the whims of vicious romantic imaginations that have lost all touch with the actual and, by virtue of their isolation, forfeited all vitality and compassion. Freezing the world into unchanging artifacts and tropes as empty as Moore's anonymous nightingale, both cultures embody the deadly detachment that the lizard-poet of "The Plumet Basilisk" tries so hard to avoid. In Egypt as in Rome, however, poets function as mere tools in the hands of those in power. Eluding a responsible commitment to fresh vision based in the actual, the artists of Rome and Egypt, in Moore's view, both create and perpetuate dictatorship.

Moving from the realms of "Too Much" to the jerboa's Africa of "Abundance," Moore presents a poetic milieu preferred by a responsible mind. Approaching the mentality of the African rat through "Pharaoh's rat, the rust- / backed mongoose," Moore states that the jerboa resembles its ancestor whose "restlessness was / its excellence; it was praised for its wit." Like the plumet basilisk, the jerboa thrives on intellectual movement and change. In distinct contrast to the artists of Egypt and Rome, the jerboa poet rests in a minimal desert purified of propaganda and washed clean of oppressive tropes—a place where the ground itself becomes visible. A digger of burrows and the color of the sand, the jerboa melds with the earth that is his home, adhering to what is real. Like the plumet basilisk who leaps from matter to mind, however, the jumping jerboa also lives by traveling between the realms of the actual and the imagination. Comparing the jerboa to a similarly inclined desert dweller of biblical times, Moore writes:

> Part terrestrial,
> and part celestial,
>   Jacob saw, cudgel staff
>   in claw hand—steps of air and air angels; his
>   friends were the stones. The translucent mistake
>   of the desert, does not make
>
> hardship for one who
> can rest and then do
>   the opposite—launching
>   as if on wings, from its match-thin hind legs, in
>   daytime or night; that departs with great
>   speed, followed by as a weight,
>
> a double length, thin
> tail furred like the skin . . .

To use Moore's quote from Bragdon, Jacob appears as an expert in "the real art of life"; reconciling his obligations to the world and the spirit, Jacob pays both his debts in full. Placing a shepherd's staff, the tool of his trade, in Jacob's hand, Moore marks him as a person of earthy occupation. Like the jerboa, Jacob eschews an aesthetic "ivory bed" and rests contentedly upon the tropeless ground, befriending the land itself. Yet, a man of spirit as well as earth, Jacob also has the power to launch violently into personal vision. The shepherd's staff doubles as a cudgel, and Moore casts Jacob as a poet who, like her ogreish Stevens, stalks toward one wielding a self-protective imaginative club. Jacob's vision, however—a

ladder between heaven and earth—is the very image of imagination ad-
hering to what is real. Even while he sees "steps of air and air angels,"
Jacob never forgets that his friends are the stones. Moore ends her com-
mentary on a famous visionary with an assertion of his grounded nature.

The jerboa, too, Moore suggests, never wholly loses contact with
the ground despite his visionary voyaging. Like Jacob and the plumet
basilisk, the desert rat can leap into the imagination and return to the sand
without becoming trapped in the visions he creates. As in "The Plumet
Basilisk," Moore invokes a shimmery water realm of fancy to make her
point. The desert mirage, the imagined space of water on the sand, brings
no hardship to one who does not "mistake" such visions for realities.
Unlike the Egyptians, the jerboa will never pursue mental reflections to
the detached point where the body dies for lack of actual sustenance. A
mixture of bird and beast like Moore's feather basilisk, the jerboa transits
between realms with similar skill. The rat soars into the imagination "as
if on wings" from "match-thin hind legs" that mark him as another
potential "living firework." With a tail as a weight, however, the jerboa,
like the plumet basilisk, remains intellectually anchored to the earth.

As the final stanzas of Moore's poem indicate, the basilisk and the
jerboa not only fly in the same way, they fly for the same reasons. Moore
ends "The Jerboa" with an image of the rat's frantic escape from the
oppressive minds of Rome and Egypt that lurk in the poem. The jerboa's
flights of fancy, Moore implies, originate in "flights from a danger," and
the rat's retreats, like the plumet basilisk's, result in a most original
music:

> By fifths and sevenths,
> in leaps of two lengths,
>   like the uneven notes
>   of the Bedouin flute, it stops its gleaning
>   on little wheel castors, and makes fern-seed
>   foot-prints with kangaroo speed.

Seeking to escape solidifying tropes, the jerboa produces a self-protective
retaliatory song that, like the basilisk's water music, specifically under-
cuts European artistic traditions with primitive verve. The jerboa com-
poses a music of fifths and sevenths, two intervals in the Western diatonic

scale that long to resolve to tonic. Valuing movement over stasis, how-
ever, the jerboa thwarts the cadences of its music and never brings its
intervals to rest in conventional Western fashion. Better suited to the
primitive Bedouin flute than to the tempered flutes of the West, the
jerboa's music sounds unending suspensions that undercut traditional
musical expectations. Like the plumet basilisk, the jerboa plays an "oc-
tave of faulty decorum" meant specifically to freshen stale European
artistic conventions. As John Slatin points out, Moore incorporates the
uneven leaps of the desert rat directly into the body of her poem.[24] Each
of Moore's stanzas begins with a line of five syllables and ends with a line
of seven, an uneven structure disconcerting to the ear accustomed to the
more traditional rhythmic patterns of rhyming verse. Moving forward
by fits and starts, Moore's verse, like the jerboa's music, avoids the
closure of conventional and, in Moore's view, anonymous forms.

As Moore's poetic self-portrait reveals, she felt that her poetic and
Stevens's had much in common in the early 1930s. Moore pictures both
her jerboa and her basilisk as responsible introspective voyagers who,
rather than escape into sealed fantasy worlds of egocentric revery, spend
their lives traveling between realms of thought and actuality in search of a
perfect balance. Menaced by restrictive and solidifying forces outside the
self, both jerboa and basilisk jump into a self-protective poetry of faulty
decorum meant to revise the oppressive tropes of detached and derivative
romanticism. Once launched, however, both creatures tire of the stasis of
their thoughts and return to the land for refreshment in a cycle repeated
again and again. The similarity of the struggle embodied in both crea-
tures becomes clear in the context of Moore's source material. In her
reading diary, Moore makes note of an article suggestively titled "The
Mastery of the Air" that appeared as part of a series by renowned natural-
ist J. Arthur Thomson in the *Illustrated London News*.[25] In his article,
Thomson addresses "the problem of flight" and catalogs four different
ways in which the difficulty has been solved in the animal kingdom.
Thomson notes insects, true birds, and bats as examples of unreservedly
successful flyers before turning his attention to the attempts of less capa-
ble creatures. Among the ranks of the weaker fliers, Thomson places
Moore's favorite of all flying lizards, the pterodactyl—the prehistoric

poetic persona that Moore took on in her correspondence with Bryher and H.D., for whom she was ever "Dearest Dactyl."[26] In Thomson's opinion, the pterodactyl could not have been a strong flier due to its lack of a prominent breastbone, or keel, to support its large wings. To illustrate his point, Thomson places a picture of the pterodactyl next to portraits of two other animals that, despite their birdlike characteristics, have trouble staying off the ground: the jerboa, identified in Thomson's caption as "a mammal that has become a biped just as the ancestors of the birds did," and the flying lizard, a close relative of Moore's basilisk. "None of these," Thomson remarks of all three creatures, "can really fly." Pterodactyl, jerboa, and flying lizard together are merely "clever parachutists that take adventurous leaps" whose "splendid failures . . . fill us with a reasonable wonder at the adventurousness of life." Casting both Stevens and herself as splendid but failed fliers, Moore leagues herself with Stevens in the creation of a limited American Romantic. Moore pictures both herself and Stevens as saved from egotistical detachment and sterility by their mutual inability to stay off the ground for long.

Yet, while both basilisk and jerboa live in leaping and landing, Moore depicts her own poetic as different from Stevens's in crucial and potentially problematic ways. The aggressive plumet basilisk, when threatened, transforms himself into a living firework, screaming meteorite, or sword whetted to fierceness. Moore pictures his poetic retaliation as loud, angry, powerful, lush, colorful, and immediately, almost hypnotically, attractive. The jerboa and its poetry, by contrast, seem utterly unassuming. Where the basilisk sports bright green and stripes, the jerboa has "pale markings" and wears a modest white and "buffy-brown." Where the basilisk has an entire midnight percussion ensemble at his disposal, the jerboa plays a single airy woodwind. The unquestioned ruler of his imagination's water world, the basilisk orders all of nature with his verse. The jerboa produces poetry by "gleaning"—an image of collecting that corresponds to Moore's habit of incorporating quotes from various sources into her verse—and making tiny "fern-seed / foot-prints" that leave little impression in the sand. Where the basilisk bespeaks Stevens's "pride in unserviceableness," the jerboa seems a model of poetic humility. Both creatures, Moore tells us, try to defend themselves against the oppression imposed by tired habits of thought, but, compared to the Stevensian basilisk, Moore's eponymous little rat appears distinctly unarmed.

Indeed, as John Slatin notices, the jerboa does not make it out of Moore's poem alive. In the final stanza of "The Jerboa," Moore pulls together a collection of images that strangely curtail the creature's poetic escape.

> Its leaps should be set
> to the flageolet;
>   pillar body erect
> on a three-cornered smooth-working Chippendale
>   "claw"—propped on hind legs, and tail as third toe,
>   between leaps to its burrow.

After arguing so strenuously for the jerboa's freedom in the image of the uneven Bedouin flute, Moore oddly ends her poem by suggesting that the jerboa's leaps be "set" to the sounds of a tempered (calibrated to the even tones of a Western scale) French woodwind of the High Renaissance. Such a proposal embodies the very sort of solidifying capture by convention that the jerboa tries so hard to escape throughout the poem. Not surprisingly, the implication that the rat can be so "set" freezes it in place. Caught on the ground "between leaps to its burrow," unprotected by the force of its own imaginative flight, the jerboa becomes the leg of a heavy ornate Chippendale chair—an immobile graven image of civilized society. Thus trapped, the quick "fern-seed footprints" of the jerboa's verse become the solid, stylized feet of the British drawing room. Where the basilisk escapes out the back end of his poem in a final flurry of "faulty decorum," the less imaginatively aggressive jerboa falls prey to the imposed refinement of over-civil stops.

So it seems that while Moore pictured her poetic project as similar to that of Wallace Stevens, she also worried that her more humble romantic flights might not be strong enough to ensure escape from old tropes and conventional habits of mind. As John Slatin correctly phrases the problem, Moore's jerboa "is a bit too polite . . . to satisfy the need for models of poetic freedom."[27] Honoring the sand by assuming its color, the jerboa pays its debt to the world, but it sacrifices too much of itself in the process. The contrast between the jerboa and the plumet basilisk concerned Moore enough to send her back to her menu of flying things in search of yet another model of poetic reconciliation—one that could guarantee escape, yet still satisfy its debts to both world and spirit. Needing a more secure poetic, Moore turned to a far better flyer than either her jerboa or her basilisk—the frigate pelican.

Moore's "fleetest foremost fairy / among birds," the frigate pelican has all the attributes that J. Arthur Thomson associates with "triumphantly successful," rather than failed, fliers. In "The Mastery of the Air" Thomson describes the most powerful birds as boats: they have "prominent keels" and can "rest on their oars"; they trace great ellipses in the sky, rising when "sailing" with the wind and sinking when turning against it.[28] Adopting the metaphor of the bird-boat (pelican-frigate) for her poem, Moore creates an image of a supremely powerful, agile, and violent imaginative voyaging. "Hell diver," "frigate-bird," or "hurricane-bird," the names of Moore's creature imply that, unlike the jerboa and the basilisk, the pelican has absolutely no fear. Named for a warship, the frigate is well protected by his art, secure enough in his individuality that, rather than spend his time fleeing from intellectual capture, he himself turns to pirating and plunder. "Air-boned" with wings that unite "levity with strength," the frigate seems to defy gravity and soars safely above the dangerous ground that both jerboa and basilisk must touch.

The frigate's poetic power, then, seems to separate it from either of Moore's more vulnerable subjects. Yet, as Moore's drafts of "The Frigate Pelican" attest, Moore's frigate marks her further consideration of what she deemed the harsh and powerful nature of Wallace Stevens's aesthetic. Moore began work on "The Frigate Pelican" in 1933, and, as with "The Plumet Basilisk," Moore's worksheets for the poem contain numerous direct references to Stevens.[29] Reiterating the comment she makes about Stevens's poetic brashness in her basilisk manuscripts, Moore writes in between draft lines of her frigate poem, "Pride in unserviceableness is not synonymous with the beauty of aloofness." Her subsequent lines reveal her early intention to include comments about Stevens's aesthetic directly in the text of her poem. In her worksheets for "The Plumet Basilisk," Moore writes that "Stevens recoils from admitting the force of basic human emotions / obliquely treats of it thru the interacting vibrations of allusive imagery." Moore recasts this comment in an early draft line of "The Frigate Pelican," writing that the frigate flies "uninterfered with by tearing emotion / Without the sensation of being disgraced in the secretly thrilling."[30] Like the Stevensian basilisk, the frigate poet lives by escaping into a private realm of the imagination that inevitably separates him from his fellows. Next to her comments about Stevens's "unserviceableness" in her worksheets, Moore creates an image of such mental evasion that directly ties the frigate to her vision of Stevens's aesthetic:

> This is how the mind works
> It is made to swell your body out
>   so that the others must fall back[31]

The picture Moore paints is one of poetic power and potential arrogance. Rising above the others, the frigate's successful mind puffs up the bird in a beautiful display inevitably tied, as the word "swell" implies, to pride— the word Moore connects with Stevens's unserviceable lyrics.

Moore thus returns to the imaginative tropics and embodies Stevens's poetic in a much more powerful flying creature than the plumet basilisk— a reflection perhaps of her own need to see some thoughts as beyond capture in an increasingly imposing world. Indeed, looking back to "The Comedian as the Letter C," Moore's pelican seems consciously modeled on the brightest, most savage spirit of Stevens's verse. The frigate pelican resides in the Caribbean, the very place to which Stevens's Crispin first travels to escape his derivative European moonlight evasions. Moore's pelican thus embodies Stevens's first instance of "green brag"—the "aesthetic tough, diverse, untamed / Incredible to prudes, the mint of dirt" that, for Crispin, eventually and inevitably fades as it "turns paradigm" in the course of the poem. "Free, elate, intent, profound," Moore's New World pelican resembles Crispin in the first flush of his escape from deadening and decadent Old World traditions. "This is not the stalwart swan that can ferry the / woodcutter's two children home; no," Moore insists. While the frigate soars in original creative splendor, less limber minds content themselves with the stale conventions of Grimm's fairy tales—an institutionalized cultural romanticism borrowed from Europe that domesticates nature, sapping its vitality in a set of solidified tropes. The mind co-opted by such ideas itself loses all power and becomes a ferryboat rather than a frigate, a mind at the service of the thoughts of others that merely transports old ideas, never getting off the ground on its own.

Free from the conformist thinking that would insist he know Gretel from Hänsel, Moore's frigate, like Crispin, sees the world in an excitingly different way. At the center of her poem, Moore repeats the pattern of "The Plumet Basilisk" and offers an extended illustration of the frigate's poetry. Following the pelican into the air as she followed the plumet basilisk into the water, Moore looks through the frigate's eyes and presents an example of his unfettered, expansive poetic vision. Once again, Moore's worksheets indicate that she had Stevens in mind when constructing the passage. In early drafts of the frigate's vision Moore writes:

> looking not seeing
> below in the blur
> the Rousseauean encounter
> ogre   jaguar
> or scuffle of peccaries in their own lust
> yucca plants[32]

Moore's notes comprise an interesting mix of her earlier comments about Stevens's poetry and snatches of "The Comedian as the Letter C." Recalling her Stevensian ogre and reprising her connection between Stevens's lush verse and Rousseau's paintings, Moore's draft lines picture the frigate's aesthetic space as a reflection of Crispin's untamed and uninhibited Caribbean amphitheater—a place of bare encounters that erases old tropes. As Stevens records Crispin's cleansed tropical vision:

> Crispin foresaw a curious promenade
> Or, nobler, sensed an elemental fate,
> And elemental potencies and pangs,
> And beautiful barenesses as yet unseen,
> Making the most of savagery of palms,
> Of moonlight on the thick, cadaverous bloom
> That yuccas breed, and of the panther's tread.
>
> (CPWS, 31)

Borrowing directly from Stevens in her drafts, Moore keeps his yuccas intact and changes Stevens's panther to a jaguar, the more prevalent cat resident of the American tropics. The Stevensian vision of Moore's frigate appears in her completed poem of 1934 in an altered, but still recognizable, form:

> he looks down and observes what went
> secretly as it thought, out of sight
> among dense jungle plants. Sent
> ahead of the rest, there goes the true
> knight in his jointed coat that
> covers all but his bat
>
> ears; a-trot, with stiff pig gait—our tame armadillo, loosed by
> his master and as pleased as a dog. Beside the
> spattered blood—that orchid which the native fears—
> the fer de lance lies sleeping; centaur-
> like, this harmful couple's amity
> is apropos. A jaguar
> and crocodile are fighting. Sharp-shinned
> hawks and peacock-freckled small
> cats, like the literal
>
> merry-go-round, come wandering into the high bird's-eye view
> of the expert for whom from the air they are ants
> keeping house all their lives in the crack of a
> crag with no view from the top. And here,
> unlikely animals learning to
> dance, crouch on two steeds that rear
> behind a leopard with a frantic
> face, tamed by an Artemis
> who wears a dress like his,
>
> and hampering haymaker's hat. [33]

Moore's chosen lines retain the image of the Stevensian frigate's aesthetic as a "bare encounter" that revises restrictive habits of mind. The animals in the frigate's vision are not the comforting domestic stock of German fairy tales, but wild, violent, and potentially dangerous creatures. Rather than recount the adventures of a make-believe knight in shining armor, the frigate prefers the "true knight," the armadillo. As Moore's line break implies, the rest of the frigate's vision strives to be similarly "like the literal." The frigate creates a poetry based in actualities, free from the solidifying gestures of old tropes—a true merry-go-round of actual animals walking in a circle rather than a false merry-go-round of domesticated figurines frozen in place as ferries for human children by the romantic intelligence in search of amusement. Moore ends her passage with a contrast between the worn romantic tropes of the groundlings and the expansive untamed vision of the high bird. "And here," Moore writes in dismay, bringing us down to earth, we have the aesthetic stuff of a bad circus. Again Moore displays the grotesqueries of a worn romantic consciousness that denies all wildness, freezing animate nature into unnatural stock artistic poses. The poet dresses as Artemis-Cynthia, Keats's moon goddess of the unfettered poetic imagination, but her romantic vision has become so derivative that she wears a "hampering haymaker's hat" over her eyes. The poet who merely recycles old romantic tropes, Moore implies, has no power to see for herself. Her tame and taming vision creates serviceable works that merely express the mottoes of the status quo: "Make hay; keep / the shop; I have one sheep." As Moore says of such circus tunes, "the steam hacks" of the old calliope "are not to be admired."

Thus, once again, Moore credits Stevens with the creation of violent and vibrant verse that undermines old romantic conventions. The frigate's successful flight from the lethargy of custom, however, leads Moore to a question of social responsibility that lies behind all three of her poems. Looking aloft, Moore wonders aloud if such a poet can ever truly serve both the world and the spirit. *"Festina lente,"* she admonishes, only to question her own grudging command, "Be gay / civilly? How so?" As John Slatin rightly notes, Moore's translation of *"festina lente"* (literally "make haste slowly") as "be gay civilly" points to her reckoning of the artist's debt to the community and the polis—the realm, as Stevens puts it, of "over-civil stops."[34] Moore's response to her self-posed question of artistic decorum marks a further revision of her sense of Stevens's verse:

> "If I do well I am blessed
> whether any bless me or not, and if I do
>   ill I am cursed." We watch the moon rise
> on the Susquehanna. In his way

> this most romantic bird flies
> to a more mundane place, the mangrove
> swamp, to sleep. He wastes the moon.
> But he, and others, soon
>
> rise from the bough, and though flying, are able to foil the tired
> moment of danger, that lays on heart and lungs the
> weight of the python that crushes to powder.

Quoting a Hindu saying that she associated with Gandhi, Moore dismisses her admonition to socially acceptable gaiety as essentially flawed. The determination of poetic value, she insists, cannot rest in the hands of those whose visions have been hampered by custom and convention. Those poets whom society damns and excludes may be blessed in their pursuit of moral imperatives higher than the comfort and pleasure of the state. Moore's reversal echoes the distinction that Shelley makes in "A Defence of Poetry" between the concept of artistic "utility" as defined by the poet or as determined by the polis. For poets, Shelley claims, "whatever strengthens and purifies the affections, enlarges the imagination, and adds spirit to sense, is useful."[35] But, he adds, for those tied to local civic conceptions of "utility," none of those poetic gifts seem functional. For those who "have their appointed office in society," Shelley complains, "utility," or reason applied usefully, means only the "banishing the importunity of the wants of our animal nature, the surrounding men with security of life, the dispersing the grosser delusions of superstition, and the conciliating such a degree of mutual forbearance among men as may consist with the motives of personal advantage."[36] The poetry serviceable to the state inevitably serves the limited perspective of those in power. As a result of such socially useful thoughts, Shelley concludes, "the rich have become richer, and the poor have become poorer. . . . Such are the effects which must ever flow from an unmitigated exercise of the calculating faculty."[37]

The "unserviceableness" of the Stevensian frigate thus marks him as a "useful" poet in Shelley's best sense—one who does not reflect old tropes and social codes, but radically seeks to change them. The final stanzas of Moore's poem indicate, however, that she does not count herself among the ranks of the "unserviceable." As many critics have noticed, Moore pulls back from the frigate's vision, plants herself firmly on the ground, and claims a community in the pronoun "We" that frankly excludes the frigate: "We watch the moon rise / on the Susquehanna."[38] Despite what many critics claim, however, Moore's position is not a happy one. Watching "the moon rise / on the Susquehanna," Moore signals her ability to join in such a communal gathering as evidence of her ongoing participation in the clichéd tropes of a worn romantic vision. The "We" of the polis still revels in the moonshine of derivative romanticism, the poetry of the sideshow Artemis, that lurks on American shores. Moving inland from the vast ocean to the Susquehanna river, Moore withdraws to the landlocked state of Pennsylvania, where both she and Stevens grew up—a potentially regressive retreat to an artistic and personal past that denies mature responsibility. The frigate, by contrast, lays waste to the old romantic moon of his youth with a new, more vital romantic vision. Once again, Moore credits Stevens's poetry with an attention to the actual world that the old Romantic of the polis ironically lacks. The frigate, like the basilisk, refreshes his vision by touching ground, resting between flights in the mundane stuff of the world—the swamp that Moore punningly implies is the grove of man. As in "The Plumet Basilisk," Moore pictures the Stevensian poetic as one of flying and landing in alternation—a cyclic romantic practice that assures that no one detached vision will dominate the poet's aesthetic.

Thus, at the end of "The Frigate Pelican," Moore suggests that her vagabond bird is the truly responsible artist in the poem.[39] When he rises from the branch, the frigate takes "others" with him, a sign that his verse serves the social function of actively releasing those oppressed by habitual and deadening thoughts. The frigate has the power to pull others up out of blindness that the basilisk and the jerboa lack. Moore thus concludes that the romantic impulse that she feared as escapist in 1932, if properly provisionalized, can and should prove a socially responsible and politically radical "foil" to the suffocating power of habit and custom. In 1932 Moore wrote to Burke that the romantic artist, indulging in solipsistic pleasure, always "elude[s] responsibility and the result is likely to be a dictatorship such as they have in Russia or in Spain or in Italy."[40] In 1934, Moore recasts the romantic artist as one who, seeking a wider and more flexible range of vision than oppressive dictates would allow, thwarts, rather than perpetuates, dictatorship.

What, then, to make of the poet left earthbound at the end of the poem? Critics tend to read Moore's separation from the bird's vision and her subsequent grounded moongazing as a brave acceptance of civility at the expense of a gayer and gaudier verse. Yet, by the end of "The Frigate Pelican," the crushing weight of limitation implied in Moore's return to earth seems also to suggest a self-critique of her own less-powerful poetic. The "we" who watch the moon rise with whom Moore makes company inevitably stay rooted in the same polis that revels in fairy tales and bad circuses—oppressive entertainments and tropes that Moore concedes the less airborne poet does not have the strength to escape or revise. The form of Moore's poem also bespeaks her growing dissatisfaction with the restrictions of poetic civility. Starting her piece with a detailed description of the frigate as seen from the ground, Moore then vaults upward in the interior stanzas of the poem and actively participates in the frigate's vision, seeing the ground through his eyes. In the closing stanzas, Moore moves back out of the frigate's vision and once again views the pelican from the ground with a renewed sense of her own position. The very structure of Moore's lyric thus proves the value of the frigate's flight. Like the "others" at the close of the poem, Moore rises under the frigate's visionary power, sees the wildness she might otherwise have missed, and frees herself for a time from the abuses of the sideshow Artemis. The frigate has the strength to pull Moore aloft, but, like the jerboa, she does not stay aloft for long. Moore returns to earth, and her fall, while it bespeaks her continued humility, also ensures her capture by the social python. Looking skyward once more at the poem's conclusion, the poet sees the frigate's flight as a "reticent lugubrious ragged immense minuet"—a now sad reflection of the limits she ascribes to her own, more grounded aesthetic. Without internal power, Moore admits, the humbler poet writes conventional courtly music fit for the polite drawing room—tunes that, compared to the frigate's, are slow, heavy, and hopelessly impoverished. In its structure, Moore's poem itself leaps and lands, but Moore implies that without the frigate's influence, the more serviceable poet may not get off the ground again.

Looking back to "The Plumet Basilisk" and "The Jerboa," then, "The Frigate Pelican" posits an important shift in Moore's conception of Stevens's verse that reflects Moore's own changing idea of poetic balance. In "The Plumet Basilisk," Moore corrects her earlier misconception of Stevens as a static aesthete—a reflection of her own anxieties about the escapist nature of poetry itself—and casts him as a provisionalizing voyager whose art depends on periodically returning to the actual in a cyclic effort to balance mind and matter. Projecting her own sense of personal threat onto Stevens, Moore excuses his, and her own, violent romantic urges as a necessary form of self-protection from the lethargy of custom. In rationalizing the plumet's and the jerboa's retreats in terms of personal vulnerability, however, Moore implies that their escapes result, in part, from weakness. The plumet dives not because he wishes, but because he must, and the result is a reluctant leap into the imagination that inevitably tends earthward. By the time she writes "The Frigate Pelican," however, she needs no such justification for romantic flights. Never at risk, the Stevensian frigate's vision clearly connotes strength rather than "nervous naked" frailty; he is active rather than merely responsive in his pursuit of higher purposes, and his poetry becomes a social rather than a purely private act. Like Moore's other creatures, the Stevensian frigate lives in leaping and landing, but his poetry, while still marginally provisionalized by his grounding, emphasizes joy and grace rather than rest, vision rather than service. Reading Stevens as a stronger and more facile romantic poet than her basilisk, Moore betrays her own growing wish to write a stronger, more spiritually incorruptible verse to counter an increasingly violent age. Looking back at *Harmonium* and particularly at Crispin, Moore rereads as a means of liberation the lines and images she once found a trap.

Thus, Moore recasts her image of Stevens and his verse from plumet to pelican, not, as Bloom would suggest, to reject his poetry, but rather to shape Stevens and his music into a more suitable artistic model for an increasingly violent time. Moore's image of the Stevensian frigate's lofty music loses much of the fluctuating and provisionalizing energy that Stevens himself found increasingly valuable to his own poetry in the 1930s, but Moore's "misreading"—or, rather, change of emphasis in her reading—reveals not her anxieties about poetic primacy, but her need for a positive model of poetic trial and imaginative success. In "The Frigate Pelican" Moore reads into Stevens's high-flying art her own persistent and deeply held wish that the duties of an increasingly ugly world might not clash so heavily with the desire to write poems. Ultimately, her projections of the growing risks of worldliness and the increasing need for poetic power speak more to her own sense of thwarting than they do to Stevens's. As Moore writes in "The Frigate Pelican," the Stevensian artist resembles "impassioned Händel," who "meant for a lawyer and a masculine German domestic / career—clandestinely studied the harpsichord / and never was known to have fallen in love." Stevens was indeed a lawyer and, at the Hartford, he engaged directly, and by most accounts comfortably, in a masculine domestic career. Moore, however, pictures Stevens, like herself, as a creature of sacrifice—one who lives without the comforts and constraints of regimented domesticity for the sake of saving music. Merging her own image with Stevens's, Moore fashions a workable likeness of a powerful, spiritual poet for a difficult age.

"A Poet That Matters": Wallace Stevens's Response to Marianne Moore's *Selected Poems*

In 1934, Wallace Stevens was appointed vice president of the Hartford Accident and Indemnity Company, and, after years of climbing through the ranks, he found himself secure in his corporate career—ironically in one of the worst years of the depression. As Holly Stevens notes, "Now, at last, he felt safe in devoting some of his time and energy to poetry without fear of being 'passed over' as an oddity" (*LWS*, 256). Free from the financial hazards of nonconformity, Stevens returned to verse and set out to collect and arrange a second volume of poems, *Ideas of Order*, partially at the urging of Ronald Lane Latimer of the Alcestis Press. Scraping together the few poems he had written since his tentative poetic rebirth in 1930 (seven in all, not counting the new set that Stevens sent to *Alcestis* for publication in October 1934), Stevens found that the act of collecting his old verses resembled that of visiting a musty intellectual archive. "Yesterday I put on ear muffs, wrapped myself in a blanket, and spent several hours in the attic," he wrote to Latimer:

> Wherever my reliquiae may have been put, they have been put for good, because I was able to find only two or three odds and ends.
> After returning downstairs and thawing out, I put together everything that I have, and I think that it will not make more than 35 pages, which could be expanded very easily by set-up to about 40. After I had made a tentative arrangement of the material, it seemed

to me that the tone of the whole might be a bit low and colorless; and, since it is the tone of the whole that is important, I might want to work on the thing, adding say, 10 or 15 pages, in order to give a little gaiety and brightness. My mind is not ordinarily as lamentable as some of these poems suggest. However, if one does not write poetry more or less constantly, it seems to fade, or to receive its impulse from circumstances which more often than not would be cheerless to anyone except the poet.[1]

In his letter to Latimer, Stevens fancifully portrays himself as one who has "been cold a long time," a version of his own snow man who, camped in a frozen space of imaginative abstinence, longs to thaw out and recover the turning spirit of an earlier self. As eager as Stevens was to restore imaginative gaiety and brightness to his lamentable mind, however, he was equally loath to duplicate what he saw as the poetic relics of his romantic past. Consigning his youthful romanticism to the attic "for good"—both forever and for better—Stevens set out in search of a new, more vital romanticism that could speak to the imaginative needs of a changing world. Between January and April 1935 Stevens experienced a flurry of creativity and wrote almost half of the thirty-two poems that appear in *Ideas of Order*. As A. Walton Litz notes, however, for all of its attempts at imaginative gaiety and brightness, *Ideas of Order* remains an elegiac volume that laments the loss of the imagination rather than revels in its return. "The experience at the center of *Ideas of Order*," writes Litz, "is one of deprivation, a sense and acceptance of 'Nothing that is not there and the nothing that is.'"[2] *Ideas of Order* thus marks a speculative and transitional period in Stevens's career. Wishing to write his way back into brightness, Stevens continued to struggle with the theoretical question of how to proceed.

At the very end of his poetic flurry of early 1935, however, Stevens managed to articulate what he deemed at least "a temporary theory of poetry"—a program for a new and better romantic poetry—in his final addition to *Ideas of Order,* "Sailing after Lunch."[3] In mid-March, Stevens sent his last-minute submission to Latimer along with instructions to place the poem at the head of his new volume. The culmination of months of creative effort, "Sailing after Lunch" tackles Stevens's dissatisfaction with a dead and derivative romantic tradition head-on. Adopting the persona of a poet in transition, one caught in the nebulous space between light and frivolous artistic fare (lunch) and a more substantive mental meal (dinner), Stevens lampoons his own position as a poet recognizing the inadequacy of his previous romantic aesthetic. "It is the word *pejorative* that hurts," the poet complains. "My old boat goes round on a crutch / And doesn't get under way." Limping about on a crutch of tired romantic tropes, the poet/pilot pictures himself as an old man propped up on a well-used aesthetic that has grown hopelessly hoary. The decorous and derivative romantic fit for the luncheon crowd leaves the poet hungry for something new.

> Perhaps it's the lunch that we had
> Or the lunch that we should have had.
> But I am, in any case,
> A most inappropriate man
> In a most unpropitious place.
>
> (*CPWS*, 120)

The poet's urbane ruminations on his incompetence show him as a member of a community rooted in the lethargy of custom—the "we" who suffer from the lunch they had, or should have had. Pulling himself away from such stodgy companions, the poet performs the initial step in finding a new aesthetic and utters the words "I am" for the first time, thereby establishing a creative identity separate from the crowd and its tropes. Yet, even while Stevens's poet recognizes his artistic failure as one of deadening conformity, he continues to cling to the pompous and elevated Latinate language of the "we" he wishes to escape. "A most inappropriate man / In a most unpropitious place," Stevens's poet has not yet learned to remake his tired vocabulary.

Resorting to prayer, Stevens's poet begs to be released from the weight of historical strictures that keep him anchored in the conventional community of the "pejorative" romantic. The "romantic," he complains, should be here, there, and everywhere, but it must never return to its current stale form, or, for that matter, to the same tropes twice. Envisioning romantic poetry as diverse in form with many sources rather than a

dull reflection of a single-minded traditional community, Stevens's poet
stumbles on the key to a new and better verse:

> It is least what one ever sees.
> It is only the way one feels, to say
> Where my spirit is I am,
> To say the light wind worries the sail,
> To say the water is swift today,
>
> To expunge all people and be a pupil
> Of the gorgeous wheel and so to give
> That slight transcendence to the dirty sail,
> By light, the way one feels, sharp white,
> And then rush brightly through the summer air.
>
> (*CPWS*, 120–21)

In the final stanzas of "Sailing after Lunch," Stevens insists that the "new
romantic" must not pretend to any permanent or predominant status.
Poetry arises from a series of internal impulses that affect the poet's percep-
tion, and the poet himself must be willing to change his tropes and his
focus to keep the mind moving. Fashioning a menu of new beginnings—
"to say . . . To say . . . To say . . ."—Stevens implies in his repetitive
structure that any of the imaginative acts the poet performs will suit as the
fount of a new romantic aesthetic as long as such acts remain provisional
and multiple. Like Moore, however, Stevens acknowledges that as the
mind grows in individual power, others must, at least temporarily, fall
back. Expunging the community that fancies the old romantic aesthetic,
the poet accomplishes the elder's dictate to the ephebe at the beginning of
"Notes toward a Supreme Fiction." The poet who discards old myths
becomes a pupil/ephebe of the sun of reality that must bear no name—the
"gorgeous wheel" equivalent to the ephebe's "gold flourisher." Stevens
thus implies that a multifaceted and ever-changing romantic poetic re-
stores some commerce with the actual world that entrenched imaginative
systems deny. "Slight," "light," "least," and "only," Stevens's proposed
poetic quivers with change that keeps the mind from completely obliterat-
ing its point of contact with the real world.

   Stevens thus arrives at the idea of a new romantic practice that, by
virtue of its radical provisionality, always remains fresh.[4] At the end of

"Sailing after Lunch," the poet's boat rushes brightly off the end of the page and out of sight, resisting any attempt to fix or define its movements—the image of Stevens's desire to keep his new poetic from turning paradigm. In calling forth such a protean aesthetic, however, Stevens was left to ponder how to sustain extreme fluidity without sacrificing intelligibility. As his gloss on "Sailing after Lunch" in his letter to Latimer betrays, Stevens felt particularly invested in his new poem even while he doubted its power to communicate. Describing "Sailing after Lunch" as "an abridgement of at least a temporary theory of poetry"—a phrase itself full of provisionalizing gestures—Stevens wrote to Latimer that the poem "should make its own point" even as he outlined his theory in detail:

> When people speak of the romantic, they do so in what the French commonly call a *pejorative* sense. But poetry is essentially romantic, only the romantic of poetry must be something constantly new and, therefore, just the opposite of what is spoken of as the romantic. Without this new romantic, one gets nowhere; with it, the most casual things take on transcendence, and the poet rushes brightly, and so on. . . . I realize that a poem, like anything else, must make its own way. Moreover, I cannot possibly change this particular one without mussing it up. It seems to me to be perfectly clear, with the explanation. I hope you will find it equally so without the explanation.[5]

Even as he wrote to Latimer, Stevens found his desire to leave his poem unfixed at war with his need to clearly define his purpose. In his letter, Stevens admits that, without an accompanying explanation, the theoretical significance of "Sailing after Lunch" may elude the audience completely. Unwilling to risk the provisional nature of his new poetic, however, Stevens resisted the impulse to "muss up" his poem by making his "temporary" theory more accessible to the squamous mind. In "Sailing after Lunch," Stevens encountered the difficulty of defining an aesthetic that, by its very nature, resisted such formulations.

Afraid that "Sailing after Lunch" would not make its point and feeling the need to explain himself more fully, Stevens came across a model for his musings that confirmed his sense of what a new sort of romantic verse could and should be: Marianne Moore's *Selected Poems*. On March 20, 1935, Stevens received a copy of Moore's book from T. C. Wilson of *Westminster Magazine* along with a request for a review. At first Stevens declined Wilson's offer, claiming that he was "planning to start a piece of work" likely to keep him "busy for some time to come"—the set of poems that was to become *Owl's Clover*.[6] Stevens's letter of refusal, however, reveals the importance of Moore's work to his emerging poetic theory. "Miss Moore is not only a complete disintegrator; she is an equally complete reintegrator," Stevens wrote to Wilson, adding by way of explanation:

> it seems to me that Miss Moore is endeavoring to create a new romantic; that the way she breaks up older forms is merely an attempt to free herself for the pursuit of the thing in which she is interested; and that the thing in which she is interested in all the strange collocations of her work is that which is essential in poetry, always: the romantic. But a fresh romantic.[7]

In Stevens's view, Moore's success as a poet was twofold. She not only blasted apart the rigid forms of derivative romanticism, but also collected the fragments into fresh poetry that seemed never to repeat the same tropes twice. In his letter to Wilson, Stevens casts Moore's verse as a series of "strange collocations" that both excite the mind and, in their oddity, resist formulaic reduction. In making something constantly new Moore suited Stevens's difficult vision of a new romantic poet.

Stevens was so taken with Moore's book that somewhere between April and late May 1935 he changed his mind about writing a review. On May 27, 1935 Stevens sent his completed note on Moore's poems, "A Poet That Matters," to Wilson along with the assertion in a subsequent letter that both "Sailing after Lunch" and the note on *Selected Poems* were "expressions of the same thing."[8] Both Stevens's essay and the marginalia that cover his copy of Moore's poems bear witness to the pleasure Stevens took in the seemingly endless and surprising variation of Moore's verse. Reworking the terms of "Sailing after Lunch"—the pejorative versus the new romantic—Stevens opens his discussion of Moore by distinguishing the quality of her spirit. "The tall pages of *Selected Poems* by Marianne Moore are the papers of a scrupulous spirit," Stevens begins: "The merely fastidious spirit *à la mode* is likely to be on the verge of suffocation from hyperaesthesia. But Miss Moore's is an unaffected, witty, colloquial sort of spirit."⁹ The pejorative romantic poet, in Stevens's terms, is "merely fastidious." Pathologically sensitive to fresh or irreverent ideas, he clings to persnickety standards and old tropes that produce musty and niggling verse. By contrast, Stevens casts Moore, the "new romantic" poet, as scrupulous rather than fastidious. Stevens's substitution grants Moore painstaking precision but distinguishes her from a closed-minded adherence to a particular style or a single set of capricious standards. Unaffected, witty, and colloquial, Moore injects language into her verse that specifically undercuts the inappropriate and unpropitious Latinate pomposities of the pejorative poet in "Sailing after Lunch."

What Stevens admires most about Moore's verse, however, is her ability to maintain the freshness she achieves. Where in "Sailing after Lunch" Stevens sends his own new romantic boat off the page, maintaining its fluidity at the risk of unintelligible formlessness, Moore, in Stevens's view, demonstrates how to write verse without sacrificing protean motion. Engaging in a lengthy discussion of Moore's formal techniques, Stevens marvels at her ability to make the most crafted verse seem unfixed. In a stanza of "The Fish," Stevens finds Moore's rhymes so light that "at first glance" her lines appear "to contain no rhymes whatever," revealing intricacies only on a second look. "The light rhymes," Stevens asserts, "please one unconsciously" rather than forcefully announcing the poet's ordering presence. Moore's musical ear strikes Stevens as similarly unoppressive. "Miss Moore instinctively relates sounds," he claims looking at the sixth stanza of "The Fish." "There is a relation between the groups of letters *ext, ks, phys*. The *i*'s in *defiant edifice* are related. As these relations change, not only the sounds change, but the colors, the texture, the effects also change" (*OP,* 217–18). Instinctive rather than regularly patterned, Moore's sounds strike Stevens as a vehicle for constant variation. Strong sounds, Stevens claims, "contrast and intermingle" with lighter sounds in Moore's verse in a way that thwarts all rhythmic expectations. Even Moore's syllabic stanzas, which Stevens admits are "rigid" in their accounting, do not mar the plasticity of her poetry. Stevens writes of "The Steeple-Jack":

The lines and stanzas flow innocently. Nevertheless, throughout the dozen stanzas the lines repeat themselves, syllable by syllable, without variation. The stanzas are mechanisms. Yet instead of producing a mechanical effect, they produce an effect of ease. In one of her poems Miss Moore writes of

> . . . intermingled echoes
> struck from thin glasses successively at random—.
>
> (*OP,* 218)

Stevens finds that even the most mechanistic of Moore's techniques produces poetry that seems artless. Her lines, like the tones of her glass harmonica in "Those Various Scalpels," appear to be made "successively at random," ordered in a way that miraculously resists attempts to discern a working pattern.

Turning to the issue of Moore's "interests," Stevens reads her verse as not only resisting rigidity in form, but also in content. Choosing "The Steeple-Jack" as an example of Moore's thematic concerns, Stevens claims that the "point of the poem is a view of the common-place." He elaborates:

> The view is that of Dürer or of Miss Moore in the mask or mood of Dürer, or, more definitely, perhaps, under the stimulus of Dürer. The common-place is, say, a New England fishing-village. Whatever the poem may do for Dürer or for the village, it does many happy things for Miss Moore and for those who delight in her. Obviously, having in mind the subject-matter of the poem, Miss Moore *donne dans le romanesque.* Consciously, the point of the poem may have been something wholly casual. It may lie in the words
>
> it is a privilege to see so
> much confusion.

Consciously, it may have had no more point than the wish to make note of observations made while in the cloud of a mood. That is Miss Moore's method. (*OP,* 218)

Engaging a commonplace subject rather than elevated abstract theme, Moore's poem once again suits Stevens's vision of a new, rather than a pejorative, romantic. What, precisely, Moore's "view" of her fishing village means to say, however, Stevens does not specify. Unwilling to fix a new romantic that, by definition, must remain unfixed, Stevens resolutely refuses to ascribe one clear meaning to Moore's poem. In Stevens's view, Moore replaces the singular elevated moral of a pejorative romantic poem with a series of points that may be "wholly casual." Eschewing the preachy poses of "the merely fastidious," Moore's verse offers a "confusion" of provisional points that Stevens finds a "privilege to see."

Stevens thus credits Moore with the same sort of poetic innocence Moore grants Stevens in "The Plumet Basilisk." In her lizard poem, Moore claims that Stevens, the "innocent gold-defending dragon," creates primal music refreshingly unfettered by the dictates of social decorum. Stevens, in turn, reads Moore as similarly "innocent" of the old rules of the pejorative romantic that pretend to govern her craft. If Stevens indeed ascribes any method to Moore, it is her stringent avoidance of method. Listing the seemingly chaotic profusion of animals that inhabit "The Steeple-Jack," Stevens claims that "subject" for Moore "is often incidental," a matter of accident rather than the planned product of the poet's eye. The flow of her images as well strikes Stevens as a by-product of unorganized esprit. In "Snakes, Mongooses, Snake Charmers, and the Like," Moore presents the cobra as an example of an object so attractive to the imagination that the poet feels inescapably moved to observe its motions. "One is compelled to look at it," she writes of the snake, "as at the shadows of the alps / imprisoning in their folds like flies in amber, the rhythms of the skating rink." From snake, to shadows, to embalmed flies, to the swirl of the skater's blade, Moore creates an exciting jumble of seemingly unrelated images in two lusty similes that playfully explore the mind's power to animate its subject. Such lines, Stevens writes, complimenting Moore in "A Poet That Matters," "might so easily have been pottered over and nullified; and how hilarious, how skillful they are!" (OP, 220) Stevens found Moore's profusion a wonderful example of her provisional romanticism, her imagination skipping from image to image with wild and unconscious abandon. Moore's vision of the fly in amber—small and immobile—collides in her lines with two spreading images of constant motion, one on a vast alpine scale. Rather than "potter" over such

connections and sap their spontaneity, however, Moore's lets the incongru-
ities stand, and her odd multiple associations keep the mind in motion.
Stevens was so taken with Moore's lines that he underlined them in *Selected
Poems* and transferred them again into the flyleaf of the book, where he
made them a metaphor for the whole of Moore's volume. "The panorama
of an imagination," Stevens declares in the flyleaf: "Pages like 'the shadows
of the alps imprisoning in their folds like flies in amber the rhythms of the
skating rink'—they are the adornments not so much of a moral as of a
pensee."[10] In his flyleaf comments, Stevens admires Moore for her ability to
create a "panorama" of imagination that remains insistently diverse.
Rather than preach a unifying and domesticating moral, Moore's pages, in
Stevens's view, conduct a complex and ongoing process of thought—the
mind in the act of finding what will suffice.

To Stevens's mind, the "people" in the poem also serve the function of
qualifying the poet's vision. As George Bornstein points out, Stevens
often employs the provisionalizing tactic of a double consciousness in his
mature lyrics.[11] Rather than present his own imaginative experience di-
rectly, Stevens often observes another, separate mind confronting the
world. As Bornstein puts it, Stevens "refracts mental action of one mind
through the apprehension of a second," distancing himself from the poten-
tially oppressive ordering force in the poem.[12] As Stevens reads "The
Steeple-Jack," Moore practices the same procedure; she does not view her
fishing village directly, but through "the mask or mood" of Dürer, putting
herself immediately at a remove from whatever ordered vision the poem
has to offer. As Stevens points out, however, Dürer constitutes only one or-
dering force among many in Moore's poem and, tracing the nested visions
of Moore's characters, Stevens revels in the multiplicity of her display:

> The people in the poem are Dürer;
>
>   The college student
>   named Ambrose sits on the hill-side
>   with his not-native books and hat
>   and sees boats
>
>   at sea progress white and rigid as if in
>   a groove;

and C. J. Poole, Steeple-Jack, with one or two references to others. Poole is merely a sign on the sidewalk with his name on it. The last stanza is:—

> It could not be dangerous to be living
>   in a town like this, of simple people,
> who have a steeple-jack placing danger signs by the church
> while he is gilding the solid-
>   pointed star, which on a steeple
> stands for hope.
>
>   (*OP*, 219)

As Stevens rightly notices, Moore does indeed fill her poem with secondary consciousnesses. In "The Steeple-Jack," Moore introduces Ambrose, her student and man of the mind, who, under the influence of ideas "not-native" to his tiny and somewhat self-satisfied village, shapes the landscape from the panoramic perspective of a hilltop. Rather than order the vista directly, Moore observes another mind in the act of ordering. Ambrose's gaze arranges the boats in the harbor into a tidy, "rigid" progression, but Moore removes herself from the potential stasis of the act, viewing the arrangement only indirectly. Moore repeats the tactic within the scope of Ambrose's vision itself. "Liking the elegance of which / the source is not bravado," Ambrose, Moore writes:

>   knows by heart the antique
> sugar-bowl-shaped summer-house of
>   interlacing slats, and the pitch
> of the church
>
> spire, not true, from which a man in scarlet lets
>   down a rope as a spider spins a thread;
> he might be part of a novel, but on the sidewalk a
> sign says C. J. Poole, Steeple Jack,
>   in black and white; and one in red
> and white says
>
> Danger.[13]

From his high vantage point, Ambrose sees the familiar shapes of the village that he cares about enough to "know by heart." His elevated

perspective allows him to glimpse C. J. Poole, the steeplejack in scarlet
who, "placing danger signs by the church," gilds "the solid- / pointed
star, which on a steeple / stands for hope." Dressed in red, Poole and his
craft embody the danger his sign proclaims. A mark of the town's bra-
vado, Poole's art reflects the needs of a community that places too much
emphasis on the material manifestations of what should be powerful
interior or imaginative sentiments. As Moore's line break in the final
stanza proclaims, "gilding the solid," the steeplejack enacts Aaron's sin of
substituting a prideful golden fixity for the mysterious idea of hope.
Poole's art of beautiful surface runs the risk of distracting from the "star-
tling inner light" that the star should bespeak. Moore's town is "not
dangerous," however, because Poole's art, too, is provisionalized within
the poem. Ambrose watches Poole at work in the same way that Moore
observes Ambrose. Ambrose knows "by heart" that the pitch of the
church steeple is "not true," and he is not seduced by Poole's, or the
town's, errors of complacency. Nesting Poole's art within Ambrose's
vision, Moore mitigates its spider's power to trap by placing it at two
removes. For both Moore and Stevens, intellectual safety involves guard-
ing against static symbols without substance.

Having discerned Moore's use of double consciousness, Stevens
rounds out his discussion of "The Steeple-Jack" by reading Moore as a
practitioner of another of his favorite provisionalizing devices—negative
rhetoric. Examining Moore's description of seaside flowers, "There are
no banyans, frangipani nor / jack-fruit trees; nor an exotic serpent / life,"
Stevens claims: "If she had said in so many words that there were ban-
yans, frangipani, and so on, she would have been romantic in the sense in
which the romantic is a relic of the imagination. She hybridizes the thing
by a negative" (*OP,* 219–20). As Michael Benamou notes, Stevens fre-
quently indulges in an imaginative "anti-rhetoric" that marks him as an
uncomfortable inheritor of romantic style.[14] In lyrics as early as "Disillu-
sionment of Ten O'Clock," Stevens presents the imagination's work in
negative terms—"People are not going / To dream of baboons and peri-
winkles." Craving the world with imagination and the world without
imagination at one in the same time, Stevens qualifies the mind's cre-
ations. As George Bornstein states, however, Stevens's reading of Moore
as an antirhetorician remains something of a self-projection.[15] Where

Moore certainly indulges in other provisionalizing tactics, the lines Stevens cites—an image of exotic undomesticated riot that the self-satisfied little town would just as soon ignore—constitute one of the only such instances of negative assertion in Moore's volume. Perhaps more important than Stevens's self-projection, however, is his self-critique. In pointing to Moore's lines, Stevens condemns the fixtures of his own unhybridized imaginative tropics—his "big finned palms," "green vines angering for life," "vivid blooms," and "wild warblers . . . warbling in the jungle"—as the relics of a tedious mind. As Stevens writes in "A Poet That Matters," the "imagination does not often delight in the same thing twice," and his comment seems specifically aimed at his own repetitive use of exotic tropical locales (*OP*, 221). Where Moore appears capable of endless diversity, Stevens fears that his own poetry may very well be going round on a crutch of expected exotic tropes.

Not surprisingly, Stevens's marginal comments in his copy of *Selected Poems* reflect his growing dislike for his own early poetic relics.[16] All throughout Moore's volume, Stevens makes note of her complaints against opaque, fixed, abstract, or overly sophisticated art—the song of the inappropriate and unpropitious aesthete that "Sailing after Lunch" hoped to dispatch for good. In "Picking and Choosing," Stevens underlines Moore's assertion that "Words are constructive / when they are true; the opaque allusion—the simulated flight // upward—accomplishes nothing." In the text of Moore's "England," Stevens marks her comments on the nature of French verse, "France, the 'chrysalis of the nocturnal butterfly,' in / whose products mystery of construction diverts one from what was originally one's / object—substance at the core." At the end of "Those Various Scalpels," Stevens underscores the question Moore makes to those aesthetes who prefer "the hard majesty of . . . sophistication" to the flexibility of artistic "opportunity": "But / why dissect destiny with instruments which / are more highly specialized than the tissues of destiny itself?" In the text of "When I Buy Pictures," Stevens highlights Moore's assessment that in artistic production, "Too stern an intellectual emphasis upon this quality or that detracts from one's enjoyment." Stevens's careful attention to Moore's ongoing critique of inflexible literary pretense points to his deep desire to eschew all stale formulaic images and language in favor of more natural and spontaneous speech. As Stevens underlined in the text of

Moore's poem "New York," it is not static plunder that the poet craves, but rather "accessibility to experience"—the ability, in a protean poetry, to always remain open to new encounters.

Indeed, on the heels of his self-critique of banyans and frangipani as relics of the imagination, Stevens again looks at "The Steeple-Jack" and admires the accessibility to experience that Moore's verse provides. Quoting Moore's observation of the fog on seaside flowers, "so that you have / the tropics at first hand: the trumpet vine . . . / or moon vines trained on fishing-twine," Stevens claims that Moore "hybridizes" her verse not only by the negative, but "by association" with the actual. "Moon-vines are moon-vines and tedious," he writes. "But moon-vines trained on fishing-twine are something else and they are as perfectly as it is possible for anything to be what interests Miss Moore" (*OP*, 220). In Stevens's view, the endless colloquial variety of Moore's images holds the mind close to the real world. Training moonvines on fishing twine, Moore consistently undercuts her, to use Stevens's marginalia from *Selected Poems*, "elans de l'imagination" with references to the common and imperfect things of every day. Moore's imagination grasps at things and, as Stevens writes, "sates itself instantaneously in them," moving on to its next subject before stale abstractions and repetitive tropes set in (*OP*, 220). The result, as Stevens writes in the flyleaf of *Selected Poems*, is a "romantic of the mundane," in touch, however fleetingly, in language and image, with the common life that Stevens felt was missing in the exotic tropical reveries of his own verse.

Stevens thus reads Moore as achieving in form, rhetoric, and content the radical provisionality that he proposes for the new romantic in "Sailing after Lunch." Throughout "A Poet That Matters," however, Stevens's need for an ally and a role model leads him to indulge in a fair amount of self-projection. The lines from "Those Various Scalpels" that Stevens borrows out of context to illustrate Moore's lively changeability function in Moore's poem as an image of irritating ambiguity. In "Those Various Scalpels" Moore critiques her urbane subject, who makes "those / various sounds consistently indistinct, like intermingled echoes / struck from thin glasses successively at random—the / inflection disguised" (*SPMM*, 57–58). As Moore points out, such random sounds have the tendency to weaken or obscure meaning. Stevens, however, ignores

Moore's complaint and turns her lines into a vision of liberating mutabil-
ity. Projecting his own concerns onto Moore, Stevens casts her as a poet,
like himself, willing to sacrifice a potentially didactic "something said"
for the riches of enhancing and sometimes difficult poetic diversity. His
reading, while partially correct, runs counter to Moore's emerging poetic
of the 1930s. As I argue in the previous chapter, early in the decade
Moore herself desired a new romantic poetic that could blast apart deriva-
tive romantic tropes without itself losing touch with the actual world.
Yet, as "The Plumet Basilisk," "The Jerboa," and "The Steeple-Jack"
attest, Moore was less sure than Stevens that an endlessly provisionalized
verse could sustain the poet, or the increasingly fatalistic populace, in
violent times. As John Slatin and Taffy Martin both point out, the confu-
sion that lurks under the surface of Moore's New England community in
"The Steeple-Jack" often threatens to overwhelm the inhabitants.[17] The
town's complacent isolation in old tropes provides only a false protec-
tion, but Ambrose's vision, while rightly provisional, may not prove
strong enough to protect the village he loves from the storms that
threaten its existence. As Moore's "The Frigate Pelican" attests, she
looked to Stevens as an example of a stronger, more secure vision that, in
becoming less rather than more provisional, could protect the poet and
resist the downdrafts and despair of hard times.

In "A Poet That Matters," Stevens thus indulges, in part, in a
"misprison" of Moore's poetry, but he does so for reasons antithetical to
those that Bloom's theory predicts. Rather than anxiously dismiss or
reject Moore as a hated rival, Stevens projects his own aims onto her
poetry so that he may claim her as a much-needed colleague in the
making of a new kind of verse. Stevens's response to Moore also goes
against the grain of Gilbert and Gubar's projections about the nature of
male/female influence among the modernists. In their book *No Man's
Land,* Gilbert and Gubar admit that in the twentieth century more than
ever before men and women, like Moore and Stevens, found themselves
joined in literary enterprises. Yet, Gilbert and Gubar insist on reading
anxiety as the primary element of such relationships. They claim that

> both men of letters and women of letters devised a variety of strate-
> gies for defusing anxiety about the literary combat in which they

often felt engaged. Among male writers, such strategies included mythologizing women to align them with dread prototypes; fictionalizing them to dramatize their destructive influence; slandering them in essays, memoirs, and poems; prescribing alternative ambitions for them; appropriating their words in order to usurp or trivialize their language; and ignoring or evading their achievements in critical texts.[18]

Point for point, Stevens's response to Moore in "A Poet That Matters" refutes Gilbert and Gubar's vision of male literary anxiety in relation to a powerful female rival. Rather than slander Moore, Stevens praises her; rather than ignore Moore, Stevens makes a serious effort in one of his few critical texts to bring her work to the attention of his peers. Rather than read Moore as a palpable threat to his own patriarchal literary authority, Stevens openly embraces Moore's verse as a working model for his own endeavors.

Indeed, looking beyond "A Poet That Matters," Stevens did, in fact, "appropriate" Moore's vocabulary, but, once again, not for the anxious and slanderous motives Gilbert and Gubar imply. Moore's seemingly endless round of fresh, provisionalized images provided Stevens with a powerful new vocabulary for reimagining and redirecting his own work. "Picking and Choosing," Moore's critique of obfuscating artistic complexity, begins with the assertion, "Literature is a phase of life." Transfixed by Moore's phrase, Stevens drew on her words to make preliminary notes for his review:

> What we have are the spiritual forces that have made Miss Moore. And one of these is the desire to be close to the truth. About what? I think about literature as a phase of life. Not about literature alone. Nor about life alone. Nor about literature and also about life. But about literature as a phase of life. And thus, of course, about life as a phase of literature. This gives her book an extraordinary value, veracity, and an extraordinary sanity. It is an exquisite book. But it does communicate literature rather than life, although it is here that the literature that is communicated is a phase of life.[19]

In the words, "Literature is a phase of life," Stevens finds yet another expression of Moore's provisional romanticism. Taking his cue from her line, Stevens reads Moore's various romantic flights as "phases," temporary interludes that occur in a cyclic progression. In keeping with Stevens's vision of a new romanticism, Moore replaces the pejorative static moon of derivative romanticism with a changing moon that waxes and wanes, forever qualifying its own brightness. Yet, the language of Moore's phrase does not directly address the issue of a "new" rather than a "pejorative" romantic poetry, but rather the relationship between life and literature. Through Moore's words, Stevens distinctly casts a provisionalized romanticism as a means of ongoing interaction with, rather than escape from, the forces of the common life. Moore's intermingling phrase grants a social component to the poet's struggle to redefine romantic verse.

Contemplating Moore's significance at the end of "A Poet That Matters," Stevens gestures toward the changing sense of the poet's role that he finds in her cyclic phrase. "Miss Moore's form is not the quirk of a self-conscious writer," he asserts:

> She is not a writer. She is a woman who has profound needs. In any project for poetry (and one wishes that the world of tailors, plasterers, barkeepers could bring itself to accept poets in a matter-of-fact way) the first effort should be devoted to establishing that poets are men and women, not writers. (*OP*, 221)

In claiming that Moore is a woman rather than a writer, Stevens insists, once more, that her poems have no "self-conscious" literary method. Rather than consciously fix her verse like a detached aesthete, Moore responds, again and again, to profound current "needs," writing whatever suits the moment. Such flexibility and spontaneity, Stevens implies, marks Moore as a proper social poet of everyday life. Like the tailor or the plasterer, Moore creates a series of provisional works that, if accepted in a matter-of-fact way like the tailor's coat, could serve the ever-changing spiritual needs of a changing society.

Abandoning the irredeemably loaded term *romantic* as a dead end in late 1935, Stevens readily took hold of Moore's phrase "Literature is a phase of life" as a means of explaining his verse. "Literature is the better part of life," Stevens wrote in his *Adagia:* "To this it seems inevitably necessary to add provided life is the better part of literature."[20] On the heels of Stanley Burnshaw's Marxist attack on *Ideas of Order,* Stevens again used Moore's words to distinguish his current poetic concerns from those of his earlier verse. Responding to the assessment of his verse as "essentially decorative," in a letter to Ronald Lane Latimer, Stevens wrote:

> I was on the point of saying that I did not agree with the opinion that my verse is decorative, when I remembered that when *Harmonium* was in the making there was a time when I liked the idea of images and images alone, or images and the music of verse together. I then believed in *pure poetry,* as it was called.
>
> I still have a distinct liking for that sort of thing. But we live in a different time, and life means a good deal more to us now-a-days than literature does. In the period of which I have just spoken, I thought literature meant most. Moreover, I am not so sure that I don't think exactly the same thing now, but, unquestionably, I think at the same time that life is the essential part of literature.[21]

From *Harmonium* to the start of *Owl's Clover,* Stevens charts his growth from a pejorative romantic poet who revels in the pure ornament of unhybridized imaginative escapes, to a poet like Moore, who provisionalizes his imaginary gardens with real toads, not allowing any one idea of order to take him far from the disorder of "life . . . now-a-days," the social confusion that it is a privilege to see.

As Stevens's rephrasing of his poetic as one of life and literature indicates, he began to equate, in the context of Moore's volume, the achievement of a radically provisional verse with the achievement of a more socially grounded poetry. As James Longenbach notes, Stevens "feared the political ramifications of certainty," and his "distrust of dogmatism runs like a refrain throughout his prose of the 1930s."[22] Indeed, in many of his lyrics penned around the time of "A Poet That Matters," Stevens foregrounds the relationship between the public and the provisional, often in distinctly Mooreish terms. In "Farewell to Florida," written immediately after his review of Moore, Stevens continues the critique of his own well-used poetic tropics that he began in "A Poet That Matters." Leaving his secondhand tropics behind, he plunges into a verse "Both of men and clouds"—a hybridized verse of fishing twine and moonvines, the actual and the poet's "cloud of a mood," that Stevens sees as the necessary mode for expressing the "shoving," "slithering," "shattered," "turbulent," "violent" mind of men in crowds. In "Sad Strains of a Gay Waltz," Stevens laments the stasis of old social forms in images that ring conspicuously close to those of Moore's "The Frigate Pelican." Where Moore pictures the measured motions of socially acceptable art as a "reticent lugubrious ragged immense minuet"—a slow, inarticulate, impoverished dance in 3/4 time—Stevens embodies his critique of decorum in a waltz, another dance in triple meter, grown equally sad. Stevens's speaker begins the poem as if correcting his, and his community's, misconceptions about such fixed forms:

> There comes a time when the waltz
> Is no longer a mode of desire, a mode
> Of revealing desire and is empty of shadows.
>
> Too many waltzes have ended. And then
> There's that mountain-minded Hoon,
> For whom desire was never that of the waltz,
>
> Who found all form and order in solitude,
> For whom the shapes were never the figures of men.
>
> (CPWS, 121)

Seeking to be, like Moore, close to the truth about literature as a phase of life, Stevens concludes that all art forms have limited life spans. Like Moore's "lugubrious" minuet, the decorous waltz is dead, a rigid social form that, unchanging, no longer adheres in any way to the actual. Invoking an expression of male-female passion, Stevens implies that the waltz once accomplished a hybridized union between a male mind and the sought-after female body of reality, but that such "desire" no longer exists in art grown static and abstract. Stevens further admits that his own exotic early poetry fairs no better as a social alternative. Never much of a dancer, Hoon offers only a static art of solitary internal reverie that, like the waltz, has grown old and impotent in its detachment from the actual. Dispatching worn artistic alternatives, Stevens thus arrives at the same question that Moore poses in "The Frigate Pelican" in her search for a social art to suit violent times: *"Festina lente*. Be Gay / Civilly: How So?" The answer Stevens gives, however, looks different from that of his role model. Where Moore imagines a stronger, less serviceable, less provisionalized moral verse as perhaps the only possible counter to the crushing power of the social python—"If I do well I am blessed / whether any bless me or not, and if I do / ill I am cursed"—Stevens imagines that, the old forms destroyed, the current "epic of disbelief" will be ordered by "Some harmonious skeptic" who, in a skeptical music

> Will unite these figures of men and their shapes
> Will glisten again with motion, the music
> Will be motion and full of shadows.
>
> (CPWS, 122)

Building on his thoughts in "A Poet That Matters," Stevens pictures an endlessly provisionalized artistic order as the source of socially relevant verse. Only the "gay" tunes of the harmonious skeptic, constantly in motion and as fleeting as shadows, can play to the spiritual needs of a violent society without losing touch with changing social realities. Strong enough to resist both the seductive stability of repetitive tropes and the materialistic fatalism left in their wake, the skeptical poet unites "these figures of men" in literature that is "a phase of life" rather than a static substitute for life. In Stevens's view, the poet can be "gay civilly" if he plays the provisional and hybridized music—the sort of music Stevens attributes to Marianne Moore.

Moore's *Selected Poems* thus serves, in part, as a stepping-stone for Stevens between the reveries of *Harmonium* and his considerations of art and society in *Owl's Clover*. Excited by Moore's endless poetic diversity, Stevens claims her as a workable model for a new, radically provisional aesthetic and commits the repetitive exotic tropes of his early verse to the dump. Making use of Moore's comments on the phases of life and literature, Stevens further reconceives the new romantic aesthetic as not merely a poetic problem, but as the potential means of creating a more socially relevant, contemporaneous verse.

Perhaps the most vivid expressions of the importance of Moore's *Selected Poems* to Stevens, however, are his continued references in the years well beyond "A Poet That Matters" to ideas he generated in the context of Moore's volume. In the spring of 1938, Stevens returns again to his reading of Moore to shape one of his most detailed prewar explorations of the new romantic poetic, "Connoisseur of Chaos." Adopting the persona of a "connoisseur" in the poem, Stevens immediately invokes Moore's lyric on the subject of "Critics and Connoisseurs"—one of his favorites in *Selected Poems*—in which she critiques an overintellectualized approach to art. As Moore sees it, connoisseurs of art who automatically despise any work that does not reflect their persnickety and stifling aesthetic standards have a tendency to miss much of the world's beauty. Addressing such stuffed shirts, Moore argues for a more flexible definition of art:

> There is a great amount of poetry in unconscious
>   fastidiousness. Certain Ming
>   products, imperial floor-coverings of coach-
>   wheel yellow, are well enough in their way but I have seen
>   something
>   that I like better—a
>   mere childish attempt to make an imperfectly ballasted
>   animal stand up,
>   similar determination to make a pup
>   eat his meat from the plate.
>   (*SPMM,* 39)

In presenting the ideas of order that intrigue her, Moore lays out the principal opposition between "enhancing diversity" and "mere fastidiousness" that defines Stevens's discussion of her verse in "A Poet That Matters." Preferring "unconscious" artistry to oppressive "fastidiousness," Moore appreciates "mere childish" or innocent attempts to order the world that demonstrate affection for the common life and make no pretence of authority or permanence. Unlike the unchanging Ming products fancied by the connoisseur, the puppy in the poem, no matter how carefully coaxed by his master to stand, will fall over. The attention lavished on the pup must be repeated again and again in a series of provisional acts of ordering that, while they can never achieve the enduring aesthetic perfection of Ming artifacts, remain lovingly and forgivingly engaged with the imperfections of the actual world. Drawing on Moore's critique of the inflexible connoisseur, Stevens's title insists, like Moore's poem, that poets must learn to appreciate the temporary, the accidental, and the incomplete. They must be "connoisseurs," not of "Ming products," but of "chaos," the necessarily unfixed process of the mind's endless search for what will suffice.

As his title suggests, Stevens's 1938 lyric on the subject of the properly provisional imagination draws heavily on his earlier reading of Moore's *Selected Poems* in "A Poet That Matters." Like Moore in "Critics and Connoisseurs," Stevens begins "Connoisseur of Chaos" by declaring his appreciation for the liberating incongruities that exist in all valid ideas of order. In the first line of "Critics," Moore admits her liking for "unconscious fastidiousness"—a paradoxical conjunction of impulsive spontaneity and meticulous thoughtful care that keeps any imaginative act from becoming oppressive. At the start of "Connoisseur of Chaos," Stevens uses the syntactical switch that he gleaned from Moore's "Picking and Choosing"—literature is a phase of life, life is a phase of literature—to phrase two similar poetic paradoxes:

> A.   A violent order is a disorder; and
> B.   A great disorder is an order. These
> Two things are one. (Pages of illustrations.)
>
> $\qquad\qquad\qquad\qquad\qquad\qquad\qquad$ (*CPWS,* 215)

Repeating the argument of Moore's "Critics and Connoisseurs" in the ironic form of a logical proof, Stevens claims that a violent order, like the conscious fastidiousness of Moore's connoisseur, is a disorder because it makes distorting demands and ignores actualities, like the tippable puppy, that do not suit its purposes. Similarly, "a great disorder is an order" in that it flexibly accommodates the variations of the actual and prefers liberating change to rigid restrictions—the hallmarks, as Stevens claims in "A Poet That Matters," of Moore's satisfying poetic.

Abandoning the illusory rhetorical structure of a single fixable proof,

Stevens's connoisseur launches instead into pages of illustrations—a great disorder of possible imaginative events that he deems casual enough to place within parentheses. The multiple examples of properly provisional poetry that follow in the second stanza display various techniques that Stevens saw at work in Moore's *Selected Poems.*

> If all the green of spring was blue, and it is;
> If the flowers of South Africa were bright
> On the tables of Connecticut, and they are;
> If Englishmen lived without tea in Ceylon, and they do;
> And if it all went on in an orderly way,
> And it does; a law of inherent opposites,
> Of essential unity, is as pleasant as port,
> As pleasant as the brush-strokes of a bough,
> An upper, particular bough in, say, Marchand.
>
> (*CPWS,* 215)

Like Moore, Stevens's connoisseur "hybridizes" his imagination by association with the actual—the imagination's impure blue contains the green of reality—and trains his moonvines on fishing twine—the lush tropical plants of the imagination that fill Stevens's poems rest upon the mundane tables of his native Connecticut. Such romantic "interminglings," while they do not "resolve the world," offer moments of change that in their disordered diversity thwart our expectations and keep the world fresh. Each new disorienting thought, like "the shade / Of a cloud on sand," produces a pleasure that is only temporary—the mental equivalent of the slight tingle derived from a nightly glass of port. Stevens further hybridizes each of his cross-fertilized propositions by mixing an intentionally conditional supposition (if such were so) with an assertion (and it is), a potential fiction with a statement of truth. The new romantic poetic, Stevens writes in "A Poet That Matters," is "an association of the true and the false." Both sit side by side in the syntax of the connoisseur's sentences.

Repudiating the implied resolution of the connoisseur's mock-authoritative opening statements, Stevens draws his poem to a close with a vision of the poet as pensive man that once again rings back to Moore's verse:

                                                        Now, A
And B are not like statuary, posed
For a vista in the Louvre. They are things chalked
On the sidewalk so that the pensive man may see.

                                                        (*CPWS*, 216)

Stevens's statement that truths are not fixed "like statuary" recalls Moore's
injunction against artistic complexity in "In the Days of Prismatic Col-
our," "Truth is no Apollo / Belvedere, no formal thing"—a line Stevens
cuts to form a more general critique of frozen abstracts and quotes promi-
nently near the end of "A Poet That Matters" as "Truth is no Apollo" (*OP*,
220). Like Moore in "Critics and Connoisseurs," Stevens rejects con-
sciously fastidious museum pieces (the static Ming products of Moore's
connoisseur) in favor of more innocent and provisional creations. Where
Moore appreciates the poetry of an owner's "mere childish" efforts to
balance a puppy, Stevens likewise envisions proper ideas of order as mere
childish pictures that boys and girls chalk in play on the sidewalk. Both
poets conceive of creative activity as temporary, spontaneous, and uncon-
scious of rules.

    In the last lines of "Connoisseur of Chaos," Stevens caps his compen-
dium of hybridizing strategies with yet another provisionalizing tactic he
found in Moore's *Selected Poems*, an act of double consciousness. Like
Ambrose, Moore's student in "The Steeple-Jack" who observes C. J.
Poole gilding the star on the church steeple, Stevens's pensive man
thoughtfully observes another mind in the act of creating an order:

    The pensive man . . . He sees that eagle float
    For which the intricate Alps are a single nest.

                                                        (*CPWS*, 216)

As George Bornstein suggests, to see the wild diversity of the Alps as a
single domestic nest constitutes an act of imaginative ordering on a grand
scale.[23] The pensive man, however, keeps his feet planted firmly on the
ground and merely looks on as the eagle arranges the landscape. The
pensive man thus observes order in the Alps only indirectly and attenuates
the eagle's vision by one remove. In the context of his considerations of

provisional verse, Stevens's image of man and bird again recalls his reading of Moore's *Selected Poems*. Floating over the landscape, Stevens's powerfully imaginative eagle mirrors Moore's acknowledgedly Stevensian bird, the frigate pelican who, full of feints, is an "eagle of vigilance." In turn, Stevens's pensive man resembles the speaker of Moore's poem who, rooted to the ground, observes the frigate's imaginative perception. Both poets provisionalize the vision of their high birds.

Yet, even while Stevens invokes Moore's verse throughout his connoisseur's catalog of provisionalizing tactics, his final image shows precisely where he and Moore part company in the 1930s. Where Stevens finds the pensive man's provisional verse the proper and necessary poetry for a violent prewar world, Moore views the pensive person's grounded position in "The Frigate Pelican" as one of difficult and dangerous sacrifice. Observing a powerful order at one remove, Moore's speaker herself remains prey to "the tired / moment of danger, that lays on heart and lungs the / weight of the python that crushes to powder." Moore implies that her provisionalized or grounded aesthetic does not supply adequate protection to defend against an increasingly turbulent society and its suffocating demands. In choosing to be civil, she doubts her ability to be gay. In Stevens's view, however, the pensive man's skeptical stance in relation to the eagle's order allows him to remain "gay civilly" in difficult times. The pensive man's multiple and changing orders, like those Stevens read in Moore's poetry, organize the chaos of society without squeezing the squirming facts into a single oppressive system. Provisionality itself, the radical provisionality Stevens reads in Moore, provides protection against the squamous minds at work in the world. What Moore conceives as vulnerability, Stevens casts as strength.

"Connoisseur of Chaos" thus ends with an image of man and bird that speaks to both Stevens's and Moore's changing senses of poetic mission in the 1930s. In her 1934 poem "The Frigate Pelican," Moore, in need of a model of artistic resistance to fatalistic materialism, envisions Stevens as a "most romantic bird" and envies the strength of his self-protected ideal flights. Stevens, in need of a model of a more socially grounded, more provisional romanticism, in turn reads Moore's *Selected Poems* as the work of a harmonious skeptic. Glancing back to Moore's frigate pelican in "Connoisseur of Chaos," Stevens makes use of her portrait of speaker and bird as an example of her properly provisionalizing aesthetic. Thus, where Moore, in her poetry, appreciates Stevens the eagle who organizes the Alps into a single protective nest, Stevens, in his, appreciates Moore the pensive (wo)man who radically provisionalizes her visions. Each poet makes the other an example of the sort of verse he or she deems appropriate in increasingly difficult times.

Pressures within, Pressures Without: Marianne Moore, Wallace Stevens, and Pangolin Poetry

For what Stevens wrote of her *Selected Poems* (1935) in "A Poet That Matters" Marianne Moore was truly grateful. As she wrote to T. C. Wilson upon reading a copy of Stevens's review: "I can hardly credit it that one so finished in his work as Wallace Stevens should say those things about my book. I can't conceive of generosity so great, as his going out of his way to do me this great kindness."[1] Watching cautiously as *Selected Poems* (her first collection since the 1924 *Observations*) made its way into an artistic milieu vastly different than that of the prosperous pre-*Dial* years, Moore feared that her "poem[s] on a persimmon" might find little support in a depression world that, as Stevens would soon write, wanted "things exactly as they are." To have Stevens as a champion, as well as T. S. Eliot in his rather eclectic introduction to *Selected Poems,* steadied her nerves. Yet, Moore's letter of thanks to Stevens reveals her doubts about the current flavor of her verse in 1935 and her feelings about the apparent solitude of her task:

> In writing for oneself as one is obliged to be doing, there is mercurial exhilaration, but even so one lapses into patience that at times is nearly morbid. Therefore encouragement takes on an air of miragelike illusion; though your matter-of-factness in counterfeiting

the essential mirage is so actual one finds oneself perhaps permanently cheered. It is a delight to feel that this legerdemain is the usual for yourself; that is to say, that you never find the gossamer assuming the texture of carpet.[2]

Moore pictures herself as one waiting alone in the desert for a sign that her work has value. Committed to the simple and difficult act of "writing for oneself" in a time of growing ideological conflict, Moore indicates that she, like her stubborn Sahara field mouse, suffers deprivations attendant to her rugged individuality. Moore humbly submits that under such solitary conditions Stevens's praise looks too good to be true. Deprecating her verse to Stevens's advantage, she credits him with a corresponding jerboalike intelligence. Not fooled by his own "translucent mistakes of the desert," Stevens can always tell the difference between what he fabricates and the reality beneath. No matter how deft the artistry or actual the mirage of praise, Moore will not take Stevens's compliment as a matter of fact.

While Moore's reluctance to accept approbation was a legendary part of her personal ethos, her comments to Stevens in July 1935 speak to a set of Moore's anxieties particular to the poetic and political milieu of the day. Isolation, hardship, the brief and "mercurial" poetic satisfactions of "writing for oneself" bounded by long intervals of "morbid patience"— Moore's words ring with fears about her potential loss of contact with the common life and the deathly loneliness of private creation. "Do you intend your poetry to be useful to yourself or others?" asked a questionnaire Moore completed for *New Verse* in October 1934. "Myself," was her emphatic one-word response.[3] Such strict attention to one's own satisfaction and standards at the expense of all utility, as Moore's letter to Stevens indicates, could lead to sincere questions of purpose in an increasingly difficult and politicized age.

Certainly those walking the lonely road of personal satisfaction had a hard time finding "encouragement" in the depression-ravaged and increasingly socially conscious 1930s. The literary world that received Moore's *Selected Poems* was fractious, dangerous, and politically charged. Everywhere around the borders of her published poems, in the *Nation,*

the *New Republic, Life and Letters Today,* and *Hound and Horn,* people were
arguing in print over the need for a politically aware poetry. Throughout
the 1930s writers committed to a Marxist view of both life and literature
launched a series of now-famous attacks against those artists who failed
to address the harsh realities of depression America and urge the country
on to an inevitable proletarian revolution. In July 1933, Michael Gold,
the self-appointed pit bull of the proletariat, published his scathing denun-
ciation of Moore's friend and fellow poet Archibald MacLeish, "Out of
the Fascist Unconscious," in the *New Republic.* Reviewing MacLeish's
Frescoes for Mr. Rockefeller's City, a volume filled with comments critiqu-
ing those who mistook polemics for poetry, Gold detected whiffs of
racial prejudice equivalent to the "mystic nationalism" of Hitler and Mus-
solini.[4] Like MacLeish, T. S. Eliot, once the darling of the avant-garde,
came under attack for both his professed conservative stand as a royalist,
Catholic, and classicist, and his frank dislike of sloppy artists bent on
turning their communism to literary account.[5] In the pages of his *Crite-
rion* Eliot pointed out the "irrational" similarities between fascism and
communism and earned his lumps for championing poetry's nobler aspi-
rations at the expense of any particular political necessity.[6] Even Harriet
Monroe's usually staid little magazine *Poetry,* the publication that housed
much of Moore's verse in the 1930s, was drawn into the fracas. In the
July 1934 issue of *Poetry,* Monroe defended her editorial policy of "aes-
thetic value" against the communist ranks in an article entitled "Art and
Propaganda." "We cannot believe," she exclaimed:

> that it is our duty to accept and spread before our readers such half-
> baked efforts at class-conscious poetry as *The New Masses, The An-
> vil, Partisan Review, Dynamo, Blast,* and other enthusiastic organs of
> the Left groups . . . may perhaps legitimately use. Stanley Burn-
> shaw, now poetry editor of *The New Masses,* has been giving a series
> of fiery talks before middle-western John Reed clubs in which *Poetry*
> is berated as a decadent in language almost unprintable, and the
> violent young poet-propagandists on his list are given extravagant
> adjectives . . .
>
> Mr. Burnshaw would strike out of the modern picture not only

Poetry but all the poets, living or dead, on our records who are not "aware of this changing world"—that is, who are not idealizing the Russian system and anathematizing our own.[7]

Quoting various reports of Mr. Burnshaw's John Reed talks, Monroe compiled a list of those authors now deemed bourgeois: Robert Frost, Edna St. Vincent Millay, Edwin Arlington Robinson—all first-generation modernists who Monroe could claim to have printed in her journal. Fighting for the preservation of her intellectual turf and those poets she helped "discover," Monroe defended an artist's right to "talk about fields, and streams, and meadows, or gallant gentlemen and ladies, or the spots on a butterfly's wings."[8] In the September issue, Burnshaw shot back in a heated response (which, to Monroe's credit, she printed in full) that outlined the social poet's position about the irresponsibility of such verses:

> It [poetry] may talk of these things if it can—but show me the poet worthy of the name who can be excited into writing about such matters when the entire social system in which he lives is bursting apart in chaos. Revolutionary poets are not any less fond of fields, streams, meadows or the spots on a butterfly's wings than are reactionary poets—but these things cannot interest them when hundreds are dying daily of starvation at the same time that food is destroyed by legislative ordinance; when a government curtails education and appropriates the largest sum in the history of mankind for war materials; when strikers are shot down for exercising the rights supposedly guaranteed them by the National Recovery Act. In such times as these a poet's themes are the best record of his sense of values; and if he continues to be primarily concerned with fields, streams, meadows and a butterfly's wing, that is all the indictment necessary.[9]

Reading such comments, Moore could safely assume that poems about pelicans, plumet basilisks, and porcelain would not, in Burnshaw's view, "pass for art."

Predictably, the critical response to Moore's *Selected Poems* reflected the stresses of the current political climate. Unlike Stevens, who found her work so full of violent feeling, the bulk of Moore's reviewers found her *Selected Poems* distinctly lacking in emotion and devoid of concern for society at large. Unfortunately for Moore, many critics took their cues on how to read her poetry from Eliot's introduction to the volume. Defending in part the "minor" nature of Moore's subject matter, Eliot wrote: "We all have to choose whatever subject-matter allows us the most powerful and most secret release; and that is a personal affair. The result is often something that the majority will call frigid; for feeling in one's own way, however intensely, is likely to look like frigidity to those who can only feel in accepted ways" (*SPMM,* 9). Once uttered, Eliot's word "frigid" took on a life of its own and supplied ample ammunition for critics—left, right, and middle-of-the-road—less than friendly to Moore's verse. Eugene Davidson of the *Yale Review* found Moore's poems "aloof," "stiff," "cool," and lacking in "progressive vitality," a poor contrast to Lola Ridge's socially conscious poems about Sacco and Vanzetti, which were "deep" in "humane sympathies."[10] John Finch of the *Sewanee Review* described her poetry as "an act of isolation, of divorce from society, the search for a deliberate loneliness" that left her "speaking a precise but unimportant monologue" that her readers could not understand.[11] The bitterest review came from the *Times Literary Supplement* and prompted Moore to write to Pound that "England does not like me and has been pouring salt on my tuft of grass."[12] The anonymous reviewer, accusing Moore, Pound, and Eliot of "a similar aesthetic and intellectual revulsion from common life and common standards," singled Moore out for special scorn:

Miss Moore carries revulsion to more elaborate lengths of exaltation. Her prosody flies full in the face of all the natural music of an English intonation, and of an American still more. Mr. Eliot is mistaken, we believe, in claiming that the cosmopolitan aestheticism her work embodies is for the life of our language. It would, we think, be truer to say that its cultivated refusals and subtle detachment are poison to us. Much nearer to the heart of English are the crooners, the slang-slingers, the lumber-jacks, in fact any men and women anywhere who are alive and immersed and in whose laughter, therefore, there will be food and fire for our next Shakespeare when he wants them.[13]

Crediting Moore with a powerful brain and a keen eye, the harshest of her reviewers in the 1930s feared that she lacked any sense of the political and social concerns of the present day. Technically proficient, coldly accurate, her difficult poems appeared aloof and detached from the common cares of the common populace. As the *Forum* summed it up in a review that Moore scrupulously copied into her reading notebook, "Revolutions in society have rather rarely their correspondences in literature, and so it happens that Marianne Moore's radical *Selected Poems* do not seem to have any connection with what is revolutionary in contemporary life."[14]

The conflict over the issue of social poetry and social responsibility in the mid-1930s, however, passed closer to Moore than the pages of the periodicals she was reading and submitting poems to at the time. Friends as well as critics brought her artistic sins before her eyes. In the mid-1930s, Ezra Pound's letters to Moore became increasingly hostile on the subject of her avoidance of "real-world" issues, namely his pet topic, economics. By 1934, Pound was frankly political, openly fascist, and making enemies anywhere he could find the space in print. Leveling his pen at Moore, he, like the host of printed arguments crossing her desk, reminded her that there was more to life than streams, meadows, and a butterfly's wings. "Wot anuvver quaker," he railed when Moore expressed frank skepticism about Mussolini's tactics:

> you allus act like a piscopal / but even if you haven't a "concern" (in technical quaker sense) with humanity, idiotic continuance of poverty disease etc.
>   FROM the mere whatnot and glass case of culture; you have got to wake up to ECON as a factor / in fact prob / the MAIN factor in the filth, garbage abomination, Sat. eve. post / american maggerzeen filth pail wherein we grew up. . . . Where does yr / "perception of relations" end or begin IF you refuse to perceive the extremely HUMAN bearing of econ / malaria and syph.[15]

Disturbed by Pound's increasingly badgering letters, Moore tried her best to patiently explain her position under his lashing tongue. "I give strict attention to anything that is said about the economic foundation on which or in spite of which we live," she responded, "but in art some things which seem inevitable ought to be concealed, like the working of the gastric juice." In Moore's opinion, a "glass stomach" might be interesting to look at, but the contents did not constitute poetry.[16]

In such a bilious environment Moore became increasingly thankful for the handful of poets she conceived as standing fast in their aesthetic beliefs. Moore's correspondence with her literary friends reflects her desire to hold on to a sense of artistic community while clinging, with less and less assurance, to an individualist aesthetic under siege. "The catnip that art is, or ignis fatuus, or drop on the cactus, does seem worth the martyrdom of pursuit, I feel," she wrote to William Carlos Williams after reading his *Collected Poems, 1921–1931,* for which Stevens supplied the preface. "So *bless* the collective wheelbarrow; with Wallace Stevens beside it like a Chinese beside a huge pair of oxen."[17] In a climate of persecution, Moore interpreted writing poetry as an outright personal martyrdom that she, Stevens, and Williams, the damned first generation, must bear together. In the face of large abstract movements like communism's masses and fascism's *Volk,* Moore fashioned Williams's wheelbarrow into a symbol of a small "collective" effort to withstand great ideological tides. The solid practicality of Williams's cart (his poetry of things), the strong determination and discipline of Moore's oxen (her poetry of animals), and Stevens's sage guidance (his resistant aristocratic ciphers that both contemplated the cart and saw beyond it) made a formidable, and still staunchly individual, team.

Moore's hopeful vision of endurance, however, was one that she clearly needed support to sustain in the 1930s. "Inner security, authority, discipline, whatever one wishes to call it, is what makes the shots go home," she wrote to Williams a few letters later, only to see her sense of security, both personal and poetic, collapse in the next paragraph:

Everyone valuable that I know, has been nearly annihilated it seems to me, by interior pressure and thwarting. It is terrible to see someone quietly suffer. Also—we must bear in mind—despite self-sacrifice and intentional renunciations; even thereby, one makes others suffer.

What is to be done! Surrounded by all this death, heaven certainly is a
necessity and I have some opinions about death and transfiguration,
though not so dogmatic as I could wish. [18]

"Surrounded by all this death," as she put it, "nearly annihilated" by a
loss of inner security in the face of public and private scorn, Moore
wondered whether her poetry could effectively fight back against the tide
of events and the pressures of ideology. Haunted by a growing sense of
evil, Moore interpreted the trend toward explicit and vitriolic verse as a
sign that poets were losing faith that there could be such things as good-
ness or beauty in the world. Moore cringed as she saw the romantic
imagination crushed steadily out of "everyone valuable" she knew, re-
placed by thoughts of war materials and details of the National Recovery
Act. "Judged by our experimental writing," Moore complained in her
1936 review of three anthologies of new poetry, "we are suffering today
from unchastity, sadism, blasphemy, and rainsoaked foppishness; and
since warnings to editors are not heeded, one would like to ask of one's
fellow-writers, is publication always better for one's talent than temporar-
ily thwarted ambition?"[19] Denouncing the host of shoddy social realist
poems rushed into print for political reasons, Moore's review, entitled
"Courage, Right and Wrong," frankly suggested that many new poets
did not have the courage or the capacity to tell right from wrong. Fasci-
nated with the foul, they had no sense of the fair.

Awash in expressions of "sadism," "blasphemy," and "rainsoaked
foppishness," Moore became all the more committed to the idea of a
poetry of spiritual resistance, and, once again, she turned to Wallace
Stevens as a model. While Moore credited both Stevens and Williams
with an all-important sense of "inner security," she often found Wil-
liams's verse more explicit and ugly than she wished. Upon reading
Williams's *Collected Poems, 1921–1931,* Moore, even though she valued his
exuberance, declared herself frankly disgusted with some of his lines.[20]
Stevens, standing in dignified lofty reserve beside the collective cart, a
creature of spirit rather than bare concrete substance, suited her better,
and Moore set out to claim Stevens as a crucial ally in her reviews of his
second volume of poetry, *Ideas of Order.*

Moore's responses to *Ideas of Order* once again show Moore defining her aesthetic concerns in concert with Stevens's verse and interpreting his work as a reflection of her own lofty poetic aims. Moore reviewed both the 1935 Alcestis Press version of *Ideas of Order* and the Knopf printing that appeared the next year, a testament to the importance of the book in her perceived battle against the dark forces haunting her world and her art. Both Moore's review of the Alcestis Press volume, "Ideas of Order," published in Eliot's *Criterion* (1936), and her review of the Knopf *Ideas of Order* and *Owl's Clover*, "Conjuries That Endure," published in *Poetry* (1937), stress Stevens's role as a consummate musician—one concerned, unlike the strident polemical poets, with sound as well as sense.[21] Moore's *Criterion* comments credit Stevens with "compactness beyond compare and the *forte agitatio* competence of the concert room," and Stevens's "meditativeness not for appraisal" reminds Moore of the "dexterousness" and "self-relish" of the great German composer Johannes Brahms (*CPrMM*, 329–30). Moore interprets "Sailing after Lunch," her favorite poem in the volume, as an example of applied music theory, noting its "principle of dispersal common to music; that is to say, a building up of the theme piecemeal in such a way that there is no possibility of disappointment at the end" (*CPrMM*, 330). In "Conjuries That Endure," Moore glances back to her Stevensian frigate pelican and once more compares the poet to impassioned Händel unrivaled "in the patterned correspondences of the Sonata No. 1" (*CPrMM*, 347). A "bold virtuoso," of "noble accents and lucid, inescapable rhythms," Stevens appealed to Moore as one who championed the beauty of words in an age of endless ugly propaganda (*CPrMM*, 347).

Yet, it is not the music alone that Moore admires in the Stevens of the 1930s, but the implicit act of faith that his melodies represent. As in her review of *Harmonium*, Moore still finds Stevens a poet of "bravura," but in *Ideas of Order*, the bravura is "bold" rather than "uneasy"—a necessarily aggressive sign that the poet's belief in beauty and order can stand up to the pressures of the age. In "Conjuries That Endure" Moore pictures the romantic impulse of Stevens's poetry as "a wall of incorruptibleness" erected against those social realist poets whose blatant and simplistic statements violate "the essential aura of contributory vagueness" (*CPrMM*, 348). The "fortitudo, frantic bass" of *Ideas of Order* marks Stevens's inner strength, his unflagging trust in the idealities of art. "Meditation for the fatalist is a surrender to 'the morphology of regret'—a drowning in one's welter of woes, dangers, risks, obstacles to inclination," writes Moore in her *Criterion* piece, chastising those poets who speak only of worldly evils. In Stevens's case, however, Moore claims that

> Poetry viewed morphologically is "a finikin thing of air," "a few words tuned and tuned and tuned"; and "the function of the poet" is "sound to stuff the ear"; or—rather—it is "particles of order, a single majesty"; it is "our unfinished spirits realized more sharply in more furious selves." Art is both "rage for order" and "rage against chaos" (*CPrMM*, 329).

Stevens's art pushes back against the evil that is with a beauty that might and should be. In Moore's view, he creates "the fairy-tale we wished might exist; in short, everything ghostly yet undeniable" (*CPrMM*, 330). In the midst of social and political pressure, Moore began to reconceive Stevens's romantic imagination not just as a delight, but as a serious protection against fatalistic materialism. Creating an "actual" that could also be a "deft beneficence," Stevens offered Moore poetic proof that "realism need not restrict itself to grossness," that a socially aware poetry need not succumb to whatever ugliness it set out to examine.

Armed with her newly reworked sense of Stevens's importance, Moore set out to transfer her thoughts about how to address the age into her verse. Moore's letters to T. S. Eliot make clear that her production of her major poem of the period, "The Pangolin," coincided with her thoughts about *Ideas of Order* for the *Criterion*.[22] Stevens's final poems for *Ideas of Order* appeared in print from late 1934 ("The Idea of Order at Key West," "Lions in Sweden," "Evening without Angels," "Nudity at the Capital," "Nudity in the Colonies," "A Fish-Scale Sunrise," "Delightful Evening," and "What They Call Red Cherry Pie" in *Alcestis*) through spring of 1935 ("Like Decorations in a Nigger Cemetery" in *Poetry* and "Sailing after Lunch," "Meditation Celestial and Terrestrial," "Waving Adieu, Adieu, Adieu," "The American Sublime," and "Mozart, 1935" in *Alcestis*), just the time when Moore was thinking hard about her armored animal.

Like her former subjects for considering the proper use of the romantic imagination—the frigate pelican, the jerboa, and the plumet basilisk—the giant pangolin poet travels comfortably between two distinctly different realms. In her worksheets for the poem, Moore copied notes from Robert J. Hatt's article on pangolins in *Natural History Magazine,* and the notes detailed her preference for the giant of the species: "Partially arboreal (the giant pangolin) while the other species are 'purely terrestrial.'"[23] Unlike its earthbound cousins, the giant pangolin appealed to Moore as a symbol of the romantic poet because he could, from time to time, get off terra firma. Yet, compared to Moore's other creatures, the pangolin spends much more of his time on the turf, a mark of Moore's growing commitment to the creation of a grounded, socially relevant verse, a task for which the pangolin poet is well suited.[24] Unlike her earlier animals, Moore pictures the pangolin, like Stevens himself, as an artist well built to resist external hazards and pressures without avoiding them. Where the jerboa and the plumet basilisk live in constant fear of capture, and the frigate in danger of losing all contact with the ground, the pangolin faces life head-on and heavily armed, able, like Moore's Stevens of "Ideas of Order," to fight back when threatened by the chaos of events with a "rage for order." Where plumet, frigate, and jerboa use their art as temporary vehicles of escape from the pressures of reality, the pangolin uses his as a direct mode of confrontation with the age. "Pangolins are not aggressive," Moore quotes from Hatt in a note she transferred verbatim into her poem, "but the giant species can do great damage with their massive axe-edged tails. Their weapons swing over the body with such force that a knife an eighth of an inch thick stabbed in the side has been doubled over."[25] The image of the giant pangolin wielding its mighty tail resembles Moore's picture of Stevens as "a big ogre stalking toward one with a knobbed club" that dates back to her review of *Harmonium.* The Stevensian pangolin of the 1930s, however, is not longer "unprovoked." Only thus self-protected can the poet go into the fray.

The pangolin's armor, then, serves the essential function of allowing the poet to face facts. Indeed, many of Moore's images of the pangolin in her poem stress the animal's ability to always remain well grounded in realities. Referring to the pangolin as "Leonardo's indubitable son," Moore implies that, like Leonardo da Vinci, he creates transcendent art that grows out of an exquisite faithfulness to biological detail.

An "artist-engineer," the pangolin melds creation with its own distinctly military sense of practical utility. Moore writes that the pangolin

> endures
> exhausting solitary
>   trips through unfamiliar ground at night,
> returning before sunrise; stepping
>   in the moonlight,   on the moonlight
>   peculiarly, that the out-
>   side edges of his
> hands may bear the weight and save the claws
>   for digging.[26]

A staunch individualist in his pursuit of poetry, the pangolin covers "unfamiliar" imaginative territory, but his sense of the nighttime, moonlit romantic task never strays far from the demands of a socially grounded aesthetic. The pangolin steps not only "in" the moonlight, but "on" it, a change of preposition that directs attention away from the silvered animal and back to the earth itself. The animals "hands" also convey its dual mission. In her review of *Ideas of Order,* Moore notes that "Mr. Stevens alludes to 'the eccentric' as 'the base of design'" (*CPrMM,* 330). The pangolin's imaginative excursions, taken appropriately on the "out- / side," or eccentric, "edges of his / hands," do not inhibit his ability to dig the soil with his claws, just as Stevens's imaginings do not compromise his contact with the real. Exerting a violence from within, the pangolin's eccentricities allow it to "bear the weight" of its own existence in a world of pressures.

"Fearful and yet to be feared," the sturdy solitary pangolin, Moore concludes, fares far better at his artistic tasks than man. Voicing her ongoing complaint about the quality of polemical poetry and prose in the 1930s, Moore states that

>   Bedizened or stark
>   naked, man, the self, the being
>   so-called human, writing-
> master to this world, griffons a dark
>   "Like does not like like that is
>   obnoxious"; and writes errror with four
>   r's.

Whether the words are gaudy or simple, Moore sees the message behind man's current writings to be disturbingly similar. Rather than create beauty or search for truth, the supposed "writing-master" of the world has sunk to the level of a monstrous griffon, squawking a series of dark messages filled with hate and death. Splitting off into angry groups with competing and hostile agendas, man forgets his commonality with others of his species. In not liking like, he hates himself. Under such conditions of self-loathing, Moore argues that poetry itself collapses. Man's dark message, twisted and repetitive, hammered out in single-syllable words that jar against the hissing Latinate "obnoxious," woefully lacks linguistic elegance. On man's lips, the pangolin's harmless hiss becomes aggressive and ugly. Where pangolins are "made for moving quietly" and "are models of exactness," man loudly proclaims his ignorance in print, misspelling "errror with four r's." Once again, in pointing to the "errror" of others of his kind, man inevitably implicates himself.

Surrounded by swarms of stinging rhetoric, the pangolin's greatest artistry lies in his ability, like Moore's Stevens of "Ideas of Order," to resist man's "morphology of regret" and not succumb to the "meditations of the fatalist." Comparing the pangolin poet to a sailboat, a humble first machine, Moore asserts that no matter what danger he faces, he never, like power-mad, angry humans, "capsizes in disheartenment"; or, to quote again from Moore's review of *Ideas of Order,* the pangolin firmly afloat, like Stevens, never runs the risk of "drowning" in his own "welter of woes, dangers, risks, obstacles to inclination" (*CPrMM*, 329). Moore's use of the sailboat here recalls her favorite piece from Stevens's *Ideas of Order*, "Sailing after Lunch," which first appeared in *Alcestis* in March 1935 in the midst of her work on the pangolin.[27] Stevens's poem begins with a famous lament about the death of romantic poetry in an unsympathetic age: "It is the word *pejorative* that hurts." Yet, rather than succumb to the hateful words of others or the weight of his own complaints, the poet on the sailboat offers up a prayer and, with a burst of feeling, grants a "slight transcendence" to his surroundings. Such an act of poetic recovery based on a direct appeal to "the spirit" offered Moore proof of Stevens's "unquenchable exaltation." Moore's heavily armored pangolin sailboat, like the poet of "Sailing after Lunch," refuses to let the age dictate his art and fights back against the thwarting of insults, self-doubt, and ennui to create something beautiful. In the midst of turmoil, neither Stevens nor the pangolin lose their sense of equilibrium.

Claiming that the pangolin is thus "made graceful" by its "adversities," Moore suggests that the thwarting contact with the grim realities of the 1930s only makes the true poet's art more precious—the harder he must fight to create his peculiar beauty, the more valuable his poems become in an ugly world. Moore stresses the importance of such visions by placing her comments on art in a religious context, frankly equating the act of creation with that of salvation. The pangolin's artistic "grace" becomes a sign of a much-doubted divine presence, the "grace of God" that, like the imagination, gives men and pangolins the inner strength to endure trial and resist temptation. Drawing a link between the pangolin's painstaking poetry and God's influence, Moore claims that "To explain grace requires / a curious hand." Reviving an obsolete sense of the word *curious,* Moore insists that to make God's grace visible, one must call upon the exacting minute inquiry and ingenious skill of the poet. Poetry, rightly written, bears witness to an ever-present power. Moore asks of her evidence of grace:

> If that which
>   is at all were not for
> ever, why would those who graced the spires
>   with animals and gathered
>   there to rest, on cold luxurious
>   low stone seats—a monk and monk and monk—
>   between the thus   ingenious roof-
>   supports, have slaved to confuse
>   grace with a kindly
> manner, time in which to pay a debt,
>   the cure for sins, a graceful use
>   of what are yet
>   approved stone
>   mullions branching out across
>   the perpendiculars?

Moore's image of the monks who built and decorated the Gothic cathedrals reflects directly on her thoughts about the pangolin's poetry. The monks, like the pangolin, were men of faith rather than skeptics. The monks, like the pangolin, were artist-engineers who, fighting the thwarting force of gravity, built gorgeous monuments by virtue of their ingenuity, reaching toward God with the imaginative splendor of spires and buttresses. If grace were not "forever," Moore asks, why would such artists have "slaved" to convince the world of God's presence? Why would those content with "low stone seats" have given themselves to the taxing creation of such ideal beauty, or kept the thought of God's grace imaginatively alive in so many worldly attributes? The language and art of "this world" stand as markers of an ideal that we can only imagine and in which we must have faith. The flying buttress becomes the visual representation of the pressure of art and imagination pushing back against the thwarting pressure of reality. The interior and exterior forces thus stabilized, man achieves equilibrium, which allows him to survive. Moore does, of course, phrase her "explanation" of grace as a question, acknowledging that there may, in fact, be other possible interpretations of the monks' industry. Yet, it is in the face of just such doubt that the poet, like the pangolin, must persevere.

Moore thus ends "The Pangolin" by suggesting that man, the now-debased writing master to this world who can no longer craft a poem, must learn how to confront his sunlit realm of realities with the same imaginative courage that the true artist-pangolin applies to his moonlit excursions. In her final stanza, Moore turns her attention to the lesser creature and gives man a new line to speak, a potential antidote to the dark phrase "Like does not like like that is obnoxious." Thwarted by dusk because he has lost the inner light of imaginative faith, man must find a way to say

>   to the alternating blaze,
> "Again the sun!
>   anew each
>   day; and new and new and new,
>   that comes into and steadies my soul."

Moore concludes that, despite his weaknesses, man must use his imagination to fight the capsizing forces of doubt and fatalism. As an example of how to do so, Moore shows man creating a small new poem of his own.

Greeting the dawn, man makes the natural sun into a poetic symbol of hope and regeneration. No matter how many times darkness falls, the natural sun always reappears—a fact that the mind, used in self-protection, translates into a sign of possibilities beyond current evils. In an imaginative act of hope, man transforms the brutalities of his actual present—"Again the sun,"—into a potential future that can be made and remade—"and new and new and new." Following Moore's prescription to see the grace of poetic artistry as a sign of the grace of God, man must perform the ultimate feat of transformative pressure against the actual and come to see the sun as a sign of the Son. Again, the issue is equilibrium. Taking in the natural light, man must make it into a force that pushes back against the actual, a belief in the Son that "steadies" the soul. As poetry, man's new words hold up better than his earlier dark griffinings. Moore not only gives man the power to make a symbol but also fills his passage with internal rhyme—again/anew, sun/come, new/into—and maintains an expanding rhythm of iambs—"Again the sun!" (two iambs) "anew each / day" (two iambs) "and new and new and new," (three iambs), "that comes into and steadies my soul" (four iambs)—the poetic equivalent of a musical crescendo. Moore again ends man's comment with a string of repeated *ss*, but here his hiss resembles the pangolin's, a graceful sound of perseverance.

The conclusion of "The Pangolin" thus offers a version of "socially conscious" poetry vastly different than that dictated by Moore's critics. Drawing in part on her reading of Stevens, Moore staunchly proclaims in "The Pangolin" that verse must confront an ugly age, not by embracing and restating its woes, but by pushing back against it with the imagination, reaffirming the power of the human spirit. In Moore's view, poetry should not ignore political and social problems, but it also should not endorse them as the only possible version of reality. Indeed, Moore's pangolin poem enacts just such a double agenda. As Margaret Holley notes, thoughts of the impending world war and the ongoing buildup of armaments permeate Moore's poem.[28] Holley cites Moore's vision of the pangolin as "*another* armored animal" alongside man "mechanicked and fighting" as proof of Moore's active concern with real-world events. Moore's equation between the pangolin and Leonardo da Vinci also brings to mind Italy and the fallen state of the birthplace of Renaissance humanism under Mussolini's increasingly aggressive fascism. If, as Holley writes, the poem "rises quickly" beyond its historical context, it does so because of Moore's sense of the poet's mission as a counterpressure to events that she, like the pangolin, must "engulf" and transform. Like the pangolin, the poem is grounded in a stinging swarm of real evils.

In the wake of "The Pangolin," Moore became increasingly convinced that her sense of the poet's mission as a counterweight to evil was one that she shared with Wallace Stevens. Shortly after "The Pangolin" was published, Stevens's *Owl's Clover* appeared, giving Moore more proof of the rightness of her approach. In her second review, "Conjuries That Endure," Moore coupled her comments on *Ideas of Order* with a discussion of *Owl's Clover,* one of Stevens's most direct attempts to deal with communism, fascism, and the events of the day, primarily Mussolini's invasion of Ethiopia. Scanning the pages of his most overtly political volume, Moore found that Stevens both dealt with pressing issues and managed to keep himself and his faith in poetry intact. "Despite this awareness of the world of sense," she wrote of *Owl's Clover,* "one notices the frequent recurrence of the word 'heaven.' In each clime the author visits, and under each disguise, the dilemma of tested hope confronts him" (*CPrMM,* 349). And in each clime, Moore implies, Stevens rises to the challenge, refusing to be "annihilated by interior pressure and thwarting" like so many of those dear to her. Throughout the final paragraph of "Conjuries That Endure," the word "hope" appears again and again. "The protest against the actualities of experience," in Stevens's verse, becomes "a protest against the death of world hope." "So long as we are ashamed," like Stevens, "of our marble victories, there is hope for the world." Stevens's poems, "embody hope that in being frustrated becomes fortitude" (*CPrMM,* 349). Using her own religious vocabulary, Moore, in late 1936, credits Stevens with a poetic scope far beyond the individual satisfactions of verse. The unserviceable jungle animal of the 1920s becomes, in the mid-1930s, the hope of the world. Moore rereads Stevens the poet as Stevens the social prophet, a reflection of the role she wished for herself in the fight against materialist despair.

Just as Moore was drawing strength for her poetic tasks from Stevens in the mid-1930s, so Stevens was drawing on Moore. In the wake of the critical response to *Ideas of Order,* Stevens began to have significant doubts about his own relationship to the concept of "social verse." Like

Moore's *Selected Poems,* Stevens's volume received its share of criticism
for its apparent detachment from the world of events. Echoing com-
plaints leveled against Moore, Babette Deutsch of the *New York Herald
Tribune Book Review* proclaimed that "Stevens is not concerned with the
present. He is too much engrossed with what is present peculiarly to
himself."[29] Theodore Roethke complained in the *New Republic,* "It is a
pity that such a rich and special sensibility should be content with the
order of words and music, and not project itself more vigorously upon
the present-day world."[30] Two of the sharpest attacks of the literary Left
came from Harriet Monroe's nemesis of the *New Masses,* Stanley Burn-
shaw, and the editor of *New Verse,* Geoffrey Grigson. Burnshaw's now
infamous review, "Turmoil in the Middle Ground," pictured Stevens as a
middle-aged poet whose harmonious cosmos of the early 1920s had col-
lapsed under the weight of world events. Pointing to the strange political
"confusion" of Stevens's latest volume, Burnshaw challenged Stevens to
scrape his turmoil of ideas into a coherent message, a single Marxist idea
of order committed to the "task of weakening the class in power."[31]
Although Burnshaw's review provoked a poem in response, Grigson's
review, "The Stuffed Gold Finch," in some ways bothered Stevens even
more. Where Burnshaw at least credited Stevens with trying to get closer
to the world of events in *Ideas of Order,* Grigson out and out hated the
volume and proclaimed that Stevens was "fixed in his 1923," a taxidermy
songbird unable to face the future.[32] The review upset Stevens so much
that he mentioned it to Moore in his letter of thanks for her first set of
comments on *Ideas of Order* in the *Criterion:*

> Just at the moment, I am very much off the English. In the last
> number of *New Verse* Grigson does a beautiful job of embalming,
> calling me a stuffed gold finch, and all that. As a matter of fact, *Ideas
> of Order* was gathered together with a few new things added. In view
> of that, I think that Grigson is justified in what he says. . . .
> Your note about *Ideas of Order* in the *Criterion* naturally gave me a
> great deal of satisfaction. I am afraid that I shall never be able to do
> much with the principle that I had in mind in my note on your
> *Selected Poems* so long as I stick to the use of the word *romantic.* The

indelible associations of that word seem to make it impossible to use it in a fresh sense.[33]

Noting Stevens's disheartened and doubtful tone, Moore interpreted his letter as a plea for support, which she readily supplied. "I have not seen the Grigson review," she responded, "but how you can think as you do, and 'think' that Geoffrey Grigson 'is justified in what he says' I don't know." She continued:

> Our good minds, Paul Rosenfeld, Mr. W. W. E. Ross, T. S. Eliot, Dr. Watson of *The Dial* and others associated with *The Dial*— William Carlos Williams, E. E. Cummings, a cohort of exacting fanaticals, hesitate to say the obvious to you or even about you for fear of seeming "wholehearted" and crass, they regarding the pinnacle of deserved triumph which a fortified author enjoys, as imperialists do the regalia in the Tower. . . . You must not honor even so much as to be aware of them, the critical shadows that darken lines and pages they cannot produce. . . . I recall hearing, through a protracted dinner, no topic discussed but your verse, and am sceptical of your not being surfeited and impeded with initiate compliments of the delicate sort. *Ideas of Order* is an enviable unity—a kind of volume-progression on certain individual poems of previous years.[34]

The urgency of Moore's roll call reflects her fear that even Stevens, the most "fortified" of pangolin poets, might be susceptible to a loss of inner security. Just as Moore was coming to think the romantic an indispensable element of poetry in a violent world, Stevens seemed to be doubting his ability to "make anything of the principle" that marked them as partners. Afraid of losing her ally, Moore was determined to shore him up in his pursuit of the ideal and insisted that his poetry was a symbol of everything valuable—the regalia in the tower—to the soldiers, like herself, in the field. Stevens responded to Moore's letter with what amounted to an apology for his moment of weakness. "The things suggested by you by way of discipline," he wrote, "are things that I dislike as much as you do. But, as we both know, being oneself is the most difficult thing in the world."³⁵

For all the difficulty involved in being himself, Stevens was not as ready to dismiss the new romantic as his letter to Moore might imply. *Ideas of Order* might be "quite inadequate from any social point of view," but Stevens pinned his doubts not on the principle behind such poems as "Sailing after Lunch," but on the words he had used to express the concept. Abandoning the term *romantic* as hopelessly weighted with old baggage, Stevens did not forsake the imaginative element of verse but rather set out to reconceive it in light of the present society of the 1930s— the task of *Owl's Clover*. Throughout his complex project, Stevens, like Moore, became increasingly convinced of the importance of poetry to a desperate and destitute age. In October 1935, Ronald Lane Latimer sent Stevens a copy of Moore's *Criterion* review of *Ideas of Order* to aid him in his poetic struggle with the point of view of the practical communist, "Mr Burnshaw and the Statue." Stevens wrote back to Latimer that Moore was "one of the angels" and ended his letter with a poet's prayer that echoes Moore's sense of the vital nature of verse in the 1930s:

> If poetry introduces order, and every competent poem introduces order, and if order means peace, even though that particular peace is an illusion, is it any less an illusion than a good many other things that everyone high and low now-a-days concedes to be no longer of any account? Isn't a freshening of life a thing of consequence? It would be a great thing to change the status of the poet.³⁶

In her review of *Ideas of Order,* Moore credits Stevens with a "rareness in peace" and a "serenity in sophistication" that resist the "wild boars of philistinism." Drawing on Moore's terms, Stevens envisions a role for poetry as a potential bid for peace in a violent age, elevating verse to a vehicle for social change, a better illusion than the ones running. "The real trouble with poetry," Stevens complained to Latimer, "is that poets have no conception of the importance of the thing. Life without poetry is, in effect life without a sanction. . . . Given the real thing, people will stop short to take it in because everyone is dependent on it."³⁷ Where in "A Poet That Matters" Stevens claimed the romantic imagination as a

"delight," an "indulgence," and a "personal satisfaction," by the time of
Owl's Clover Stevens recognized poetry as an official social "sanction," a
blessing that legitimizes all life. Following the same lines as Moore,
Stevens began to wonder if poetry, rightly written, could satisfy the
imaginative needs, not just of the individual, but of a whole society.

Yet, as *Owl's Clover* reveals, Stevens considered the creation of such
"stop short" poetry a difficult task in light of present conditions. Given
the sad nature of the depression era, the depleted state of the available art,
and the flashy attractions of fascism and communism, Stevens lamented
that "those phases" of the social situation that he regretted as "merely
violent" might prevail in the long run over any glimpse of the beautiful
or any hope of change. Where Moore pictured Stevens as a well-fortified
poet, capable, like the regalia in the tower, of standing for the hopes of a
whole society, Stevens was less sure about the power of his art, or anyone
else's, to resist the onslaughts of the general populace bent on listening to
the wrong voices. Stevens begins *Owl's Clover* not with a statement of
hopeful resistance, but with a grand pronouncement of artistic incapacity
in the form of an old woman's encounter with a group of marble Pegasi
in the park. Posed for takeoff that implies transcendence, "white forelegs
taut / To the muscles' very tip for the vivid plunge," the apparently
muscular fantasy is powerless to animate its depression-ravaged audi-
ence.[38] Confronted with a "bitter mind / In a flapping cloak," the statue
collapses, reduced to rubble by the pressure of the woman's black
thoughts. As James Longenbach notes, "The Old Woman and the Statue"
presents a double critique of both the irrelevance of the monumental
marbles and of the gross incapacity of the audience.[39] Like other Ste-
vensian statues, the mythical horses, posed and fixed, have outlived their
usefulness and must change if they are to revive the age. In Stevens's
view the horses, however beautiful, are a common cliché. "Another
evening in another park, / A group of marble horses rose on wings,"
begins "The Old Woman and the Statue." If this is just "another evening"
in just "another park," then this statue is just "another" group of horses,
an undifferentiated symbol that does not speak to or for its particular
environment.

Dissatisfied with his horses, Stevens creates images throughout *Owl's
Clover* that ask whether the romantic can be remade to offer elevation

without escape, whether, in Moore's terms, pangolin poetry is possible. In "A Duck for Dinner," Stevens searches the Bulgar's bleak socialist park for a potential poet/savior, evaluating possible performers based on their ability to maintain grace under pressure:

> It may be the future depends on an orator,
> Some pebble-chewer practiced in Tyrian speech,
> An apparition, twanging instruments
> Within us hitherto unknown, he that
> Confounds all opposites and spins a sphere
> Created, like a bubble, of bright sheens,
> With a tendency to bulge as it floats away.
> Basilewsky's bulged before it floated, turned
> Caramel and would not, could not float.
>
> (*OP*, 93–94)

Like Moore, Stevens hopes for an armored individual, one who can both touch the day and press back against it—a relationship between the poet and the world at large that Stevens expresses in terms of concentric circles. The social orator will not do as a transformative force because, despite his lovely elocution, he is all style and no substance. Ignoring real-world conflicts, the orator's frivolous words constitute a mere fragile soap bubble of deforming thoughts that, rather than engage the time, simply float away. Basilewsky, the communist composer of such social realist works as Concerto for Airplane and Pianoforte, also fails in his attempt to properly confront his day. Like the orator's, Basilewsky's bubble deforms what it reflects, but not in an attempted act of transcendence. The communist artist's single-minded perspective forms a sticky coating that obscures the particularities of the actual under a thick, monochromatic, political glaze. In adhering so closely to the social and political reality it attempts to portray, Basilewsky's balloon loses its poetic power to rise above the grossness of its subject and cannot push back against the age.

The specter of two clear artistic failures prompts Stevens to wonder if any poetry, however much the "real thing," could withstand the force of practical pressures:

                              And yet
In an age of concentric mobs would any sphere
Escape all deformation, much less this,
This source and patriarch of other spheres,
This base of every future, vibrant spring,
The volcano Apostrophe, the sea Behold?

                                                    (OP, 94)

Stevens's gloss on the passage reads:

> Given the mobs of contemporary life . . . it is impossible to project
> a world that will not appear to some one to be a deformation. This is
> especially true when the projection is that of the volcano Apostro-
> phe, the sea Behold: poetry. At a time of severely practical require-
> ments, the world of the imagination looks like something distorted.
> A man who spouts apostrophes is a volcano and in particular the
> volcano Apostrophe. A man full of behold this and behold that is the
> sea Behold.[40]

Stevens's query about the possibility of poetry may be full of doubt, but
the images he uses to phrase his question suggest what a truly resistant
and transformative poetic entails. As Margaret Dickie argues in her book
Lyric Contingencies, Stevens's image of the poet/volcano "unites creation
and destruction, equates animation with violence. . . . when it erupts it is
more truly explosive than anything the hot-air social orator can imag-
ine."[41] Countering the pressures outside the singing self, the true poet of
our time pushes back against the concentric mobs with multiple spheres
of his own making. Rather than blow fragile bubbles, the true poet, the
"base," the "spring," the "source," generates energy that thrusts upward
from the center of the self with the creative violence of a volcano and the
surging power of the sea. Stevens finds the metaphors for the true poet's
activity in the passions of earthly processes, a sign that his verse must
begin in the real and, like the sea and the volcano, remain in motion,
issuing forward from the actual, then drawing back to base. As in
Moore's pangolin poem, the stakes in the creation of a more powerful
poetry range beyond the preservation of the self to become nothing less

than our collective future. "To think of the future is a genius," writes
Stevens, and the poet is "He from whose beard the future springs, elect"
(*OP,* 94, 95). In such weighted, nasty times, those who can imagine
better days ahead are poets of rare vision. Only they, with the power of
the mind, make the world, as Moore puts it, "new and new and new,"
countering a static present with a range of fresh possibilities.

Thus, the concept of a socially conscious poetry that Stevens creates
concurrently with Moore's pangolin, far from abandoning the imagina-
tion, reflects an ongoing need for ever-more-powerful transformative ex-
periences to meet a violent age—volcanic blasts that, Stevens laments,
might never come. Plagued with doubts, Stevens goes cowering forth in
Owl's Clover, attempting to generate the resistant social poetic he projects.
Like Moore's pangolin poem, *Owl's Clover* begins in contemporaneous
realities. The specters of communism, fascism, depression, machine guns,
infantry movements, and Mussolini's aggression in Ethiopia haunt Ste-
vens and form the basis of his poem—the context for the art of the age.
Like Moore's poem, however, *Owl's Clover* quickly rises beyond its base,
transforming events in a way that fulfills, if not entirely successfully, Ste-
vens's proposed double agenda. As Helen Vendler notes, Stevens's rheto-
ric throughout the *Owl's Clover* shows significant signs of strain. The
ballooning music of the poem's mythical transformations clashes uncom-
fortably against the sardonic low tone of its actualities, and Stevens's lyric
leaps seem forced and unnatural.[42] As his rampant cutting of his original
poem indicates, Stevens certainly sensed that his flights fell short of the
volcanic poetry the age so desperately needed. Indeed, throughout *Owl's
Clover,* as James Longenbach points out, Stevens remains tentative about
the poet's ability to ever truly transform the age, questioning the common
denominator between the poet and the audience.[43] Try as he might to drag
the world up after him with lyric explosions, Stevens finds himself, like his
marble horses, thwarted in the attempt.

Yet, in true pangolin style, Stevens does not wholly abandon the
prospect of a romantic counterpoetry on the basis of his own failures.
Indeed, throughout his prose accompaniment to *Owl's Clover,* "The Irra-
tional Element in Poetry," Stevens insistently trumpets the importance to
the age of the volcanic romantic he fears he cannot fashion and grants his
old theory of the "new romantic" a specifically social significance. In his

commentary, Stevens dispenses with the troublesome word *romantic* in favor of the term *irrational,* but the field of his inquiry remains the same— "the transaction between reality and the sensibility of the poet from which poetry springs." His remarks show that, in the same way that Moore uses her reading of Stevens to bolster her belief in the romantic and shape her pangolin' poetic, so Stevens looks back to his reading of Moore in "A Poet That Matters" to reconsider the poet's role and maintain his faith in the imagination's power. As I argue in the previous chapter, Stevens saw Moore's provisionalizing poetry and aesthetic vocabulary as keys to the creation of a flexible, socially grounded verse— the radically provisional song of a harmonious skeptic that could change endlessly to suit the age. Considering the importance of Moore's provisional poetic to the present day in "A Poet That Matters," Stevens claimed that Moore's verse disclosed a romantic intelligence that "means in a time like our own of violent feelings, equally violent feelings and the most skillful expression of the genuine" (*OP,* 220). In "A Poet that Matters," Stevens's general sense of artistic embattlement, the need for "violent feelings," had not yet coalesced into an overt expression of political and social struggle.

By the time Stevens pens "The Irrational Element in Poetry," however, his sense of the poet's mission is more clearly defined. Looking back to "A Poet That Matters," Stevens builds on his sense of the need for "violent feelings" to face a world of "violent feelings" and brings the new romantic into a political and social context:

> It is one thing to talk about the end of civilization and another to feel that the thing is not merely possible but measurably probable. If you are not a communist, has not civilization ended in Russia? If you are not a Nazi, has it not ended in Germany? . . . We are preoccupied with events, even when we do not observe them closely. We have a sense of upheaval. We feel threatened. We look from an uncertain present toward a more uncertain future. One feels the desire to collect oneself against all this in poetry as well as in politics. If politics is nearer to each of us because of the pressure of the contemporaneous, poetry, in its way, is no less so and for the same reason. Does anyone suppose that the vast mass of people in this country

was moved at the last election by rational considerations? Giving
reason as much credit as the radio, there still remains the certainty
that so great a movement was emotional and, if emotional, irratio-
nal. The trouble is that the greater the pressure of the contemporane-
ous, the greater the resistance. Resistance is the opposite of escape.
The poet who wishes to contemplate the good in the midst of confu-
sion is like the mystic who wishes to contemplate God in the midst
of evil. There can be no thought of escape. . . . These are fortify-
ings, although irrational ones.[44]

In "The Irrational Element in Poetry," Stevens recasts his time of "violent
feelings" as one of apocalyptic menace, replacing a vague sense of unrest
with a list of real-world political threats (the rise of Nazi Germany) and
recognizable historical evils (communist Russia). Stevens argues that,
placed in such a context, romantic poetry functions not just as a personal
satisfaction, but as a form of political resistance—a vision of possible
beauty with the potential to move vast numbers of people to emotive
action, just as the promise of the New Deal moved people to vote for
Franklin Roosevelt. When confronted with an increasingly specific sense
of social threat, Stevens, like Moore, claims that poetry can be a vehicle
for social change rather than a mere indulgence. In his restructuring of
the new romantic, Stevens, by association, rewrites Moore as a poet who
"matters" not to Stevens alone, but to the world at large. The violent
emotions that Stevens finds in Moore's poetry in "A Poet That Matters"
become the "fortifications" (a word Stevens borrows directly from
Moore's supportive letter) of the soul. Where in "A Poet That Matters"
Stevens pictures Moore as a maker of "delightful" and "truthful" lyrics,
in "The Irrational Element in Poetry" Stevens recasts poets like Moore as
indispensable keepers of the good.

Thus Stevens, like Moore, endows the poet of the late 1930s with a
weight of moral responsibility. In a time of evil, the poet must undertake
a quest for good—a noble search for truth and beauty that for Stevens,
like Moore, becomes a matter of faith. Pausing in "The Irrational Ele-
ment in Poetry" to ask the question, "why does one write poetry?"
Stevens answers at first in ways that echo his sentiments in "A Poet That
Matters." Impelled by "personal sensibility," poets write to escape the

monotony of their own imaginations. Yet, rather than end the discussion on a note of personal need, Stevens draws on Bremond and, like Moore, links the poetic impulse to the search for God:

> All mystics approach God through the irrational. Pure poetry is both mystical and irrational. If we descend a little from this height and apply the looser and broader definition of pure poetry, it is possible to say that, while it can lie in the temperament of very few of us to write poetry in order to find God, it is probably the purpose of each of us to write poetry to find the good which, in the Platonic sense, is synonymous with God. One writes poetry, then, in order to approach the good in what is harmonious and orderly. (*OP,* 227–28)

Stevens thus relates the irrational element in poetry, the part of verse that tends toward the pure poetry of the imagination, to an impulse toward the ideal that strongly echoes Moore's sense of the religiosity of verse. In "The Pangolin," Moore pictures the poet's graceful turnings in an ugly age as an act of faith in an ideality beyond the self. In times of trial, poetry becomes a hopeful prayer, an imaginative statement of belief in beauty that Moore interprets as a sign of God's grace. Stevens, too, extends the writing of poetry into the realm of the sacred. Poetry equals the good, which imaginatively equals God—the abstraction, as Stevens puts it, "upon which so much depends."

Yet, despite the similarities apparent between Stevens's concept of the good and Moore's sense of pangolin grace, the consideration of the abstraction upon which so much depends prompts Moore and Stevens to part company. Where both poets picture the writing of romantic poetry as sacred activity in the mid-1930s, they locate the looked for ideal in subtly different places. In Moore's view, poetry represents a quest for an ideal presence that clearly lies outside the self, a quest that, because of our fallen natures, we can never fulfill. Moore's sense of poetic "thwarting" issues from her desire to believe in something she can never know and to maintain a faith in a goodness that, by definition, cannot be realized on this earth. The imagination's constant freshening—and new and new and new—thus becomes a stay against ever-present doubt, an imaginative fighting back that marks an uneasy hope in a divinity beyond the self that must be remade again and again. For Stevens, the battle for belief is no less intense, but differently placed. Stevens locates the ideal within the self rather than outside it, a product of an internal imaginative pressure that rises up, like volcanic steam, and pushes outward. Whatever divinity Stevens contemplates remains strictly a product of human making, a god equivalent to a new and tremendously powerful poem subject to imaginative change. Stevens's sense of poetic "thwarting" issues from an ongoing sense of dissatisfaction with the products of the mind—the ideals he creates do not remain ideals for long. The imagination grows stale and a once-beautiful vision becomes a restrictive trap that must be opened by a return to the real from which all poetry springs. The imagination's constant freshening—"and new and new and new"—thus reflects, for Stevens, the poet's inability to craft a perfect poem in which to believe, one that will keep changing, moving from abstraction to the real—the supreme fiction, that, by definition, can never solidify beyond its notes. For both poets God and the imagination are ultimately one, but for different reasons. God and the imagination are one for Moore because God can only be approached through the imagination in a fallen world. In Stevens's poetic philosophy, God and the imagination are one because God is only a product of the human mind subject to change. For both poets the result is the same. Both live in a world without a present God in which the issue of belief in the possibility of a God becomes the equivalent of beautiful verse.

Thus, the mid-1930s proved a time of intellectual accord for Moore and Stevens, although their poetic philosophies ultimately led them in different directions, a turn that would become even more apparent during the years of the Second World War. Given the sacred sense of romantic poetry that evolves in the work of both poets throughout the period before the war, their gravitation toward one another in a time of poetic trial seems apt. Both were attacked by the literary Left for the same reasons and both countered their critics by insistently reiterating their sense of the importance of the imagination to an age sorely lacking in beauty. Both insisted that the romantic imagination had a potential social value as a counterweight to evil. Yet, neither poet emerged from their experiments of the mid-1930s firm in the conviction of their social romanticism. Dissatisfied with his forced romantic flights in *Owl's Clover,* Ste-

vens cut away at the poem, eventually discarding the piece from his
Collected Poems. The poem that follows *Owl's Clover*, "The Man with the
Blue Guitar," signals a rhetorical move away from the high-blown verse
of romantic counterpunching to a simpler bareness of plain speaking.

Moore, too, apparently suffered pangs of doubt about her confronta-
tion with the age in the pangolin, and she did not publish a single new
poem between 1936 and 1940. Instead, she wrote a novel, eventually
rejected for publication by Macmillan, which bore a telling title bor-
rowed from Anthony Trollope, *The Way We Live Now*. Convinced of the
importance of beauty in poetry, Moore turned to prose to do her own
plain speaking about the evils of the age. For Moore, as for Stevens, the
advent of the Second World War and America's entry into that war
proved another important aesthetic turning point—another opportunity
to redefine their poetry in relation to the world and each other. For both
Moore and Stevens, the trade of romantic violence for actual violence
seemed less viable in a world actually, rather than hypothetically, at war,
and both poets again set out to find a poetic that would suffice for the
1940s.

Chapter 6

Singing the Soldier Home: Wallace Stevens's "About One of Marianne Moore's Poems" and the Trials of Postwar Poetry

In August 1943, after years of correspondence and mutual attention, Stevens and Moore finally met on a broad lawn in front of Mount Holyoke College in Massachusetts. The occasion that brought them together was the Entretiens des Pontigny, a ten-day gathering of French and Belgian intellectuals exiled by Nazi occupation and determined to keep their cultures alive on foreign shores. Invited to attend the event by the Sorbonne philosopher Jean Wahl, himself a survivor of a Nazi concentration camp, Moore and Stevens traveled to Mount Holyoke to add their American voices to the conference's call for worldwide intellectual resistance. On August 11, Stevens, seated outdoors on the bright green grass behind a small desk under a tree, delivered his paper entitled "The Figure of the Youth as Virile Poet" with Moore and her mother in attendance. Later in the conference, Moore read her essay "Feeling and Precision" under the same boughs. The setting for the poets' talks was idyllic. Struck by the beauty of the scene and the participants, Moore recorded in her travel diary her first impressions of Stevens and his friends Henry Church, editor of the French literary magazine *Mesures,* and his wife Barbara:

> Wallace Stevens! The poet and his art. . . . Mrs. Church in navy
> blue crepe with white touches, blue shoes, white hat w/ wings—

sumptuous white tweed coat and a little wristwatch, platinum with oblong dial the size of a pencil eraser. Henry Church dark brown suit and shoes and pork-pie panama hat— . . . straight fine nose and great decorum. Wallace Stevens w/ no hat, a maltese gray suit with changeable or invisible pinstripe of blue and green and a pale blue foreign neck tie—black shoes—a remarkable hair cut; not sheared to thinness in a line with his ear—but sculptured down yet with a close short effect.[1]

As her diary attests, Moore found Stevens and the Churches images of elegance. Sumptuously dressed, decorous, sculptured, straight, and fine, aesthetically unique and pleasing, they seemed to embody the intellectual and cultural refinement under attack in Europe at the time. Throughout her life, Moore told the story of her first meeting with Stevens many times, and she always made note of the elegant accoutrements and lovely setting that gave the day its emblematic quality. In an interview with Donald Hall seventeen years later, Moore recalled:

> During the French program at Mount Holyoke one afternoon Wallace Stevens had a discourse, the one about Goethe dancing, on a packet-boat in black wool stockings. My mother and I were there; and I gave a reading with commentary. Henry Church had an astoundingly beautiful Panama hat—a sort of pork-pie with a wide brim, a little like Bernard Berenson's hats. I have never seen as fine a weave, and he had a pepper-and-salt shawl which he draped about himself. This lecture was on the lawn. Wallace Stevens was extremely friendly.[2]

In Moore's memory, the day remained one of happy accord—beautiful people in a beautiful place—poets brought together to trade ideas in a sort of Shangri-la far from the physical hardships and deprivations of the war. As she recorded later, Stevens struck her on their first meeting as an "extremely friendly" man of "scientific unevasiveness."[3] He answered questions precisely with a sense of personal integrity, and Moore admired both his directness and his desire to be accurate. Their first encounter remained enshrined in Moore's recollection as something high and true.

Yet, in all of Moore's remembrances of the occasion, one element seems strangely absent: the intellectual content of the day. Where Moore recalls the exact look of Henry Church's hat to Donald Hall seventeen years after the event, she has a hard time recollecting Stevens's lecture; in "The Figure of the Youth as Virile Poet" it is Coleridge, not Goethe, who dances in black wool stockings on the packet. Moore mistakes the one image she recalls from Stevens's talk, and her error points to a gap in her earlier record of the event. Moore usually took meticulous notes whenever she attended a lecture, yet her travel notebook remains empty of comments on Stevens's remarks. She follows her description of Stevens behind his desk on the lawn with two words, "His lecture—," only to leave the rest of the page conspicuously blank.[4] Moore's blank page reflects an ongoing attitude toward Stevens's Entretiens lecture. While Moore made frequent references to many of Stevens's prose pieces in her letters and commentaries throughout her career, particularly "The Noble Rider and the Sound of Words," on the subject of the virile youth she remained uncharacteristically quiet.

One possible interpretation for her empty page and fading memories is that Moore did not find many useful ideas in the lecture Stevens read that day. Indeed, Moore's enduring portrait of her happy personal concord with a gracious and elegant Stevens overshadows the fact that the papers the two poets delivered at the Entretiens were very different. Moore's lecture, "Feeling and Precision," consisted primarily of technical comments about poetic form and diction. Within her essay, Moore argues the importance of formal control to poets who, in the midst of the horrors of war, find themselves consumed by violent feelings. "Feeling at its deepest," Moore contests, "tends to be inarticulate. If it does manage to be articulate, it is likely to seem over condensed, so that the author is resisted as being enigmatic or disobliging or arrogant."[5] Taking issue in part with the proliferation of bombastic and sentimental war poetry in the early 1940s, Moore makes an equation between the true sincerity of a poet's feeling and the precision of his or her verse. Those poets who pay close attention to technique, labeled disobliging and dispassionate by their critics, in fact care more deeply about the war than those who spout excessive and easily accessible rhetoric. Recalling Stevens's image of poetry as a lion in "Poetry Is a Destructive Force," Moore agrees that "It can kill a man," but only if the cat has sharp claws. Without his weapons, "the lion's leap would be mitigated almost to harmlessness . . . ., so precision is both impact and exactitude, as with surgery" (*CPrMM*, 396). Drawing on Stevens's 1938 lyric, Moore thus fires another round in her ongoing argument that poetry defends against dangerous times. Agreeing with Stevens's earlier wartime aesthetic of "The Noble Rider and the Sound of Words," Moore maintains throughout "Feeling and Precision" that poetry is a violence from within that protects us from a violence from without. A good war poet, Moore announces at the end of her essay, modifies his or her feelings with "moral and technical insights" and creates an ordered pressure against the chaos of reality that preserves the freedom of the soul.

Given her continued appreciation of Stevens's figure of the noble rider, Moore must have been somewhat surprised at the Entretiens to meet his successor, Stevens's virile youth. As Allen Filreis points out, "The Figure of the Youth as Virile Poet" marks a significant departure from Stevens's pre–Pearl Harbor aesthetic of "The Noble Rider and the Sound of Words."[6] In "The Noble Rider," Stevens seeks an internal imaginative pressure to press back "against" the pressure of reality, a poetic counterforce that, like Moore's cathedral in "The Pangolin," implies a relation between the imagination and the real that is one of "precise equilibrium." In "The Figure of the Youth," Stevens seeks instead an "agreement with reality" that places an even greater emphasis on the poet's wartime attachment to the facts of his day.[7] Filreis's comments dovetail with James Longenbach's argument that Stevens's increasing desire to be grounded in the experience of the manly soldier led him to define his poetic ever more sharply along the axis of gender. Longenbach suggests that during the period of America's involvement in the Second World War, Stevens became increasingly anxious about the decorative elements of his verse—the rosy light that turned all muscle to fanciful mush. In response to his fears of poetic effeminacy in wartime, Stevens reimagined "the real" and factual world as something masculine, undermining his earlier wartime visions in "Notes toward a Supreme Fiction" of poetry as a marriage between the feminine "real" and the masculine imagination.[8] In "Notes toward a Supreme Fiction," Stevens's Ozymandias courts the contemplated spouse of the real in Nanzia Nunzio, the "great captain" joins in "mystic marriage" with the bawdy body of the maiden Bawda, and the poet himself ultimately mates with the Fat Girl, terrestrial. Poetry issues from a union of male and female forces in which "the real" is feminine.

In "The Figure of the Youth as Virile Poet," however, Stevens exchanges his concept of "mystic marriage" for the image of an unwed manly poet of fact. Boldly announcing that "the centuries have a way of being male," Stevens claims that present poets, like the active male "heroes" of history, must work to endow their times with a specifically masculine flavor. Setting the factual creations of the virile youth in scornful opposition to earlier, more decorative, attempts at verse, Stevens genders the poetic imagination of the past as female. Looking back to the poetry of previous centuries he writes:

> In effect, what we are remembering is the rather haggard background of the incredible, the imagination without intelligence, from which a younger figure is emerging, stepping forward in the company of a muse of its own, still half-beast and somehow more than human, a kind of sister of the Minotaur. . . . It is the imagination of the son still bearing the antique imagination of the father. It is the clear intelligence of the young man still bearing the burden of the obscurities of the intelligence of the old. (NA, 52–53)

The antique imagination appears in Stevens's wartime essay as a she-beast, a feminized burden of obscurities and old myths that the young male poet must grudgingly bear and, Stevens implies, attempt to do without. To be a truly manly poet of fact, the virile youth must say: '*No longer do I believe that here is a mystic muse, sister of the Minotaur. This is another of the monsters I had for nurse, whom I have wasted. I am myself a part of what is real*' (NA, 60). Of course, the virile youth, like all of Stevens's poet figures, cannot ultimately sustain himself wholly in the real, but the exchange the youth enacts with the unreal at the end of the essay is an exchange with a monstrous female figure who leads him into a maze where he would rather not linger. If the poet dwells apart in his imagination, Stevens warns, "the masculine nature that we propose for one that must be the master of our lives will be lost" (NA, 66).

Having come to know Stevens in the prewar period as a poet of imaginative hope, Moore may have found it hard to adjust to Stevens's

1943 picture of the poet as a masculine creature of fact. Indeed, there is evidence to suggest that Stevens's emphasis on virility and actuality at the expense of the balm of the imagination struck Moore as part of a dangerous national trend. In an interview in 1945 for the series "Poets Are People" broadcast from the Brooklyn Public Library, Moore responded to the question "What do you most dislike in present-day American tendencies?" with the curt remark, "I detest our tendency to glorify American virility."[9] Poets in wartime had the habit of extolling the very sorts of "heroic" manly exploits that Moore found most problematic. Power, for Moore, was a matter of the spirit. As the war deepened, she remained convinced that the violence without could only be conquered by the pressure of the moral imagination, by a faith in and commitment to higher values and purposes—the strategy of her Stevensian pangolin.

Yet, looking back over her own prewar verse, Moore began to question whether an emphasis on the poet's violent imaginative resistance might be misplaced in wartime if untempered by other virtues. Moore's war poems suggest that, in response to her anxieties about the glorification of virile strength, she, like Stevens, considered her poetry more closely in terms of gender during the years of the conflict. Paying homage to Stevens in her prewar poem of 1936, "The Pangolin," Moore makes her perfect poet beast a strong male. Covered with impenetrable scales and heavily armed, the male pangolin poet is a solitary creature with an unshakably steady soul who can fight back against the pressure of reality with killing force. In 1941, on the brink of America's entry into the Second World War, Moore republished "The Pangolin" in her book of war poems *What Are Years*. Where "The Pangolin" is the final poem in her 1936 volume of the same name, in *What Are Years* (1941) Moore moves "The Pangolin" to a penultimate position, ending her volume with a 1940 poem, "The Paper Nautilus." Another image of the poet with a shell in a violent world, Moore's paper nautilus answers and modifies her vision of pangolin verse directly in gendered terms. Where the pangolin is male and solitary, the paper nautilus is female and a mother. Moore begins "The Paper Nautilus" by posing the question, why do poets write in wartime? Her answer is that true poets write not for politicians or for critics, but for children:

For authorities whose hopes
are shaped by mercenaries?
    Writers entrapped by
    teatime fame and by
commuters' comforts? Not for these
    the paper nautilus
    constructs her thin glass shell.

    Giving her perishable
souvenir of hope, a dull
    white outside and smooth-
    edged inner surface
glossy as the sea, the watchful
    maker of it guards it
    day and night; she scarcely

eats until the eggs are hatched.[10]

Both Moore's pangolin and paper nautilus use verse as a form of protection. Yet, while Moore pictures the pangolin's art as a suit of armor that protects only the wearer, the paper nautilus spins a "thin glass shell" that cradles and preserves her young. In "The Paper Nautilus," the poet's self-preservation and the virtue of strength take a backseat to the virtue of self-sacrifice and the preservation of the species. The maternal artist seeks to shield others, not only the self. The nautilus's struggle ends only when those in her charge can enjoy true liberty—"the intensively / watched eggs coming from / the shell free it when they are freed." Saddled with a weighty sense of obligation, the nautilus poet sacrifices the "freedom" of her own art until such time as the world becomes a safer place for her offspring.

Moore's "The Paper Nautilus" thus begs poets caught up in violent times of virile force not to neglect gentler and, in Moore's view, more feminine virtues, such as motherly love. Looking back on her masculine pangolin, Moore concludes that the image of the impregnable solitary poet must be tempered to suit the growing need for compassion and obligation to others in troubled times. Where the masculine pangolin, secure behind his impregnable armor, confidently defends himself against the pressure of reality, the feminine paper nautilus, protected only with a "thin glass shell," lives in constant fear of being crushed by the pressure without. The shell the nautilus spins, both fragile and "perishable," speaks to Moore's sense that true peace begins with an admission of general weakness and vulnerability—an acknowledgment, as she writes in "What Are Years?" that "all are naked, none is safe." The contrast between her two poet figures, however, suggests that while the pangolin might be too strongly masculine and self-reliant to prove a working image of the compassionate war poet, the paper nautilus, in turn, might be too frail to withstand the pressures of the day. Moore's positioning of "The Pangolin" next to "The Paper Nautilus" in her volume *What Are Years* suggests that the perfect poet of wartime lies somewhere in between her two creatures. The ideal war poet must be both strong and compassionate, both self-protective and protective of others, both manly and maternal—a union of male and female forces.

Thus, Moore and Stevens first came to know and like each other personally at a time when, poetically, they had markedly different agendas. Convinced of the wartime importance of an increased contact with masculine reality, Stevens arrived at the Entretiens armed with his figure of the virile poet in the hopes of dismissing the more feminine and decorative elements of his own poetic. Moore, however, came to the Entretiens convinced of the wartime value of a poetic integration of feminine and masculine virtues and remained faithful to her sense of the poet's moral imagination as a saving grace in troubled times. Stevens thus traveled to Mount Holyoke to disrupt the equilibrium in his poetic that Moore found most valuable. The blank pages in her Entretiens travel diary and her uncharacteristic silence on the subject of Stevens's lecture perhaps reflect Moore's sense that Stevens had lost his balance. The virile youth made up a page of Stevens's poetic that Moore decided she would rather not record, and the artistic dissonance between the two poets was a matter only the end of the war could resolve.

The summer of 1946 in Connecticut was, by Stevens's account, a beautiful one. Under the clear skies and bright sunshine of the first full summer after the war, Stevens rediscovered a number of simple pleasures. His table once again held fresh vegetables and unrationed butter, an abundance that caused him, as he put it, to "double" his "normal size."[11] Elsie grew large, beautiful roses in their garden, and the house was filled through the season with their scent. Yet, the summer of 1946 for Stevens was both one of plenty and of doubt. As James Longenbach points out, Stevens faced the postwar world with trepidation, afraid that any sense of ordinary life might be impossible to retrieve in the wake of the destruction.[12] Having identified himself with and championed the manly soldier during the last years of the conflict, Stevens wondered, once the hostilities were over, how to sing once again of peace. In keeping with his own poetic credo, "It Must Change," Stevens set out in search of a new figure for the poet. The image he found to suit his needs was not that of a virile youth, but of a small woman with a very big hat—his friend Marianne Moore.

Stevens turned back to Moore's poetry at the war's end with a renewed and vital interest and again made her the subject of his theoretical ruminations on the nature and the role of verse. In July 1946, Stevens sent "Credences of Summer" to Jose Garcia Villa, editor of *Viva,* along with a note that indicated that he was once more thinking of Moore's poetry. "Some time ago you wrote to me about a note on Marianne Moore," Stevens remarked to Garcia Villa. "What is the deadline for her number?"[13] No record remains of Stevens's efforts for *Viva,* but he pursued the project and the essay that resulted, "About One of Marianne Moore's Poems," eventually appeared in the summer 1948 issue of Theodore Weiss's *Quarterly Review of Literature.* In the meantime, Stevens spent the summer of 1946 making Moore the subject of his verse. Stevens's set of thirteen poems penned just after "Credences of Summer," "More Poems for Liadoff," contains the lyric "The Prejudice against the Past," Stevens's direct response to Moore's wartime poem "A Carriage from Sweden."[14]

Such a concentrated flurry of attention in Moore's direction speaks to Stevens's changing artistic agenda in a postwar context. In part, the explanation for Stevens's renewed interest in Moore lies in his own anxieties about the possibility of finding a poetry to confront the devastation of the age. As James Longenbach notes, "More Poems for Liadoff" is a dark set of lyrics in which Stevens struggles to put the Second World War behind him and to find a poetry capable of recuperating a wasted world.[15] The poems of "More Poems for Liadoff" tell of a postwar imaginative and emotional poverty—of small, poor people, "raggeder than ruin," making their way in a depleted atmosphere, trying, as Stevens puts it in the title of his final lyric, "to discover life." Thoughts of the war's lasting and difficult legacy permeate the set. In "Burghers of Petty Death," Stevens laments that individual death has become routine and meaningless in the face of mass extinction, eclipsed by

> a total death,
> A devastation, a death of great height
> And depth, covering all surfaces,
> Filling the mind.
>
> (*CPWS,* 362)

War leaves behind the empty landscape of Stevens's snow man, a field of emotional numbness in which the only possible poetry comes from "a wasted figure, with an instrument," who "propounds blank final music." "Human Arrangement" echoes Stevens's fear that the war has left the world trapped in a "final" state of depletion beyond poetry's reanimating power:

> Place-bound and time-bound in evening rain
> And bound by a sound which does not change,
>
> Except that it begins and ends,
> Begins again and ends again—
>
> Rain without change within or from
> Without.
>
> (*CPWS,* 363)

The elimination of violence without leads to stagnation within, leaving the poet chained to everyday reality with a starkly limited and repetitive vocabulary. After the war, "without"—the realm outside the self—becomes a keen expression of deprivation, the equivalent of "doing without." In "Mountains Covered with Cats," Stevens reflects that the war poet returns from battle an "invalid personality / . . . outcast, without the will to power," and "impotent" before the jumble of reality (*CPWS,*

368). With the poet in a depleted condition, war lingers on unresolved by soothing music.

Against such a bleak backdrop, Stevens struggles in "More Poems for Liadoff" to find tentative solutions to the problem of a postwar poetic. Throughout the set, Stevens half-heartedly continues his search for a poet/hero to transform the age with a blast of Nietzschean will, only to decide that such a creature cannot, and ultimately should not, come.[16] As the title of Stevens's set proclaims, the songs of the postwar are for Anatole Liadoff, a little-known Russian musician and composer of the late nineteenth and early twentieth century whose career speaks directly to Stevens's emerging sense of a poetry of lesser, more ordinary, things. A student of Rimsky-Korsakov's at the great conservatory at St. Petersburg, Liadoff reputedly made a name for himself chiefly by wasting his talents, forgoing large-scale works for small, unassuming piano pieces and minor orchestral sketches. While other composers, like Mussorgsky, Rimsky-Korsakov, and, later, Prokofiev and Stravinsky, engaged in avant-garde tonal experiments, Liadoff, disdainful of his colleagues modernist endeavors, contented himself with works based on humble Russian folk songs and composed variation sets on simple pastoral themes. In writing poems for Liadoff, Stevens creates lyrics of limitation that profess a desire to stay close to the ordinary experience of everyday folk, poems that ultimately reflect Liadoff's craving for simple variations on common themes.

Like Liadoff, Stevens opts for a poetry of small satisfactions, scaled down to suit the times. The first poem of Stevens's group, "A Woman Sings a Song for a Soldier Come Home," points to Stevens's desire for a gentler and simpler chant that, while not offering much in the way of grand flights, will grant some solace. As the title suggests, Stevens's poem depicts the poet's mental homecoming—a move back to the more familiar ground of peacetime poetics after long years preoccupied with thoughts of bloody conflict. Lacking nurse or kin, the soldier/poet comes back to his old village and, severed from his past and oppressed by the memory of the war, he "walks and dies" from a wound that "does not bleed." Stevens pictures the soldier as doomed to suffer unless a new sort of poetry can be made to replace the thoughts of war:

> unless
> One person should come by chance,
> This man or that,
>
> So much a part of the place, so little
> A person he knows, with whom he might
> Talk of the weather—
>
> And let it go, with nothing lost,
> Just out of the village, at its edge,
> In the quiet there.

(CPWS, 360–61)

The words that heal issue not from a hero, but from a noncombatant with no particular distinguishing features—"this man or that"—a figure so ordinary that he looks strange to the soldier/poet. Rooted in a particular physical place, the villager speaks of local and normal things rather than apocalyptic events. Such conversation establishes a continuity between the poet's pre- and postwar village life and frees him of his painful wartime burden. The poet's recuperation, however, is not merely a matter of relearning the speech of his place. As the title of Stevens's initial poem suggests, a woman must sing the soldier home. The soldier's potentially saving contact with the ordinary man lies nested in a woman's compassionate lyric—a coupling that reflects Stevens's renewed willingness to see poetry as an act of union between male and female poetic forces, simple fact wed with soothing song. The once autonomous virile youth of brutal fact returns to his village a battered wreck, and a female poet restores him with a song that doubles as instruction. She teaches him to temper his violent thoughts and believe again in poetic grace.

The need for a return to a more feminized poetic echoes throughout "More Poems for Liadoff," and, in such a context of recovery, Stevens's poem to Moore, "The Prejudice against the Past," becomes particularly important. Placed directly after his picture of poetic impotence—"the invalid personality . . . without the will to power"—in "Mountains Covered with Cats," Stevens's poem to Moore signals a shift in his set from male to female voices. Collapsing the "father-fire" of "The Red Fern" and the Nietzschean maleness of "The Dove in the Belly" into the complaints of "Mountains Covered with Cats," Stevens ends "More Poems for Liadoff" with Marianna's Swedish cart ("The Prejudice against the Past"), a mother's song to her daughter ("Extraordinary References"), and a waitress's colorful bouquet ("Attempt to Discover Life")—poems in which the creative forces, gendered female, restore peace to a land of war. Stevens's rediscovery of Moore's poetry in "More Poems for Liadoff" thus appears as a function of his renewed interest in the feminine force of his own postwar poetic. Rejecting the lopsided puffery of solitary virile maleness, Stevens turns back to Moore's verse as a model of how to write simpler lyrics to restore the age. Hers is the woman's song that will sing the soldier home.

In an act that reflects his disenchantment with his own wartime aesthetic, Stevens chooses in "The Prejudice against the Past" to pay direct homage to one of Moore's war poems, her 1944 lyric "A Carriage from Sweden," published in her lean book of the same year, *Nevertheless*. Inspired by an antique Swedish carriage housed in the Brooklyn museum, Moore's poem reflects the tone and style of many of her war lyrics. Crafting a carefully detailed description of her subject, Moore gradually reveals what such a cart means to a world at war and grants the carriage a moral value that reaches far beyond its decorative surface. A product of one of the few countries to maintain armed neutrality during the Second World War, Moore's Swedish cart, both "responsive and responsible," becomes a symbol of compassion, "stalwartness," and resistance to evil that reminds Moore of "Denmark's sanctuaried Jews."[17] Moore thus revives a put-away museum piece and, moving from past to present, makes it an important current reminder of those who refuse to sacrifice their integrity to wartime aims. Rather than address the soldier's movements or the brutalities of the Holocaust directly, Moore offers up a past product of a hopeful aesthetic intelligence that pushes back against the current pressure of hate and destruction.

Removed from Stevens's late wartime poetic of, as Longenbach puts it, "no-nonsense engagement with reality," Moore's carriage provides Stevens with a living example of the sort of poetry needed to heal the postwar world.[18] As the title of his response suggests, Stevens feared that the war had in fact created a "prejudice against the past," a sense that the world was so changed and depleted that all expressions of beauty or belief would seem nothing more than naive nostalgia for a prewar world. In Stevens's view, however, Moore's carriage from Sweden argued against such a pessimistic vision of years gone by and suggested a relationship between the past and the present vital to recovering a sense of peace. Casting "day," the sunlit solid present, as "the children's friend," Stevens begins "The Prejudice against the Past" by reflecting that today is not entirely bleak for those creatures, like Moore and children, who can see beyond the wasted surface:

> Day is the children's friend.
> It is Marianna's Swedish cart.
> It is that and a very big hat.
>
> Confined by what they see,
> Aquiline pedants treat the cart,
> As one of the relics of the heart.
>
> They treat the philosopher's hat,
> Left thoughtlessly behind,
> As one of the relics of the mind . . .
>
> Of day, then, children make
> What aquiline pedants take
> For souvenirs of time, lost time,
>
> Adieux, shapes, images . . .
>
> (*CPWS*, 368–69)

Stevens's short lyric begins by presenting two competing interpretations of the present. In the first stanza, Stevens suggests that both Moore and children use their imaginations to find peace in the dismal here and now. For "Marianna," the beauty of the old Swedish cart still exists in the present—living proof of unflagging current virtues. Referring to Moore's signature tricorne as a "philosopher's hat," Stevens implies that Moore brings a specifically moral intelligence to bear on the depleted present—a belief in the invisible that amounts to hope. Pedantic literalists, on the other hand, look around and see a present utterly corrupted by the war—a place where the good things of the past no longer apply. To the unimaginative pedants of the postwar, Moore's cart and hat, as well as children's games, are examples of pure nostalgia, relics of dead sentiments and beliefs.

As the simple rhymes (that/hat, cart/heart, behind/mind, make/take) and childlike, monosyllabic diction of the lyric indicate, Stevens clearly sides with the children and Moore in the dispute, and he devotes the remainder of his poem to a refutation of the pedants' pessimistic stance. In the last two stanzas of "Prejudice against the Past," Stevens argues that not all products of the imagination constitute mere nostalgia. Children, he writes, make things:

> not of day, but of themselves,
> Not of perpetual time.

> And, therefore, aquiline pedants find
> The philosopher's hat to be part of the mind,
> The Swedish cart to be part of the heart.

> (CPWS, 369)

Stevens reminds the pedants that children are not "of perpetual time" and have no memory of the world before the war. The romantic images that children create are therefore not merely nostalgic memories of a golden past, but the living product of the present. Unaware that the world is fallen, children make out of dust shapes and images that jaded adults, overcome by a sense of loss, find inappropriate. The imagination of the postwar child thus becomes an argument for the relevance of Moore's poetry. The present-day hopeful thoughts of children prove that Moore's verse is not merely a souvenir of prewar sentiments and beliefs long dead. Her compassion and moral intelligence remain, like her Swedish cart, part of the living heart and mind of the present. In the face of ruin, Moore's poetry, like children's play, proves that the postwar world is not wasted beyond imaginative recovery.

Stevens's poem of homage thus suggests two principle reasons he turned back to Moore's poetry as a model for his postwar verse. First, Stevens's lyric casts Moore as a poet of ordinary things who captures the postwar poetic ideal he sets out in "A Woman Sings a Song for a Soldier Come Home." Starting with a simple, real subject—an old

pony cart—Moore creates an unassuming, yet satisfying lyric suitable
for children—a song of an ordinary object that counters wartime de-
spair and, as Moore says of her cart in "A Carriage from Sweden,"
makes one "feel at home." Second, dispelling the prejudice against the
past, Moore's verse grants Stevens an all-important sense of continuity
between his own past and present imaginative experience. Reading "A
Carriage from Sweden," Stevens concludes that Moore's use of the
past constitutes more than mere nostalgia. Her poetry makes the past
meaningful to the present, a move that opens the door for a recovery
of the imagination in a depleted postwar context. In Stevens's view,
Moore's simple cart provides a healing link between the pre- and
postwar world that releases the poet from the bleak final music of
unremitting fatalism.

Indeed, the vital importance to Stevens of Moore's unnostalgic link
between the past and the present becomes apparent in the poem that
follows "The Prejudice against the Past" in "More Poems for Liadoff,"
"Extraordinary References." A companion piece to "Prejudice against
the Past," "Extraordinary References" again speaks to the relationship
between the pre- and postwar world. Modeling his poem on Moore's use
of a historical subject in "A Carriage from Sweden," Stevens selects one
of his own—his family history. During the war years, Stevens became
fascinated with his ancestry and prodigiously traced his family tree at a
great cost of time and money.[19] On his mother's side, Stevens followed
his line of descent back to the Zellers of the Tulpehocken region of
Pennsylvania, the site of "Extraordinary References." A potpourri of
incidents borrowed from his own past, Stevens's poem constitutes his
own potentially nostalgic Swedish cart, his "put-away museum-piece"
that he must make meaningful to the wasted present. Picturing a mother
telling her daughter about her family history, Stevens juxtaposes images
of his past with an account of the present. "Your great-grandfather was
an Indian fighter," the mother tells her child, only to reveal, in the story
of a second soldier, why this bit of history is relevant:

> *My Jacomyntje! This first spring after the war,*
> *In which your father died, still breathes for him*
> *And breathes again for us a fragile breath.*

In the inherited garden, a second-hand
Vertumnus creates an equilibrium.
The child's three ribbons are in her plaited hair.

(CPWS, 369)

Recalling his reading of Moore's cart, Stevens concludes, as James Longenbach points out, that the story of his own past "is not simply nostalgic."[20] The mother tells a history that, like Moore's account of the Swedish carriage, becomes an image of "stalwartness" that reflects directly on the present. In spite of wars and deaths, the family recovers and will recover from the father's death in the most recent war, finding a fragile "spring," Stevens's season of imaginative rebirth, in the depleted present. Echoing "Prejudice against the Past," Stevens links the family's recovery to the creation of an ordinary song to take the place of "extraordinary references." The poems of the postwar spring from scaled-down subjects and simple acts of compassion suitable for children: "The mother ties the hair-ribbons of the child / And she has peace." Again, as in "Prejudice against the Past," Stevens suggests that children of the "inherited garden" remain happily unaware of the fall. The daughter has three ribbons in her plaited hair. For her, this simple act of ordering is enough, and her contentment points the way to the renewal of shapes and images and a fragile poetic future. The inherited garden may be dilapidated, but the imagination, the ordering impulse, lives on.

"Extraordinary References" thus suggests a further, more personal, reason Stevens took Moore's poetry so to heart after the war. Certainly, the "unannoying romance" of the Swedish cart both underlines Stevens's move toward a postwar song of ordinary things and proves to Stevens that the imagination is not a souvenir lost to the present day. In making the past relevant to the present, however, Moore's poetry also, in Stevens's view, endorsed and supported his wartime passion for genealogy, an interest that could seem a mere nostalgic retreat in desperate times. The coupling of "Prejudice against the Past" and "Extraordinary References" suggests that Stevens perhaps considered Moore's work a justification of his own intense interest in past things in a time when the world seemed consumed with present losses. As Stevens writes of the postwar world in "A Woman Sings a Song for a Soldier Come Home,"

> Nothing survives
> Except what was,
>
> Under the white clouds piled and piled
> Like gathered-up forgetfulness,
> In sleeping air.

$$(CPWS, 360)$$

In a world erased and obscured by "gathered-up forgetfulness," remembering the past becomes a vital step to restoring the present. For Stevens, Moore's poetry proved that "what was" still is. Her verse established a sense of continuity that gave Stevens hope for the continuation, not only of his poetry, but, on a deeper human level, his family.

The connection that Stevens crafted between Moore's poetry and the use of his own past did not end with "More Poems for Liadoff." During the same summer in which he composed his poems for Liadoff, Stevens happened upon a paper by H. D. Lewis in the July 1946 number of *Philosophy*.[21] Seeing Moore's image in the piece, Stevens coupled Lewis's thoughts with Moore's poetry to explain, once again, why her verse was vital to the postwar age. The title of Stevens's resulting essay, "About One of Marianne Moore's Poems," is deceptively simple. The essay is a hodgepodge of Stevens's reading of Moore's ode to the ostrich, "He 'Digesteth Harde Yron,'" his comments on Lewis's broad poetic theory, and, in a seemingly unrelated middle section, an account of his August 1946 trip to visit the old Zeller household in the Tulpehocken region of Pennsylvania. Located in the midst of his poetic and philosophic reflections on Moore's verse (parts 1 and 3), Stevens's travelogue (part 2) seems out of place. Why would Stevens, launched on a close reading of Moore's poem, indulge in such a strange and seemingly incongruous interruption? The answer lies in his companion poems in "More Poems for Liadoff." Read in the context of "The Prejudice against the Past" and "Extraordinary References," the relationship Stevens draws in his essay between Moore's poetry and his postwar return to his family past becomes both clear and poignant.

The themes Stevens addresses in "About One of Marianne Moore's Poems" echo the concerns of "The Prejudice against the Past" and "Extraordinary References" so closely that all of Stevens's considerations seem inescapably of a piece. In parts 1 and 3 of his essay, Stevens bases his analysis of Moore on H. D. Lewis's paper, "On Poetic Truth," from which he clips and transplants relevant phrases verbatim into the body of his own discussion. Stevens's cut-and-paste technique often condenses Lewis's argument beyond recognition, but a glance back to the full text of "On Poetic Truth" provides clues to why Stevens felt Moore and Lewis so closely linked. Placing poetic "veracity" at the opposite pole of scientific reason, Lewis's paper argues that the present-day populace has been duped into thinking that science deals in facts. In Lewis's view, scientists are abstractionists. They attempt to reduce all reality to a "collection of universal qualities," sets of cold purely intellectual equations that ignore the "particular" and "concrete" aspects of reality.[22] Reversing the usual sense of the conflict, Lewis concludes that poets, rather than scientists, are the age's true "realists." Poets confront "the irreducible data" of the world and their engagement with the particulars of reality results in "the revelation of something 'wholly other' by which the inexpressible loneliness of thinking is broken and enriched."[23] Where scientists examine facts only to confirm or deny general intellectual rules, thereby subjugating the endless variety of the real to familiar sets of ideals, poets approach a chaotic reality "which the mind can never tackle altogether on its own terms."[24] Pulling a Stevensian maneuver, Lewis rounds out his discussion by distinguishing between "real life" and the reality revealed by the artist. "Warning may be entered here," he writes, "against the foolish but prevalent belief that, if art is realistic, it must cling very closely to objects as we normally see them. That is precisely what art cannot do."[25] Lewis argues that it is the job of the poet's imagination to make the familiar unfamiliar, creating a "particular" and "individual" reality that dislodges the rational scientist's comfortable, habitual perceptions and shows us the true "otherness" (irreducibility) of things outside the conceptions of our minds. Reality, in Lewis's terms, is distinctly unorderable in its particularity—a strangeness only poetry's irrational magic can touch.

Like Marianne Moore, Lewis thus proved an ally in Stevens's postwar argument against those who believed that poetry, a mere relic of the imagination, no longer suited the age. Citing the limits of rational science, Lewis's paper insists that poetry remains a critical point of contact with irreducible, irrational realities in a disillusioned postwar world given to cold calculations. Lewis's essay thus echoes Stevens's sense of the importance of Moore's poetry as set forth in "The Prejudice against the Past." In his poem to Moore, Stevens claims that her verse proves the importance of poetry to "aquiline pedants" bent on reducing the depleted present to a series of bald scientific observations. Lewis's sense of poetry as point of contact with an individual reality "at the opposite pole to science, and out of its reach," thus reflects Stevens's reading of Moore as a poet of reality (the Swedish cart) who, donning her philosopher's hat, does not succumb to the bareness of a relentlessly rational context.

Given the thematic resonances between Lewis's piece and Stevens's poem to Marianna and her Swedish cart, Stevens's application of Lewis to Moore's "He 'Digesteth Harde Yron'" in "About One of Marianne Moore's Poems" seems a natural continuation of his earlier argument about Moore's artistic significance. Like Moore's "A Carriage from Sweden" (1944), "He 'Digesteth Harde Yron'" (1941) is a war poem, and Moore's argumentative strategy in her ostrich ode resembles that of her other lyric. Depicting an unassuming poetic subject, the "strange" and "comic camel-sparrow," Moore's poem presents a detailed description of the beast that, like her description of the Swedish cart, doubles as a wartime lesson in resilience and compassion. Stevens devotes the first section of "About One of Marianne Moore's Poems" to pointing out the important contrast between Moore's poetic "realism" in "He 'Digesteth Harde Yron'" and the age's wasted rationalism. Reworking the terms of "The Prejudice against the Past," Stevens quotes from the bible of aquiline pedantry, the *Encyclopedia Britannica,* placing its entry on the ostrich next to Moore's lines on the same subject. "Somehow," Stevens ruminates, "there is a difference between Miss Moore's bird and the bird of the Encyclopaedia." He explains:

This difference grows when she describes her bird as

> The friend
> of hippotigers and wild
> asses, it is as
> though schooled by them he was

the best of the unflying
pegasi.

The difference signalizes a transition from one reality to another. It is the reality of Miss Moore that is the individual reality. That of the Encyclopaedia is the reality of isolated fact. Miss Moore's reality is significant. An aesthetic integration is a reality. . . . To confront fact in its total bleakness is for any poet a completely baffling experience. Reality is not a thing but the aspect of the thing.[26]

As in "The Prejudice against the Past," Stevens pictures Moore as a poet who makes the pedants' bare facts uniquely meaningful. Granting value to otherwise useless details, Moore rises above the "total bleakness" of the age. Again borrowing a thought from "The Prejudice against the Past," Stevens implies that Moore's poetic power lies in her moral imagination, her "philosopher's hat." Noting that she avoids naming the subject of her ostrich poem directly, Stevens suggests that Moore, in small part, joins in Plato's love of abstraction and allusion. Stevens concludes, however, that while Moore shares Plato's "desire to engage objects apprehended by thought and not sense," she "does so only as it may be necessary for her to do so in order to establish a particular reality or, better, a reality of her own particulars" (*NA, 95*). As in "The Prejudice against the Past," Stevens insists that Moore's hat remains a modest postwar hat, one not so big or wide as to obscure her view of ordinary realities.

Thus, reworking the terms of his earlier poem, Stevens again makes Moore his model for a less imaginatively extravagant, yet elevating, postwar verse. The aesthetic combination of Moore's concrete Swedish cart and her philosopher's hat reappears in Stevens's essay as a factual ostrich with a smattering of philosophical abstraction. Moore's philosophical realism defeats the bleak pedants of postwar rationalism in both works. The similarities between the analytical sections of Stevens's essay and his earlier poem to Moore, however, tell only part of the story of Moore's importance to Stevens's postwar poetic recovery. Mirroring his presentation of "The Prejudice against the Past" and "Extraordinary References" in "More Poems for Liadoff," Stevens sets his analysis of Moore's "He 'Digesteth Harde Yron'" in "About One of Marianne

Moore's Poems" next to a lengthy account of his visit to his maternal ancestral homestead in Pennsylvania. Stevens's analysis of Moore's poetry abruptly ends and the poet announces, "During this last September, I visited the old Zeller house in the Tulpehocken, in Pennsylvania" (*NA*, 99). Read against the background of his pair of poems, Stevens's apparent digression comes to light as a further poignant consideration, inspired by Moore's verse, of the postwar prejudice against the past.

The postwar poet's relationship to the past may seem a buried issue in the analytical sections of Stevens's essay, but occasionally it bubbles to the surface. "To see things in their true perspective," Stevens writes at the beginning of his reading of "He 'Digesteth Harde Yron,'" "we require to draw very extensively upon experiences that are past. All that we see and hear is given a meaning in this way" (*NA*, 93). Moore's poem, Stevens suggests, grants its ostrich significance in the present by recalling its past—a compliment that recalls Stevens's praise of Moore's insistence on the value of past things in "A Carriage from Sweden." As Stevens undoubtedly recognized, the argumentative strategies of Moore's two poems are similar. Just as Moore proves in "A Carriage from Sweden" that her museum piece is not a silly romantic relic, so she proves in "He 'Digesteth Harde Yron'" that the primitive ostrich, the last large bird of its kind, is not a relic of evolution. The ostrich, like the carriage, still has something to say to the present age. Throughout "He 'Digesteth Harde Yron,'" Moore traces the history of her subject and plays on the relationship between the past and the present, between the historical and the modern ostrich, in order to question man's current values. Her poem begins:

> Although the aepyornis
> or roc that lived in Madagascar, and
>   the moa are extinct,
>   the camel-sparrow, linked
> with them in size—the large sparrow
> Xenophon saw walking by
>   a stream—was and is
>   a symbol of justice.[27]

The only animal of its kind to escape extinction, the ostrich carries a special message to humans bent on self-extinction in a time of war. The ostrich's survival becomes a lesson in human behavior as Moore lists the qualities that have saved the bird from the fate of its ancient fellows, qualities she hopes humans will adopt before it is too late to save the lesser species. Compassionate, careful, swift, and strong, the ostrich "watches his chicks with / a maternal concentration," doing everything in his power to ensure the safety of his young. Debunking the present notion of the ostrich as a comic coward—he is "never known to hide his / head in sand"—Moore applauds the ability of a past culture to see the bird's true value. The ancient Greeks piously worshiped the ostrich as a "symbol of justice," and Moore argues that the compassionate, vigilant bird should be so valued again in the present context. In Moore's view, the ostrich "was and is" a symbol of justice, and greedy present-day "externalists," drawn only to the bird's fine feathers, must learn to see the ostrich's deeper meaning if the world is to survive the war. The value granted the bird in the past still applies to the present.

Thus, like "A Carriage from Sweden," "He 'Digesteth Harde Yron'" argues the relevance of a historical subject to a current crisis, insisting that the values of long ago live on in the here and now. Stevens's choice of "He 'Digesteth Harde Yron'" as a critical subject thus speaks to his continued interest in Moore's recuperation of the past for present purposes. The distinction between poetry (Moore's ostrich) and pedantry (the encyclopedia's ostrich) that Stevens makes on Moore's behalf in his essay remains a contrast between a poet who keeps faith with an imaginative past and those who live only in a starkly factual postwar present. Part 1 of Stevens's essay thus reiterates the argument he makes in "The Prejudice against the Past" against those who dismiss Moore's poetic link with the prewar imagination as romantic nonsense.

Given the continued attack on those who ignore the past that runs through the analytical sections of Stevens's essay, the apparently digressive second section of "About One of Marianne Moore's Poems" makes compelling sense. Just as his reading of Moore's Swedish cart in "The Prejudice against the Past" paves the way for his use of family history in "Extraordinary References"—Moore's poetry proves that the romantic shapes and images of the past still speak to the present, therefore Stevens's personal and poetic past still speaks to the present—so Stevens's commentary on Moore's ostrich poem prepares the way for his return to his ancestral roots in "About One of Marianne Moore's Poems." "He 'Digesteth Harde Yron'" convinces Stevens that a connection with the prewar world remains crucial to a postwar revival of the imagination. Inspired by Moore's sense of the importance of the past to a scarred and unimaginative present, Stevens returns to his own past in the second section of "About One of Marianne Moore's Poems" and, following the pattern of "The Prejudice against the Past" and "Extraordinary References," argues the relevance of his ancestry to a postwar present convinced that all history is worthless.

As in "Extraordinary References," the issue that lies behind part 2 of Stevens's essay is his own poetic recovery. On the heels of his appreciation of Moore's ostrich in "He 'Digesteth Harde Yron,'" Stevens selects his own historical subject and, following Moore's example, attempts to forge a link with the imaginative past that will reanimate the aquiline present and revive his verse. Stevens begins his tour of Tulpehocken in part 2 of "About One of Marianne Moore's Poems" with a visit to the old Zeller homestead. Set against his sense of an imaginatively depleted postwar world, Stevens's description of the place and his vision of those who lived there seems initially only to mark the irretrievable distance between the present and the past:

> Over the door there is an architectural cartouche of the cross with palm-branches below, placed there, no doubt, to indicate that the house and those that lived in it were consecrated to the glory of God. From this doorway they faced the hills that were part of the frame of their valley, the familiar shelter in which they spent their laborious lives, happy in the faith and worship in which they rejoiced. Their reality consisted of both the visible and the invisible. (*NA,* 100)

Reworking a line from "He 'Digesteth Harde Yron'"—"The power of the visible / is the invisible"—Stevens pictures his ancestors as the happy inhabitants of a reality, like Moore's, made significant by the imagination. As Stevens's account of his journey reveals, such a dual reality still exists for some of the older residents of the region. During a visit to Christ Church near Stouchsburg, Stevens receives a tour from a "stout

old Lutheran" whose attention to the physical structure of the church
strikes Stevens as a metaphor for the old man's faith:

> When the committee of the church in charge of the building was
> making its plans last spring, this true lover of his church agreed to
> paint the fence around the adjoining graveyard. In part, this fence
> consisted of cast-iron spears. He painted the spear-heads silver and
> the staves black, one by one, week after week, until the job was
> done. Yet obviously this man's reality is the church-building but as a
> fellow-existence, of a sort. (*NA,* 100)

Painting the fence around the church graveyard, the old man saves the
sad ground from desolation with an act of artifice that reflects his belief in
the invisible. His imaginative touch makes the graveyard a thing of
beauty, and Stevens regards the old man's handiwork with a kind of awe.
Painting "one by one, week after week," the attention the man gives to
the physical spears of the fence seems evidence of an imaginative recov-
ery no longer possible in a postwar world stripped of belief by aquiline
pedants who see all art as romantic reliquary. Time has passed the old
man by.

The question Stevens poses in the remainder of his account is whether
such a fellow existence can speak to, and potentially aid, the poet of the
present. Following the account of his encounter with the old Lutheran,
Stevens recalls a visit to a second church, the Trinity Tulpehocken Re-
formed Church, and a second graveyard. Untouched by the loving hand of
the painter, the Trinity graveyard appears a much grimmer place:

> The wall was of limestone about four feet high, weatherbeaten,
> barren, bald. In the graveyard were possibly eight or ten sheep, the
> color of the wall and of many of the gravestones and even of some of
> the tufts of grass, bleached and silvery in the hard sunlight. . . .
> There were a few cedars here and there but these only accentuated
> the sense of abandonment and destitution, the sense that, after all,
> the vast mausoleum of human memory is emptier than one had
> supposed. Near by stood the manse, also of limestone, apparently

vacant, the upper part of each window white with the half-drawn
blind, the lower part black with the vacantness of the place. Al-
though the two elderly men were in a way a diversion from the
solitude, there could not be any effective diversion from the reality
that time and experience had created here, the desolation that pene-
trated one like something final. (*NA*, 101)

In Stevens's account, the Trinity graveyard is a space of unremitting
reality—a bleached, colorless ruin utterly untouched by the grace of the
imagination. Unlike the tended graveyard of Christ Church, the Trinity
graveyard, "abandoned" and given over to the sheep, belongs wholly to
the postwar present that sees fit to neglect the past. Throughout his
description, Stevens transforms the wasted graveyard into a working
metaphor for the larger, more desolate graveyard of the entire postwar
world. The equation Stevens makes between local death and mass death
harkens back to his lyric in "More Poems for Liadoff," "Burghers of
Petty Death." Stevens begins that lyric with the two figures he spies in
the yard—these "two by the stone wall" for whom the "grass is still
green"—the potential diversion from the solitude. As in his travelogue
description of the Trinity graveyard in "About One of Marianne Moore's
Poems," however, Stevens concludes that nothing can relieve the sadness
of devastation and "total death" that haunt the scene:

> These are the small townsmen of death,
> A man and a woman, like two leaves
> That keep clinging to a tree,
> Before winter freezes and grows black—
>
> Of great height and depth
> Without any feeling, an imperium of quiet,
> In which a wasted figure, with an instrument,
> Propounds blank final music.
>
> (*CPWS*, 362)

In Stevens's poem, as in his prose account, the poet's greatest fear is that
the devastation of the postwar world has become something permanent—
a blank that the mind can no longer fill. If read in the context of Stevens's

travelogue, then, the "wasted figure, with an instrument" who can no longer enliven the real in "Burghers of Petty Death" becomes an autobiographical representation of Stevens's own poetic uncertainties. As Stevens laments in his travelogue as he looks out on the haunting vacancy of the Trinity graveyard, "There could not be any effective diversion from the reality that time and experience had created here." Doubting his power to poetically recover the space from "the desolation that penetrated one like something final," Stevens admits that he himself might be the wasted poet figure of his poem, too overcome by the postwar ruin to ever recover his voice.

Yet, Stevens's prose account of his visit to the Tulpehocken region does not end with his vision of emptiness. Stevens punctuates his complaint about the unremitting reality of the Trinity graveyard with comments that show he has learned something of poetic recovery from Moore's example:

> Later, when I had returned to New York, I went to the exhibition of books in the Morgan Library held by the American Institute of Graphic Arts. The brilliant pages from Poland, France, Finland and so on, books of tales, of poetry, of folk-lore, were as if the barren reality that I had just experienced had suddenly taken color, become alive and from a single thing become many things and people, vivid, active, intently trying out a thousand characters and illuminations. (*NA*, 101–2)

Looking at the imaginative products of some of those countries hit hardest by the war, Stevens closes the second section of his essay with an assertion that art still has the power to revive the postwar world. Under the animating touch of tales and folklore and poetry, the mass grave of the present, the barren reality, springs to life. Stevens thus proves at the end of his account that he has discovered the value of his own past. Forging a link with his imaginative ancestors, Stevens decides that their belief in the invisible still applies in the present and finds the faith to reimagine the wasted landscape of the postwar world as "vivid," "alive," crowded rather than empty, and constantly changing. Rather than perpetuate his identification with the wasted figure of "Burghers of Petty

Death," Stevens comes to identify with the old Lutheran who paints the spears of the Christ Church graveyard. For Stevens, as for the patient old man, reality ultimately consists of both the visible and the invisible. Stevens thus learns the lesson of his history, which is also the lesson of Moore's verse: The recuperation of the postwar present depends on the poet's ability to keep faith with the imaginative past. For the people of Poland and France and Finland, the "isolated facts" of their situation after the war proclaim a horror so complete as to render all existence meaningless. The job of the poet in such a world is to keep the past alive—to restore a sense of "fellow-existence" with the invisible and find a way to make the present facts significant without ignoring their physical reality.

The second section of "About One of Marianne Moore's Poems" thus says far more about Stevens's quest for poetic recovery than it does about Moore's verse. Yet, the journey that Stevens undertakes in the middle section of his essay is one built on Moore's example, and, as such, it pays Moore a high compliment. In the outer sections of his essay, Stevens credits Moore with the kind of poetry he hopes to write, the perfect poetry of fellow existence for the postwar age. Nesting his own search for imaginative recovery inside Moore's model, Stevens shows that Moore's verse has given him a hopeful guide for his own postwar poetic. Stevens's essay thus tells the same story as his first lyric in "More Poems for Liadoff," "A Woman Sings a Song for a Soldier Come Home." Both his essay and his poem recount a homecoming. The soldier in the poem, like Stevens in his journey to the Tulpehocken, returns to a village that represents a forgotten past, a place where "Nothing survives / Except what was, // Under the white clouds piled and piled / Like gathered-up forgetfulness, / In sleeping air." Empty of nurse or kin, the village recalls the desolation of the Trinity graveyard, and the question Stevens poses is whether he, the wounded poet/soldier, can make a connection with the past that will allow him to sing again and recuperate the postwar present. The answer to his question and the lesson he must learn lie in the woman's saving song: Remember what was before the war, remember the speech of the place and the imagination of the past, and you will be healed. The tale of the soldier/poet and the woman poet who helps him to feel at home in the postwar world thus resembles the story Stevens tells of himself and Moore in his essay. If Stevens is the soldier/

poet come home to a wasted world, then Moore is the woman who, in telling him to remember his past, teaches him how to sing of present realities.

Stevens's postwar appreciations of Moore in "More Poems for Liadoff" and "About One of Marianne Moore's Poems" thus reveal a profound shift away from Stevens's earlier wartime poetic of "The Figure of the Youth as Virile Poet." Where Stevens's 1943 remarks cast the ideal poet as a virile young man of fact, his postwar works reimagine the arbiter of poetic truth as a compassionate woman with a philosopher's hat. Where Stevens's manly poet of wartime considers the feminized minotaur of the past as nothing more than a monstrous nuisance, Stevens's poet of the postwar returns to the maternal imaginative past as a source of succor and inspiration. Where Stevens claims in 1943 that the centuries, taking their character in part from poets and philosophers, "have a way of being male," in 1946 he applauds Moore as the poet of her time and gladly follows her example. In returning to Moore's poetry as a model after the war, Stevens freely admits that his wartime poetic of mighty solitary maleness no longer applies. In Moore's verse, he finds a quieter poetic for a sadder day.

Chapter 7

The Final Years of Friendship

In July of 1950, an errand at Trinity College brought Marianne Moore and her brother Warner to Hartford, Connecticut—home of the Hartford Accident and Indemnity Company and its poet–vice president, Mr. Wallace Stevens. Moore and her brother discovered that they had some free time to spend in the city, and, as Moore recalled in a written tribute to Stevens some years later, Warner asked his sister what she would like to do:

> I hesitated, then said, "I'd like to call on Wallace Stevens, but have no appointment." My brother said, "Here's a nickel; call him up." I said, "With Wallace Stevens, you aren't haphazard . . ." and deliberated. "He is formal." My brother stepped into a telephone-booth, saying, *"I'll* call him up." The door of the booth was open and I heard him say, "Have you had lunch, Mr. Stevens?" He came out. "What did he say?" I asked. "Said 'Come right over.'"[1]

The result of Moore's wish and Warner's impetuous phone call was a short meeting between the two poets at Stevens's office. Escorted down the wide corridors of the Hartford's imposing white edifice, Moore and her brother met Stevens in front of his massive mahogany desk "with nothing on it"—an impeccably clean surface that reminded Moore of the phrase "order is mastery." Stevens, Moore, and Warner spent some minutes chatting, and then Stevens gave his guests a formal tour of the building that Moore remembered in detail:

> We crossed the corridor and through a short connecting one, enter-
> ing a large room with many windows, its desks not too near to-
> gether and not too small. As we passed the many desks, each of the
> persons working on papers or at a typewriter looked up at Mr.
> Stevens with a pleased smile, reminding me of a visitor to a writing-
> conference I had attended who said when Hartford insurance was
> mentioned, "They aren't bothered with strikes there; the girls at the
> Hartford have it nice." (*CPrMM*, 581)

After some pleasantries, brother and sister departed. By Moore's ac-
count, the entire interview took less than half an hour.

Despite its brevity and formality, her meeting with Stevens left a
deep impression on Moore. As Moore's account reveals, she saw the
Hartford as a high, clean, well-ordered place free of strife. She was taken
with the ample and industrious surroundings, "the desks not too near
together and not too small," and the "pleased smiles" of respect and
deference that greeted her friend and fellow poet in the work place.
Moved by her admission into Stevens's sanctuary, Moore wrote a poem
to Stevens thanking him for her visit. The lyric of eight short lines,
"Pretiolae" (little pretzels), ultimately expresses Moore's appreciation for
much more than her short tour of the Hartford. Within the poem, Moore
creates a complex image of affection that predicts the course of the two
poets's increasingly personal poetic conversation of the 1950s.

As Patricia Willis points out, Moore drew on a number of sources to
create "Pretiolae."[2] After her visit to Stevens's office, Moore wrote to the
Hartford Accident and Indemnity Company to gain more information
about the building. The company sent her postcards of the imposing
structure along with a letter describing the Hartford's classical facade: six
columns and a pediment, all of solid granite. Moore also saved an adver-
tisement for the Hartford that pictured four firemen with hoses battling a
blaze next to the superimposed image of an insurance policy bearing the
name of Abraham Lincoln. Both the Hartford's building and its advertise-
ment consciously projected a corporate image of unshakable and lasting
security. In spite of all calamities and through all ages, the Hartford—the
trusted insurer of Honest Abe—would stand and protect those who

needed aid. Drawing on her sources, Moore transferred the Hartford's image of helpfulness and stalwartness to the subject of her poem—Wallace Stevens:

> The dutiful, the firemen of Hartford,
> Are not without a reward—
> A temple of Apollo on a velvet sward

> And legend has it that small pretzels come,
> Not from Reading but from Rome:
> A suppliant's folded arms twisted by a thumb.

Having praised Stevens's verse throughout the years as a wall of poetic incorruptibility, Moore found the Hartford Insurance Company and its mighty edifice fitting metaphors for Stevens and his art. Like Stevens's imagination, the Hartford offered protection against the unpredictable vicissitudes of the actual world—a pressure within to push back against the pressure without. Recasting Stevens as Apollo, the master musician of the Greeks, Moore makes the classically facaded Hartford building into his temple. The protective work of the insurance man and the creative work of the poet have, to Moore's mind, much in common. Both provide potential buffers against tragedy.

In the second stanza of her lyric, Moore shifts her metaphor and expands the range of her compliment. Moving from Apollo to *pretiolae,* Moore playfully invokes the town of Reading, Pennsylvania—the birthplace of both Wallace Stevens and, by coincidence, America's first pretzels. The jump seems abrupt, but, as Moore hints in her published notes that accompany her poem, little pretzels have something in common with the Hartford's massive structure:

> Pretiolae are thought by the *New York Times* to have been originally Roman—little pieces of baked dough symbolizing the folded arms of a suppliant, presented to children for dutifully said prayers. "Little Pretzels" were introduced to America in the 18th Century from Germany, by bakeries in Lititz and Reading, Pennsylvania, in accordance with a secret recipe—hand-twisted for factory ovens.[3]

The themes that connect the two stanzas of Moore's poem are those of duty and reward. The beautiful temple of Apollo rewards or pays tribute to the "dutiful" firemen of Hartford in the same way that the *pretiolae* of legend reward the dutiful children of Rome for saying their prayers. Moore's connection implies that both Stevens and his verse, like the Hartford temple and the Reading pretzels, are ample rewards for the hard work and attention they demand. By 1950, Moore well knew that Stevens could appear as reserved and as difficult as his poems. Yet, as Moore's account of her trip to the Hartford and her subsequent lyric confirm, she found his company and his verse well worth the extra effort they required. Moore's poem insists that, like the *pretiolae*, both Stevens and his poems are unique and special gifts. Moore ends her poem to Stevens with a humble pretzel bow in his direction that doubles as an embrace: "A suppliant's folded arms twisted by a thumb."

Written in the wake of her visit with Stevens, Moore's "Pretiolae" seems a profuse thank-you for less than a half hour's time at the Hartford. Yet, looking back over the years leading up to Moore's trip to Stevens's office, the depth of her gratitude and her particular desire to call on Stevens in 1950 acquire a certain logic. The years immediately following the Second World War were not happy ones for Marianne Moore. The end of the war marked the beginning of weakening health for Moore's mother, Mary Warner Moore, with whom Moore had lived since the day she was born. Mrs. Moore suffered from throat and stomach problems, both of which increasingly inhibited her ability to speak and to eat from 1944 until her death in 1947. Under the strain of her mother's constant care, Moore often became ill herself, and her correspondence during the period reveals her growing sense of trepidation and depression. In the summer of 1946 she wrote to Ezra Pound, who, after a literal postwar "trial" of his own, had just entered St. Elizabeth's Hospital:

> I sound dull because I am dull. You know our propensity for illness. . . . This time it is hard. My mother is having a battle to eat; or rather swallow (because of an injury to the nerve controlling the palate). I have been telling people I cannot write letters or even receive them; but we think of you, Ezra, and wish you could be

comfortable. Don't be embittered. Embitterment is a sin—a subject
on which I am an authority.[4]

Angered by her mother's undeserved suffering, Moore struggled to
keep her bitterness at bay and her literary life intact. Early in 1945, Moore
accepted, with W. H. Auden's urging, the prodigious challenge of trans-
lating the fables of La Fontaine, a project for which she initially had great
enthusiasm.[5] As her mother worsened, however, so did her ability to
work, and Moore began to question both the wisdom of her effort and
her talent as a poet. When, in March 1947, Stevens sent Moore a copy of
his volume *Transport to Summer,* which included his poem of homage to
Moore, "The Prejudice against the Past," she barely had the energy or the
heart to reply to his praise. "Dear Mr. Stevens," she wrote:

> The title, *Transport to Summer,* is in itself a gift, and I thank you for
> giving my Swedish cart the savor of poetry.
>   This use of words—strange but also natural—makes me realize
> why I used to think I would like to be a writer.[6]

While acknowledging gratitude for Stevens's attention, Moore's note
also revealed, in part, her waning enthusiasm for her own work. Over-
whelmed by personal sadness and difficulty, Moore had to be reminded
why she once wanted to write, why poetry once seemed important. Her
letter to Stevens suggests that, by 1947, what she "used to" think about
the pleasure of her profession no longer applied.

On July 9, 1947, Mrs. Moore died, and Moore fell into a state of
depression that lasted several years. Between 1947 and 1950, Moore pub-
lished only five poems. Without the comments of her mother, Moore's
best editor and her most valued critic, Moore found that poetry itself
seemed beside the point. As she wrote to Pound in response to questions
about her work, "At best [I] am barely managing 'to live and think.'"[7]
Moore's questioning of literary purpose was further fueled by Mac-
millan's lack of interest in her manuscript-in-progress of La Fontaine's
fables, a blow that prompted her to change publishers for the duration of
her career. In the midst of her grief, Moore received another gift from
Wallace Stevens; his essay "About One of Marianne Moore's Poems"

appeared in the summer 1948 issue of the *Quarterly Review of Literature*. Again, Moore's response to his kindness was brief and poignant:

> I ponder what you have from time to time said about life, its largesse and its deprivations. There is the enchantment of accuracy, which seems more imperative than the personal—"heliotrope, inconstant hue. Be sure the audience beholds you, not your gown." All of which is to ask you to infer thanks for your thoughts in the *Quarterly Review of Literature*.[8]

The full extent of Moore's thanks may be difficult to infer from her note, but as in her earlier letter, Moore linked Stevens's thoughts with the possibility of her own poetic recovery. Just as Stevens's verse reminded Moore of why she once wanted to write, so his verse restored her sense that life could be largesse as well as deprivation. In her note, Moore quoted from Stevens's poem "In a Bad Time," a lyric that speaks directly to the role of poetry in times of tragedy. The poem makes clear the root of Moore's gratitude to Stevens. How "mad" would "he," the snow poet in search of essential reality, have to be, Stevens wonders at the start of his poem, to say "'He beheld / An order and thereafter he belonged / To it?'" By way of considering the point, Stevens invokes the image of a beggar:

> But the beggar gazes on calamity
> And thereafter he belongs to it, to bread
> Hard found, and water tasting of misery.
>
> For him cold's glacial beauty is his fate.
> Without understanding, he belongs to it.

> (*CPWS*, 426)

The question Stevens poses in "In a Bad Time" resembles the query he makes throughout "More Poems for Liadoff": How does a poet write about, and in, bad times? The poet who speaks only of the world's destitute reality becomes a beggar—a ragged man who has no internal resources of his own. Those who gaze only on calamity belong to it, and such poets exist on a miserable prisoner's diet of bread and water, unable to free themselves with the power and plenty of the imagination. In rejecting the poet who begs, however, Stevens finds a disturbing similarity between his own quest for a snowy poetry of ultimate reality and the ragged man's aesthetic of disaster. "What has he that becomes his heart's strong core?" Stevens asks of the glacial poet who beholds nothing that is not there: "He has his poverty and nothing more."

> A forgetfulness of summer at the pole.
>
> Sordid Melpomene, why strut bare boards,
> Without scenery or lights, in the theatre's bricks,
> Dressed high in heliotrope's inconstant hue,
>
> The muse of misery? Speak loftier lines.
> Cry out, "I am the purple muse." Make sure
> The audience beholds you, not your gown.
>
> (*CPWS*, 427)

The poet who revels in poverty, belonging only to the mind of winter, fares no better than the beggar at one with calamity. Recasting the glacial poet's icy field as a bare theater of misery, Stevens concludes that a poetry of impoverished reality alone is an aberration. The tragic muse's gown, covered with earth and dirt—Stevens specifically describes it as "sordid"—cannot maintain its imaginative coloring. Dressed in "the heliotrope's inconstant hue," the impoverished poet, like the flower that gives his gown its color, is fated to follow the motions of the earthly sun rather than to replace it, like Hoon, with a burst of mental energy. Stevens urges the poet mired in misery to speak loftier lines and, as much as possible, leave the muddy gown behind.

In a bad time herself, Moore appreciated Stevens's assurances that misery need not leave an indelible mark on an author's verse, that poetry could replace poverty as the heart's strong core. Longing to write of more than the "personal heliotrope's inconstant hue" of her own sadness, Moore took Stevens's admonition to "write loftier lines" as a call to poetic recovery and struggled to throw off Melpomene's faded shroud. Stevens provided Moore, once again, with a sense of the imagination's role as a saving pressure against the thwarting deprivations of the actual world.

Thus, read in the context of her postwar turmoil and her exchanges with Stevens, Moore's trip to the Hartford and her subsequent pretzel poem seem less impromptu afterthoughts than the culmination of years of perceived postwar indebtedness. In casting Stevens's office as the beneficent shrine of Apollo in "Pretiolae," Moore draws on Stevens's "In a Bad Time" and consciously chooses the golden lyre of Apollo's poetry over the bare chants of Melpomene, the muse of misery. Moore's lyric thus thanks Stevens for his continued appreciation of her poetry and, as she saw it, his unflagging belief in the imagination's balm. The folded praying arms of the suppliant pretzel at the end of "Pretiolae" show Stevens that, despite her difficulties, she, thanks to him, has not lost her faith in verse.

Moore's trip to the Hartford, however, ultimately resulted in far more than just a poem to Stevens. Her visit marked the beginning of a period of close personal friendship between the two poets that grew, in part, out of loss. The year 1947 was for Stevens, as well as Moore, a year of bereavement. In April 1947, Stevens's close friend and confidant, Henry Church, suddenly died. He left behind his wife, Barbara, who, in Stevens's words, was "so completely crushed" by Church's death that Stevens feared for her health.[9] In the painful years that followed, Stevens and Barbara Church grew to be frequent correspondents and friends in their own right. A bit of a nomad after her husband's death, Church divided her time between visits to her home in France, extensive European tours, and long stays in New York during which she frequently entertained Stevens and her other literary acquaintances. Following Moore's visit to the Hartford in the summer of 1950, Stevens, perhaps sensing that Moore and Church might ease each other's loneliness, suggested that Church invite Moore to a luncheon she was arranging to celebrate a reading he planned to give at the Young Men's Hebrew Association (YMHA). Moore accepted Church's invitation, and her letter reveals that, even before they became reacquainted, Moore felt she and Church shared a common bond:

> I have often thought of you since the day at Mt. Holyoke when you and Mr. Church, my Mother and I, sat listening to Wallace Stevens on the lawn beneath the trees. I remember so well your white coat

(made by Hermes as I am interested to know) your little brilliant watch and what you said to me of Mr. Church and how he would give you things.

How good of you to invite me to your party for Wallace Stevens after his reading at the YMHA. . . . Now that I am no longer closely at home to take care of my Mother, I do go to New York sometimes.[10]

Invoking the memory of Henry Church alongside that of her mother, Moore linked herself with Church in a mutual understanding of personal loss.

As Stevens had perhaps predicted, the two women quickly became devoted friends, and, as a result, Stevens and Moore met socially with increasing frequency. Both Moore and Stevens were, by accounts, somewhat shy and private individuals, uncomfortable at social gatherings, yet loyal to those few souls they found like-minded. James Johnson Sweeney, the director of the Guggenheim Museum and a friend of Church's, recalled his impression of the two poets's relationship for Peter Brazeau: "I think he [Stevens] was aloof until he found his way, found a sympathetic response. Both Stevens and Marianne Moore were very quiet. I thought that they were really sympathetic."[11] The three-way correspondence between Church, Moore, and Stevens supports Sweeney's claim of sympathy. Each time either Stevens or Moore praised or appreciated the other in a letter to Church, Church would pass the compliment on to its proper recipient, helping to cement the personal bond between the two poets. As Stevens wrote to Church some months after he and Moore became reacquainted, "She [Moore] is a woman of natural goodness, sympathy, consideration for others, which people may not always notice in the face of her prowess in other respects. She is the true connoisseur, who expertises everything she does. Her willingness to make friends charms me."[12]

As the poets became better friends, Stevens grew to appreciate not only Moore's poetry, but her integrity, honesty, and simplicity—a combination he often found astonishingly and happily incompatible with the literary scene of his day. "How good she is as compared to most literary people!" Stevens exclaimed to Church, "None of the egotism and nerves."[13] Stevens also feared, however, that the very qualities of goodness and sympathy he valued in Moore might make her life difficult in a

harsh world. In January 1952, Moore captured the Bollingen Prize in
Poetry for her *Collected Poems* (1951). The award, however, brought her
little joy. Still struggling with La Fontaine and grieving for her mother,
Moore looked on her collected poems, many of which her mother had
critiqued and edited, as painful reminders of happier days. Church sent
Moore a bouquet of white roses to celebrate her success, and Moore
replied from the depths of her depression, "I do not believe in sadness—
only in indelible memory—but if I were too sad, this kind of bestowing,
as by a hand from Heaven, would revise my darkened outlook."[14]
Church relayed the news of Moore's melancholy to Stevens, who had
served on the committee awarding Moore the prize. He, in turn, sent
Moore his own message of congratulations, stating, "Your poems, the
creations, not to say creatures, of wit, would be the adornment of any
literature. But they are chiefly the adornment of yourself."[15] Moore, not
to be roused, responded: "That you are not indifferent to my animals is
both a pleasure and a reprieve; for deify them intrinsically as I may, upon
glancing at any but a few of my pieces, Miss Dryasdust is the inevitable
impression, I can but say."[16] Touched by Moore's frustration and sorrow,
Stevens wrote to Norman Holmes Pearson, "She [Moore] belongs to an
older and much more personal world: the world of closer, human intima-
cies which existed when you and I were young—from which she and her
brother have been extruded like lost sheep. As a matter of nature they
stick together. What she has she has tried to make perfect. The truth is
that I am much moved by what she is going through. It is easy to say that
Marianne, the human being, does not concern us. *Mais, mon Dieu,* it is
what concerns us most."[17] Something in Moore's character reminded
Stevens of his own happier days of human intimacy—a kinder world
from which he also felt "extruded"—and he often pictured himself and
Moore together, gallantly making their way in an unfamiliar place.
"When you think of what her life might be and of what it is," Stevens
remarked to Church, "you feel as if you and she were a pair of sailors just
off the boat, determined to see things through."[18] Stevens found Moore
the person as compelling as Moore the poet.

    Moore, in turn, cherished Stevens's friendship and sensed a common
bond between them in Stevens's complex mixture of personal frankness
and reserve. She admired his matter-of-fact openness and "scientific

unevasiveness," although she knew that Stevens's abrupt manner of speaking his mind often made him seem sharp and threatening. In her 1964 tribute to Stevens, Moore recalled an incident during a luncheon with her friend that she felt exemplified his character:

> Anecdotes were mentioned which were considered amusing—one, about goats, which Mr. Stevens had told previously, and he was asked to tell it again. He shook his head—insistently begged to tell it—and said, "Do; I'd like to hear it." He said with almost intimidating emphasis, "You need not look at me with eyes of entreaty. I shall *not* tell it." "Order is mastery"—his own words; also, perceptiveness heightened, might describe him. (*CPrMM*, 582)

Reiterating one of the common themes of her poetry, Moore's anecdote suggests that behavior that seems merely unaccommodating and asocial can be more fittingly explained as a form of self-protective integrity. Moore admired Stevens for being true to his nature and not consenting to amuse his companions on request. Stevens did not share his thoughts unselectively or easily, but Moore attributed such traits, not to coldness, but to Stevens's "heightened perceptivity." "Feeling at its deepest," she wrote in "Feeling and Precision," "tends to be inarticulate. If it does manage to be articulate, it is likely to seem overcondensed, so that the author is resisted as being enigmatic or disobliging or arrogant" (*CPrMM*, 396). Moore found Stevens the walking embodiment of her own painful paradox. A man of deep feeling, his affection for Moore rested side by side with his harsher moments, and Moore was grateful for his kind and often protective gestures on her behalf. On March 6, 1951, Stevens received the National Book Award for *The Auroras of Autumn* with Marianne Moore in the audience. After the ceremony, the two poets sat down to a small celebratory dinner with Lloyd Frankenberg, another poet friend of Stevens's, and Frankenberg's wife at the Drake Hotel. Their meal over, Stevens insisted that Moore take a cab home to Brooklyn at his expense rather than risk the subway. Moore appreciated Stevens's thoughtfulness and wrote to him soon after, "You did us a great deal of good. Brevity is not adapted to expressing what I feel about your thoughtfulness at the time of my departure."[19] Moore recorded her cab ride in large letters in her daily diary. His small act of generosity was just the sort of considerateness she appreciated. Just as her brother had not been too "self-determined" to preface their visit to the Hartford by inquiring, "Have you had lunch, Mr. Stevens?" Stevens was not too self-determined to inquire of Moore after their dinner, "Do you have a ride home?"

As Moore and Stevens became personally closer, so the quality of their poetic interaction changed to reflect the growing confidence between them. The sense of league that Stevens felt with Moore resulted in one of the most significant signs of trust that Stevens could bestow upon a fellow poet. Always shy of totalizing moments, Stevens had a particular horror of collecting or selecting his poems for publication, fearing that a single final gesture would supersede, and thereby undercut, years of complex poetic growth. In 1950, however, in order to avoid issuing a collected volume, Stevens agreed to draw up a list of selections for Knopf.[20] Knopf, however, decided not to pursue a selected poems, opting instead to reissue Stevens's earlier volumes. Hearing of Knopf's decision, Moore stepped in and suggested to her friends at Faber and Faber, Peter du Sautoy and T. S. Eliot, that they publish an English selection of Stevens's poems. Du Sautoy responded enthusiastically, promising to "actively pursue" the project, and Stevens, agreeing to the switch, began planning an English volume in the fall of 1951.[21] Uncomfortable with his initial list for Knopf (Stevens felt that if he enshrined some poems himself, he would only slight others), Stevens requested that Moore compile his poems. On November 5, 1951, Stevens wrote to Herbert Weinstock at Knopf:

> If Marianne Moore is free to make the selection [for an English edition], I should rather have her do it. . . . I shall be perfectly willing to let Miss Moore have the copy of my own selection. That might save her a lot of work. She and Mr. Eliot are very good friends. Apparently he would like the idea, and I am certain that I would, not only on account of the typing problem but because I am a great admirer of Miss Moore. Moreover, I have considerable doubt whether I should be likely to pick the same things that other people would pick.[22]

Trusting Moore's judgment implicitly, Stevens was willing to leave his poetic fate partly in her capable hands. Acknowledging that Moore and he might not pick the same poems, Stevens was nonetheless content to appear as whatever sort of poet she ultimately found him to be.

Perhaps feeling the potential weight of his request, Moore respectfully left the list of selections to Stevens, who grudgingly complied. He insisted, however, that Moore pass on to Faber and Faber that his choices be considered not as pieces the author wished to "preserve," but as poems "representative" of his career. With Moore acting as Stevens's go-between, Faber and Faber received his new list of poems late in November 1951. Moore, however, contributed one striking and significant change to Stevens's selection. On November 26, 1951, when the two poets met for tea at Church's apartment in New York, Moore suggested that Stevens add to his list one of his most recent lyrics, "Final Soliloquy of the Interior Paramour," and place the poem at the end of his volume.[23] Stevens took Moore's advice, thereby altering his *Selected Poems* to reflect Moore's sense of his career.

Moore's vision of Stevens's poetic of the 1950s, however, was quite different from Stevens's. As "Pretiolae" implies, in the postwar years Moore, for personal and poetic reasons, longed to read Stevens as a poet of unshakable imaginative fortitude whose spirit could insure protection against actual calamities. Some months before she approached Faber and Faber about Stevens's selected volume, Moore wrote a review of *The Auroras of Autumn* that reiterated her sense of the imaginative bent of his late poetic. In her review, "The World Imagined . . . Since We Are Poor"—the title itself a line from Stevens's "Final Soliloquy"—Moore cited Stevens's belief that "happiness of the in-centric surmounts a poverty of the ex-centric."[24] Stevens's poetry, she wrote, "substitutes for poverty, abundance, a spiritual happiness in which the intangible is more real than the visible and earth is innocent; 'not a guilty dream' but a 'holiness' in which we are awake as peacefully as if we lay asleep" (*CPrMM*, 428). Borrowing a line out of context from "An Ordinary Evening in New Haven," Moore concluded that Stevens's verse tells us "'If it should be true that reality exists / In the mind,' one has it all" (*CPrMM*, 430).

To quote Moore herself, "omissions are not accidents." In her review of *Auroras of Autumn,* Moore chose to ignore such contrasting lines from "Ordinary Evening" as

> We seek
>
> The poem of pure reality, untouched
> By trope or deviation, straight to the word,
> Straight to the transfixing object, to the object
>
> At the exactest point at which it is itself.
>
> (*CPWS,* 471)

Indeed, in Moore's review, the word *reality* appeared only once. Needing an Apollo, she decided to gloss over the part of Stevens's poetic of the 1950s that longed, once again, for the world without imagination. Moore's suggestion that Stevens add "Final Soliloquy of the Interior Paramour" as the final lyric of his selected poems reflects the strength of her decision. Prior to Moore's proposal, Stevens planned to give the important final position in his selected volume to the poem "Angel Surrounded By Paysans," the same poem that ends *Auroras of Autumn.* Moore's review of *Auroras of Autumn* contained no references to "Angel Surrounded," a reflection of the fact that the poem did not fit her reading of Stevens's poetic. In "Angel Surrounded," Stevens once again considers the relationship between poetry and poverty. Where Stevens casts the poet of "In a Bad Time" as a beggar, in "Angel Surrounded" he imagines the poet as a peasant, a poor man of the countryside. Yet, the angel that comforts the impoverished soul is not a projection of the indomitable imagination, but rather "the angel of reality," "the necessary angel of the earth." Stevens's lyric converts what was for Moore in the postwar era a symbol of spiritual fortitude into a figure of the elusive, flickering world of mere being that the poet seeks beyond the distortions of the mind. Stevens's poem implies that the impoverished poet is blessed, for he shall witness the angel of the real; only the mind stripped of decoration will "see the earth again, // Cleared of its stiff and stubborn, man-locked set" (*CPWS,* 496–97).

As Harold Bloom points out, Stevens's poem undoubtedly problematizes the presence of the angel of reality, phrasing the angel's final assertion of identity in language so tentative and qualified that, to use Bloom's phrase, the verse imparts "an anxiety unable to achieve an identifiable form."[25] Stevens himself worried that most of his readers would miss the point. "For nine readers out of ten, the necessary angel will appear to be the angel of the imagination," Stevens complained, "and for nine days out of ten that is true, although it is the tenth day that counts."[26] Moore, however, felt that the first nine days outweighed the tenth. The Stevens she valued was one for whom the angel of mercy was the angel of the imagination, as her proposal to substitute "Final Soliloquy of the Interior Paramour" for "Angel Surrounded by Paysans" suggests.

In "Final Soliloquy," Stevens pictures the impoverished poet's reunion with the "interior paramour," the imagination whose loving embrace, like that of Moore's paper nautilus, is so close that the poet and his imagined world become one. A warm shawl, a restful room, a dwelling, a boundary, a light, a power—the poet's imagination in "Final Soliloquy," as in so many of Moore's poems, becomes a self-protective shield against the poverty and despair of the actual world. Stevens's interior paramour ultimately makes an equation between the grace of poetry and a saving faith in deity. The imagination allows the poor man to intuit an order in obscurity, granting a beneficent touch of the supreme fiction: God and the imagination are one.

Once again, however, Stevens hints that he is not completely satisfied with the paramour's soliloquy. Stevens ends the line "We say God and the imagination are one . . ." with a tantalizing ellipses, indicating that there might be something beyond this pronouncement that remains, for the moment, unsaid. The ellipses undercuts the sense that the poet has found a final answer to his poverty. The paramour's room may only be a place where the poet rests rather than a place where the poet resides. As Stevens's paramour states, we think the world imagined is the ultimate good "for small reason." Moore, however, admired Stevens's poem for its statement of protective faith. In a 1952 speech on Stevens's poetry that she delivered at Bryn Mawr, Moore indulged in a bit of self-cribbing and, quoting from "Final Soliloquy," used Stevens's lines as proof for statements she had made earlier about "The Auroras of Autumn": "Thus happiness of the in-centric surmounts a poverty of the ex-centric. For poverty, poetry substitutes a spiritual happiness in which the intangible is more real than the visible."[27] The Stevens Moore wished to read in the 1950s was a Stevens who believed, once and for all, that the world imagined was the ultimate good.

Given a choice between the soliloquy of the interior paramour of the imagination and the monologue of the seraphim of reality, Moore chose to remember Stevens as the lover rather than the angel. Just as importantly, however, Stevens chose to follow Moore's advice about which role suited him best. "Final Soliloquy of the Interior Paramour" stands as the final utterance in Stevens's only sanctioned volume of selected poems—a sign that Stevens respected Moore's insights into his poetry enough to potentially alter the look of his career.

The Stevens of the 1950s, however, was never as much a poet of the imagination as Moore wished him to be. Indeed, Stevens felt that Moore, not he, demonstrated a faith in the imagination's power and goodness that, as the addition of "Final Soliloquy" to his selected volume suggests, he perhaps wished he could sustain. As Stevens wrote to Barbara Church, Moore struck him as "a moral force 'in light blue' at a time when moral forces of any kind are few and far between."[28] Properly cloaked in Stevens's color of the imagination, Moore resembled the poet wrapped tightly in the paramour's shawl, able to press back against spiritual poverty with strong belief. For his own part, however, Stevens remained more skeptical about the light, power, and miraculous influence of the paramour's garb, as a lyric penned around the time of Moore's editorial work on Stevens's behalf, "How Now, O, Brightener . . . ," indicates. The title of Stevens's poem constitutes an apostrophe to the imagination, the "brightener" that brings color to the black-and-white world of fact. Stevens sets his lyric in spring, the season of the imagination's rebirth when, as Stevens writes in "The Sun This March," the early sun "re-illumines things that used to turn / To gold in broadest blue" (*CPWS*, 133). Yet, in "How Now, O, Brightener . . . ," the imagination's resurrected brightness does not bring "voices as of lions coming down." Something intervenes to foil the lion's leap—a "trouble of the mind" that stays "in the sight, and in sayings of the sight" even as the imagination's spring returns:

Trouble in the spillage and first sparkle of sun,
The green-edged yellow and yellow and blue and blue-edged green—
The trouble of the mind

Is a residue, a land, a rain, a warmth,
A time, an apparition and nourishing element
And simple love,

In which the spectra have dewy favor and live
And take from this restlessly unhappy happiness
Their stunted looks.[29]

The "trouble of the mind" in the poem is the nagging presence of reality. For the poet of "How Now," the green of the actual and the imagination's blue bleed endlessly together, neither color able to usurp the other. The anticipated "broadest blue" of "The Sun This March" remains a feeble "blue-edged green," and the imagination is reduced to a mere halo around an indissoluble and inescapable something. What remains of reality in "How Now," however, proves comforting and not threatening to the poet's power. Reversing his sentiments of "In a Bad Time," Stevens here depicts the real as a sensual realm of natural opulence rather than a site of unbearable external poverty and pressure. The dewy residue/dew of time and place may "stunt" the poet's imagination, but without it, Stevens implies, too much would be lost. Using alliteration to make his point, Stevens compares the poet's sight and sayings of sight and the spillage and sparkle of sun to the less poetic joys of his earthly catalogue—"a land, a rain, a warmth, / A time, an apparition and nourishing element / and simple love." The sliding s of the poet's sparkling spectra dies out of the third stanza, but the rich and evocative vocabulary that replaces the hiss leaves no doubt that Stevens's sympathies lie with the land. The simple love of the real that troubles the poet also brings him happiness.

Stevens's late career includes many such small lyrics that uphold a simple love of the real and question the turning spirit of the poet's earlier self. Moore, however, remained convinced that the interior paramour was an important part of Stevens's poetic and took every opportunity to remind him of his better half. On November 27, 1951, the day after Moore and Stevens discussed "Final Soliloquy of the Interior Paramour"

over tea, Moore sent Stevens an inscribed copy of the English edition of
her own recent volume, *Collected Poems*. Between the pages of the book,
Moore placed a postcard of a modern painting that caught her fancy and
reminded her of her friend. Entitled "Zoo Picture" and attributed by
Moore to "Mary Meigs," the painting depicts an odd confrontation be-
tween a primitively rendered roaring lion in a cage, all claws and teeth,
and three small children who seem curiously calm in its presence. In the
background, four monkeys, endowed with human smiles, oversee the
encounter.[30] Moore's choice of postcard speaks once again to her impres-
sion of Stevens and his verse. Throughout her career, Moore associated
Stevens, to varying degrees, with the dangerous jungle cat that appeared
in so many of his poems. From her very first review of *Harmonium*, "Well
Moused, Lion," in which Moore cast Stevens as a "ferocious jungle
animal," to her assertion in her review of *Parts of a World* that Stevens
"does not speak language but mediates it, as the lion's power lies in his
paws," the lion struck Moore as a consistent emblem of Stevens's
poetic—the animal violence within pressing back against the pressure of
reality.[31] Stevens's lyric "Poetry Is a Destructive Force" was one of
Moore's favorites, and she was in the habit of quoting his lines about the
poet and his art:

> He is like a man
> In the body of a violent beast.
> Its muscles are his own . . .
>
> The lion sleeps in the sun.
> Its nose on its paws.
> It can kill a man.
>
> (*CPWS*, 193)

The association between Stevens and the lion was one that Moore shared
with Barbara Church. In an invitation to one of her many parties,
Church wrote to Moore, "I hope Wallace Stevens will come, he usually
does—you see 'there will be Tigers' and perhaps Lions even."[32] Moore
also alluded to her often-used image of Stevens in a note to the king of the
poetic jungle himself. In response to a series of congratulatory telegrams
that Stevens sent Moore on her receipt of the Bollingen Prize and the

National Book Award, Moore playfully complained to Stevens: "You are trying to make a lion of a dandelion."[33]

Given her appreciation of Stevens's leonine imagination, Moore most certainly sent Stevens a postcard of Mary Meigs's "Zoo Picture" hoping that he would see a reflection and an appreciation of his poetic of violent protection in the print. Moore also, however, added another level of potential interest to her gift. The card Moore sent was black and white and, in keeping with her penchant for accuracy, Moore described the colors of the original painting on the back of the postcard in exquisite detail so that Stevens could get the full flavor of the work. Underneath the title of the painting, she wrote:

apes—left to right: royal blue, crimson, steel grey and brown, beige

the lion: dark green

the floor of the lion's cage: scarlet

the floor of the lion's zoo: cabbage-rose pink

wall of the zoo: watermelon pink

left to right: the children wear: scarlet + bluish claret, dark blue, garnet.[34]

In his letter of thanks to Moore for her volume and enclosure, Stevens implied that he found both Moore's card and her colors particularly interesting:

Thanks for the copy of the English edition of your *Collected Poems*, which has now reached me—and for everything else: du Sautoy and the promptness of your letter to him. . . . Halliday has issued a little book-list in which he describes your collection as the best collection of the year. I love its watermelon pinkness as an object. . . . Your description of the little picture which you inserted in your book gives me a poem of my own.[35]

Having dismissed the lion of the imagination in favor of the warm residue and stunted colors of reality in "How Now," Stevens nonetheless found

Moore's insertion, with its colorful description and violent subject, in-
triguing enough to offer a poem in response. The image inspired by
Moore's postcard appears in the second section of Stevens's 1952 poem
"Prologues to What Is Possible," a visionary quest for the supreme fiction
in two parts. In part 1 of "Prologues," Stevens pictures the poet as a
seaman who, traveling alone, seeks "a point of central arrival, an instant
moment, much or little, / Removed from any shore" (*CPWS*, 516). In the
second part of the poem, Stevens reimagines the poet's voyage as the
search for a visionary metaphor to take the poet "beyond resemblance"
into an intuited realm of a purely transcendent poem. Stevens's speculation
on just what sort of poetic self such a language might release indicates that
he discerned his reflection in the roaring beast of Moore's postcard. As his
response to Moore's offering makes clear, Moore once again prompted
Stevens late in his career to see himself as a poet of imaginative prowess:

> What self, for example, did he contain that had not yet been loosed,
> Snarling in him for discovery as his attentions spread,
> As if all his hereditary lights were suddenly increased
> By an access of color, a new and unobserved, slight dithering,
> The smallest lamp, which added its puissant flick, to which he gave
> A name and privilege over the ordinary of his commonplace—
>
> A flick which added to what was real and its vocabulary,
> The way some first thing coming into Northern trees
> Adds to them the whole vocabulary of the South . . .
>
> (*CPWS*, 516–17)

With Moore's image before him, Stevens wondered aloud whether her
snarling lion might still speak to the heart of his aesthetic purpose. In
Moore's description of her postcard, Stevens saw a keen example of the
poet's ability to suddenly and magically increase the ordinary by "an
access of color." The poetic brightening that Moore granted her card
perhaps reminded Stevens that his commitment to "what was real and its
vocabulary" could never entirely substitute for the beauty of the mind,
the blue force he found in Moore's poetry. In "Prologues to What Is
Possible," Stevens defines the lion of the imagination in the legal lan-
guage of peerage, granting the beast "a name and privilege over the
ordinary of his commonplace," as a king might ennoble a subject and

give him power over the commoners. Reversing his earlier assessment in "How Now," that reality's residue grants "dewy favor" and brings happiness, Stevens declares in "Prologues" that the imagination, the noble rider, rules the land. The leonine Stevens of "Prologues" proposes a poetic of "addition" (Stevens uses the word four times in the stanza) rather than subtraction, placing emphasis on what the poet gains through an increase of imagination rather than, as in "How Now," what "remains" of the real in the equation. Stevens ultimately envisions the poet's discovery of the interior paramour as a warmly human encounter, a "look or a touch" that "reveals its unexpected magnitudes" and seems a prelude to a relationship that will prove an exalted and worthy trade for the "simple love" of real things. Responding to Moore's reading of his poetic, Stevens suggests that if the snarling lion of the self were set free, the world imagined might well be the ultimate good.

Stevens finally leaves the poetry of the lion's leap as a matter of speculation and simile, offering only a provisional prologue to an event that might never come. Yet, as Moore's addition to Stevens's *Selected Poems* and her postcard suggest, Moore kept Stevens wondering what might still be poetically possible toward the end of his career. Attracted to the picture Moore painted of him in the 1950s as a consummate poet of imagination—a lion, an Apollo, and a paramour—Stevens continued to consider the visionary possibilities of his verse partly at her prompting.

Just as Moore felt moved to shape Stevens's late poetic in response to her own aesthetic needs, so Stevens, as the two poets became closer, felt increasingly comfortable offering Moore advice about her work and her career. Throughout the late 1940s and early 1950s, Moore continued to do battle with her translations of La Fontaine's fables, as she watched what she initially thought would be a minor project grow into an eight-year struggle. In 1950, the year she made her trip to the Hartford, Moore took time away from her fables to prepare the text of her *Collected Poems*. Once her collection was complete, she agonized about whether to return to her translations or to move on to fresh tasks, finally deciding in 1951 that she had invested too much of her time and heart in La Fontaine to leave the work unfinished. As Moore and Stevens met with increasing frequency in the early 1950s, Stevens found he had a front-row seat for Moore's creative exertions on behalf of the French poet. Throughout the period, Moore sent Stevens many of her fables, including "The Crow and the Fox," "The Dragon with Many Heads and the Dragon with Many Tails," and one of her wolves.[36] At first, Stevens attempted to be supportive of Moore's efforts. In March of 1951, Stevens sent Moore an edition of La Fontaine's fables graced with delicate and detailed drawings by Hans Fischer, adding by way of encouragement "there is an affinity between your keen eye and Fischer's."[37] Moore was charmed by the exquisite gift and wrote that she felt a "criminal" in keeping it since she had "no ivory ottoman with swansdown cushion on which to lay it while looking at it."[38] At the end of her appreciation, she informed Stevens that she planned to consider the lovely book a loan: "You had not written your name in this; neither have I written mine; and though I ought not of course to tell you my plans, I regard it as an omen,—that when I send you my fables, I may send you yours too."[39]

Moore's plan to return Stevens's volume, however, did not prove an omen of the speedy completion of her project. Through revision after revision, Moore wrestled with her fables while enduring frequent bouts of illness, depression, and doubt. She wrote to Barbara Church in January 1952:

> I have not worked on my Fables—really worked—for about ten days. Now I am assiduous again and hoping that circumstances will favor me and that I can advance beyond my frustrations and dissatisfactions. As I look at the French, I pale with dismay—realizing the gravity of my attempt. . . . Never before that I remember have I wished to hasten the seasons; but I am impatient for my brother's house to be done, and to have finished my La Fontaine and be attempting something else; and to have resumed summer clothes.[40]

Stevens perhaps sensed Moore's frustration, and, as time wore on, he too became impatient for her to move on to other tasks. As prize after prize rained down on Moore's *Collected Poems,* culminating in the Pulitzer Prize in May 1952, Stevens became increasingly convinced that Moore was wasting both her time and her talent on her translations. In February 1952, Moore became ill after a trip to visit her mother's grave in Woodlawn Cemetery, and she was bedridden for several weeks. Concerned about

Moore both poetically and personally, Stevens began to formulate a plan with Barbara Church for their friend's recuperation. On March 20, Moore was again well enough to go out, and Stevens, Church, and Moore attended a brunch hosted by James and Laura Sweeney. In a letter to Church the next day Stevens remarked, "I thought M. M. looked charming (for a poetess) and on the train I toyed with images of her *after Paris* with a forêt of her own and, perhaps, her own corniche."[41] Knowing that Church was going to France in a few months, Stevens decided that Moore must go with her and spend the summer at Ville d' Avray.

Once Stevens envisioned Moore in Paris, he found the image hard to let go, and as Church's sailing date approached in late May, Stevens apparently took every opportunity to press the point of Moore's departure. Just why Stevens so vehemently wished to send his friend abroad remains a complex question. Although he too had a standing invitation with Church at Ville d' Avray, Stevens himself never traveled to Europe, preferring to see the postwar world through Church's letters and postcards. In *Wallace Stevens and the Actual World,* Alan Filreis argues that Stevens's reluctance to tour a devastated Europe springs from his "characteristically American" need in the 1950s to remain hopeful about the possibility of European postwar regeneration and the containment of communism. In Filreis's view, Stevens "felt the need to breathe easily again in the postwar years" and consciously chose to stay at home and imagine "his" Europe rather than travel abroad and experience actualities that might prove threatening to his American optimism about reconstruction.[42] In such a context, Stevens's insistence that Moore take the trip he refused to make again reflects on his reading of her poetry. Having cast Moore in the years after the war as a poet whose gracious philosopher's hat rescues the postwar world from its relentless waste, Stevens perhaps felt Moore's poetic well suited to the task of tackling an actual Europe with hopeful moral fortitude. In sending her to France with Church, Stevens may have hoped to jar Moore loose from the allegorical fables of La Fontaine and send her back to a poetry of her own particulars—the significant digestion of the "harde yron" of reality that Stevens found important to his own production.

If Stevens was hoping to see France through Moore's eyes, however, he was not destined to get his wish. No matter how he and Church enticed Moore with the promise of a Parisian adventure, Moore would not leave home. As Church's boat left the dock, she sent Stevens her analysis of Moore's refusal:

> I think she [Marianne] is afraid of all sorts of things, mostly afraid of too much excitement, and she loves that too. It is a wonderful thing for me to know her and to feel that she likes me. I can talk with her easily, freely. She believes me when I tell her that all the routine things about travelling would be taken care of by me and Suzanne we are such seasoned hard boiled travelers, but at the last instance she always finds reasons, hesitations—La Fontaine, her brother, other things, even clothes, and she decides against. Perhaps one has to get into the habit of moving around. [43]

While Moore was trepidatious about disruptions in her routine, another explanation for her reluctance may lie in her affinity with the very poet attempting to secure her passage. What both Stevens and Church failed to notice was that Moore, like Stevens, was for the most part an intellectual traveler who saw the world through the pictures of the *Illustrated London News* and who preferred to journey between the covers of books and in the halls of the New York museums. She was, as she herself claimed, an observer, but she also valued the perspective and calm of her study. In the years after the war, particularly those following her mother's death, even such intellectualized concentration on the actual world proved taxing, as Moore's decision to translate La Fontaine's fables attests. Rather than engage in a reality of her own particulars, Moore chose to face the actual world at more than her usual distance. Donning the mask of La Fontaine, Moore returned through his poems to Aesop's allegorical bestiary, voicing her dissatisfactions with the greed and cruelty of human nature under the deep cover of someone else's words and someone else's creatures—the obvious protective political strategy behind La Fontaine's gift of his fables to the Dauphin. Shunning for a time a more direct approach to the actualities and difficulties of her postwar world, Moore stepped into the past, from La Fontaine back to Aesop, to show that the simplest of human lessons known to the Greeks still remained unlearned. As Laurence Stapleton points out, Aesop's animals

differ from Moore's in that they behave like people, while Moore's crea-
tures, never wholly subsumed under any allegorical function, behave like
animals.[44] Moore's fascination with La Fontaine in the postwar years
perhaps speaks to her sense that, in the wake of the Second World War,
humans needed, more than ever, to be instructed about the sins of their
nature—a feat best accomplished through morals and fables rather than
the actual particularities of detailed description.

Moore's decision not to tour a Europe under reconstruction, then,
may have stemmed from a fear similar to Stevens's that the "harde yron"
of the actual devastation overseas might be too hard for even the best of
poetic ostriches to digest. Moore's fables, while a burden, were also a
shield against more difficult postwar poetic encounters. Stevens, how-
ever, remained convinced that if Moore was not enjoying her work, she
should cut her losses. In June 1952, Stevens received an honorary degree
from Columbia University with Moore in the audience. Following the
event, Stevens and Moore met over cocktails, and Stevens could not
resist raising the issue of Moore's aborted trip once again. As Moore
reported the conversation to Barbara Church: "Wallace Stevens asked
with the greatest interest about your departure, (your sailing) and as you
admit, I am not a raconteur of few words—He then said why he had
wanted me to go along—namely that 'you are just the right person for
me with whom to go'!"[45]

Convinced of the "rightness" of Church's invitation, Stevens contin-
ued to hope throughout 1952 and into the following year that Moore
would trade the trials of La Fontaine for the excitement of Paris and the
rewards of her own verse. Determined that Moore should not waste any
more valuable time on translations he felt detrimental to her career, Ste-
vens raised the issue again as Church prepared her travel plans for the
summer of 1953. The result was the closest thing to an argument the two
poets ever had. On March 19, 1953, Moore, Stevens, Church, and the
Sweeneys again met for lunch in New York. After the party, Church sent
Stevens and Moore home in her chauffeured car, and Stevens, his tongue
loosened by alcohol (he subsequently promised Church that he would
hereafter "stick, chiefly, to anchovies"), proceeded to tell Moore pre-
cisely how she was wasting her talents. Stevens's lecture set off a flurry of
letters between Moore, Church, and Stevens that grant insight into the

quality of the two poets's friendship. Attempting to inject the event with
a bit of humor, Moore wrote to Church:

> You would have smiled if you had heard him [Wallace Stevens] in
> the car, saying, "Mrs. Church is <u>real</u>. You should do what she <u>asks</u>
> you to do, and forget all those things you hate to do." And of
> course I said as was requisite, "I must do what I do, for the same
> reason you said I must be certain that I myself like my fables. I
> must be satisfied that <u>I</u> think I am doing what <u>I ought to do</u>. So
> don't feel that I am victim and a pitiful worm. I do what I am
> satisfied is for the best."[46]

In forcefully announcing "Mrs. Church is real," Stevens revealed in part
why he so passionately wished Moore to travel. In committing herself to
La Fontaine at the expense of earthly pleasure, Moore was, in Stevens's
view, trading real life for art, a trade that, even during the most transcen-
dent of poetic moments, Stevens found problematic. Fearing that he
himself may have lived "a skeleton's life as a questioner of reality," Ste-
vens wished Moore to grasp Church's offer of happiness with both
hands. To trade life for translations, in Stevens's view, was folly. The
response Moore quotes herself as offering, however, defines happiness
quite differently. Moore claimed she was happiest doing not what she
pleased, but what she "ought," finding satisfaction in the fulfillment of
duty that Stevens both respected and found hard to comprehend. "The
more I see of her the more certain I am that some question of integrity
enters into everything she does and is decisive of it for her," Stevens
remarked to Church, adding "personally, I do not think as she does and
do not feel that my integrity is involved."[47]

On receiving Moore's letter, Church read more sting in the ex-
change than Moore was willing to admit. Attempting to smooth any
ruffled feathers, Church wrote:

> And don't mind what Wallace Stevens says—I know he means you
> to be happy, he thinks and says we are both in good company when
> we are in each others company—he does not approve translations,
> he is afraid some of your precious energy might get lost in your

translating the fables and he has quite a trace of dictatorship—but he really wants you to do exactly what you want to do, in your time too—he should go to Europe.[48]

To which Moore replied:

A "bit of a dictator," yes, and of an eclectic. Two things Thursday, made me feel that we must exercise our sensibility protectively, knowing that a little tug of the nerves makes one say a strange thing that one's judgement would avoid and not mind. And Wallace Stevens loves you very much; in fact each of us, I think.[49]

Ultimately the rift between the two friends over Moore's fables lay in Moore's perception of Stevens, not so much as a dictator, but as an "eclectic." In assigning Stevens to such a philosophy, Moore implied that he had a tendency not to follow any particular system or code of behavior when determining right conduct, preferring to select doctrines that suited his needs. Where Moore felt bound by an unshakable sense of personal honor and obligation to others—she had a contract, she would fill it—to finish her fables, Stevens believed that Moore should do as she liked and abandon the project. Stevens saw the issue of completion as one of personal will, while Moore saw it as a matter of upholding a code of conduct to which the needs of the self were subordinate. Nearing the end of her fables, Moore's attitude toward her translations became a study in her conception of the poet's duty to things transcendent. "I didn't ask to do the work," she wrote to Church, eliding her initial hand in launching the project, "I was given it." Picturing the fables as the dubious gift of a power greater than herself—a cross to bear—Moore equated the completion of her work with the fulfillment of some higher purpose.

As the above exchange between Moore and Church indicates, however, both women decided they admired and cared for Stevens in spite of his flaws. He obviously loved them both, they concluded, and should be forgiven. Having put the event in perspective, Moore longed to show Stevens that no permanent damage had been done to their friendship. Sometime during the week of their disagreement, Moore received a copy of Stevens's now-published *Selected Poems* from Faber and Faber, the book she had initiated, deputied, and helped to shape. The volume on which the two poets had worked together provided a ready bridge between them, and Moore used the book as an excuse to send Stevens a note that, in warmly praising his poems, implied the continued importance of their fellowship. Quoting her favorite lines from many of Stevens's lyrics, Moore ended her letter with a touching gesture of forgiveness to the poet himself. Such poems, she wrote to Stevens, were:

> indispensable—together with a few verbal pineapples
> such as you see fit to share with certain friends
>   of whom I hope I am one.
>   Marianne M.[50]

Stevens breathed a sigh of relief upon receiving Moore's note and responded immediately with a somewhat embarrassed and grateful apology:

> Dear Marianne:
> I was in rather a chaotic state when we separated the other evening and may have been dog-gone informal. Your note tells me, in effect, that you have no grudge. The web of friendship between poets is the most delicate thing in the world—and the most precious. Your note does me immense good.[51]

Read in the context of Moore and Stevens's conflict over the fate of La Fontaine, Stevens's letter offers apology for much more than his too many martinis. In pushing Moore directly about her work and her life, Stevens realized that he had overstepped his bounds and, afraid of damaging the web of trust between them, he acknowledged that Moore must be herself.

Stevens issued a perhaps more profound apology to Moore through Barbara Church some months later. In June 1953, Moore capped off her astounding year of prizes by winning the M. Carrie Thomas Award of Bryn Mawr College. Stevens wrote to Church that the cash award of five thousand dollars that Moore received was "a handsome prize for an honest working girl," and he took the opportunity of Moore's success to fire one last shot in the battle of Moore's fables:

> All of these awards recognize her faithfulness to the exquisite standards she sets for herself. Personally, I cannot help thinking that she ought to let it go at that; and that the La Fontaine is a mistake, since it is next to impossible to please people by translations. Yet she may be able to step into La Fontaine's skin and speak his words, and, if she does, she might add to his prodigious success and her own.[52]

Church instantly recognized Stevens's "yet" as a bow in Moore's direction. For the first time on record, Stevens admitted that "if" Moore could do well by her fables, she "might" create something marvelous, a weakening of his earlier unilateral disapproval. Emphasizing Stevens's acknowledgment of possibility, his magic "if," Church copied Stevens's statement verbatim into her next letter to Moore, who replied:

> Is it not kind of Wallace Stevens to take my fables so to heart? Only a friend could ponder the matter in that way. As for me, I am long past saving. A folly perhaps to have undertaken it—the impossible feat and when I see the rhymes: could and would; then and men (or when); he and me!; I am in despair. Furthermore in my present "absolutely faithful" undigressing version, much dash and color are lost. But it has to come out—I can't retreat; nor am I despondent. . . . How like you Barbara, to speak of the "if" as you do, Wallace Stevens's "if."[53]

Moore had, by the end of her project, become resigned to a product less than perfect, but, to both Moore and Church, Stevens's "if" proved an important concession.

In July 1953, Moore finally pronounced the manuscript of the fables finished and, after eight long years of difficult work, she faced the inevitable question of whether the project had been worth the energy and the sacrifice it had demanded. Had she made a mistake in not accompanying Barbara Church to Europe? Had Wallace Stevens been right in pointing

out the folly of trading life for art? Moore considered these questions and
ultimately uttered the last word in the disagreement over the value of her
fables in the form of a poem. In her first piece of verse published in the
wake of her fables, Moore answered Stevens's image of the precious
"web" between the two poets with a web of her own—"The Web One
Weaves of Italy." Moore's short four-stanza lyric serves as an explanation
to both Church and Stevens for her reluctance to sacrifice her fables for a
European tour. Italy was one of Barbara Church's favorite destinations, a
country that, denying Church her company and Stevens his wish, Moore
would never see in person. Drawing on a *New York Times* article on the
"Festivals and Fairs for the Tourist in Italy," however, Moore crafted a
poem that frankly stated her preference for intellectual touring over ac-
tual travel. Moore's lyric begins:

The Web One Weaves of Italy

grows till it is not what but which,
blurred by too much. The very blasé alone could
    choose the contest or fair to which to go.
    The crossbow tournament at Gubbio?

For quiet excitement, canoe-ers
or peach fairs? or near Perugia, the mule-show;
    if not the Palio, slaying the Saracen.[54]

    The web one weaves of Italy is a web created by the mind—the Italy
of the imagination—and, as Moore's first two stanzas imply, it, like the
web of friendship, is fragile. Confronted with a list of fairs and festivals, a
barrage of events that the tourist in Italy might witness, Moore finds that
the Italy of her imagination becomes "blurred by too much" informa-
tion. Too many observed details threaten to obscure the clarity of her
ordered internal conception and leave the sensitive poet unable to decide,
as Moore's question marks indicate, where to focus her attention or how
to define her subject. As Margaret Holley notes, Moore's poem displays
her fear that "observation of the external world, its sensuous and factual
details, can extend indefinitely," often to the point of overwhelming the
sensitive observer.[55] In the third stanza of the poem, Moore pulls back

from the thought of actual tourism and, looking at the catalog of fairs and festivals again, appreciates:

> —its nonchalances of the mind,
> that "fount by which enchanting gems are spilt."
> Are we not charmed by the result?—
>
> quite different from what goes on
> at the Sorbonne;
>
> (*CPMM,* 164)

Reading the list again, Moore "salutes" the glittering spectacle of its unmanageable and purposeless details, "the nonchalances of the mind," even while she critiques its confusing and indiscriminate jumble. Moore's description of the mind that makes the list, "that fount by which enchanting gems are spilt," issues from her own translation of La Fontaine's fable "The Monkey and the Leopard." La Fontaine's fable depicts a contest between a well-dressed, fancy-furred leopard and a clever monkey who each attempt to attract an audience at a fair. In the end, the monkey, a symbol of the active mind, draws more attention than the leopard, the "ostentatious dunce" of the body's exterior beauty. Moore translates La Fontaine's moral: "Exterior diversity / Can never charm as the mind can, to infinity— / That sparkling fount by which enchanting gems are spilt."[56] Here, then, is the moral of Moore's poem and her message to Stevens and Church. No matter what the real Europe has to offer, its "exterior diversity," while distracting, can never "charm" like the mind's travels. Moore implies that an encounter with the haphazard exterior details of the actual Italy might restrict her imaginative conception of the place, bloating her image with spectacles that, while entertaining, would inhibit her more profound thoughts—the studious life of the Sorbonne. Given a choice, as in La Fontaine's fable, between the monkey's carnival and the leopard's, between the fairs and festivals of the mind and the fairs and festivals of the actual Italy, Moore chooses the monkey.

Thus, in "The Web One Weaves of Italy," Moore defends her decision to stay home at the same time that she confirms her faith in her fables. Using La Fontaine's moral as her proof of the mind's superiority

to exterior detail, Moore shows Stevens and Church that her fables them-
selves have proved a more valuable journey than any proposed actual
travels, no matter how pleasant. More than mere literary spectacles or
collections of observed details, Moore's fables, as all of her poems of the
1950s, have morals. The fable of the monkey and the leopard is a carnival
that not only entertains but instructs, drawing the mind away from the
glittering surface of the details to ponder profounder lessons of human
experience. Juxtaposing the moral of the fair in her fable with the charm-
ing but meaningless fairs of the actual Italy, Moore suggests in the 1950s
that the role of poetry is not merely to observe, or record, but to seek
universal truths and transcend actual details with a sense of higher pur-
pose. Choosing the infinity of the moral imagination over the limitations
of the actual world, Moore ends her disagreement with Stevens by show-
ing him in "The Web One Weaves of Italy" that she has, in hindsight,
done exactly the right thing in staying at home and sticking to her fables.

The long and revealing exchange between Moore and Stevens over
the issue of the fables of La Fontaine thus ultimately speaks to the differ-
ing poetic agendas of the two poets in the 1950s. Faced with the waste of
the war and the death of her mother, Moore turned from a reality of her
actual particulars to poems concerned with eternal mysteries, ethical ques-
tions, and the power of the moral mind. Faced with his seventieth birth-
day and concerned that "real" life may have passed him by, Stevens
turned more often to poems that longed for the residue of the actual
world. Just as Moore attempted to shape Stevens's career to suit her
needs, wishing him to maintain his faith in the imagination's nobility and
the power of the spirit, so Stevens attempted to shape Moore's career,
and her life, to suit his continued sense of the importance of the poet's
connection to the actual world—the plain sense of things he felt might be
missing from his own verse. Stevens needed Moore the actual traveler;
Moore needed Stevens the interior paramour. Certainly neither poet
changed completely to accommodate the other's vision. Stevens agreed
to end his *Selected Poems* with "Final Soliloquy of the Interior Paramour,"
but he chose to close his *Collected Poems* with a scrawny cry outside the
mind that undercuts the paramour's "vast ventriloquism"—"Not Ideas
about the Thing, but the Thing Itself." Moore never did travel to Europe
or return to the plethora of concrete detail evident in her earlier poems.

Yet each poet, in response to the other, rethought the position and the purpose of poetry in the 1950s. The lively personal conversation between Moore and Stevens inspired shifts and adjustments, actions and reactions, in a poetic dialogue between friends that constituted a vital form of influence.

Notes

Introduction

1. I am indebted to both Bonnie Costello and Celeste Goodridge for their useful assessments of the importance of Stevens's work to Marianne Moore's production. In her article "Marianne Moore's Debt and Tribute to Wallace Stevens," *Concerning Poetry* 15, no. 1 (Spring 1982): 27–33, Bonnie Costello points to some of the resonances of tone and imagery between Stevens's and Moore's verse and, tracing Moore's general appreciation of Stevens's poetry, points to instances of Moore's Stevensian diction. Costello's *Marianne Moore: Imaginary Possessions* (Cambridge: Harvard University Press, 1981) also offers an important first glimpse of Moore's notes about Stevens that appear in worksheets for her poem "The Plumet Basilisk" (149–50). In *Hints and Disguises: Marianne Moore and Her Contemporaries* (Iowa City: University of Iowa Press, 1989), Celeste Goodridge devotes a chapter to explicating Moore's complex reviews of Stevens's verse. I hope to build on the work of these two scholars and to suggest that Stevens, too, drew on Moore's work to shape his art.

2. Harold Bloom, *The Anxiety of Influence* (Oxford: Oxford University Press, 1973), 5.

3. Harold Bloom, *A Map of Misreading* (Oxford: Oxford University Press, 1975), 10.

4. George Bornstein directly addresses the inability of Bloom's theory to accommodate a more cooperative view of poetic influence in "Four Gaps in Postromantic Influence Study," the introduction to his *Poetic Remaking: The Art of Browning, Yeats, and Pound* (University Park: Pennsylvania State University Press, 1988). Bornstein's introduction argues that Bloom's vision of literary historical agon ignores four pivotal points: the importance of the work of Victorian poets to the work of modernist poets, the social-historical circumstances in which modernist poets worked (primarily their perceived position as outsiders to, rather than anxious inheritors of, literary tradition), the textual circumstances of modernist

poets' literary production, and the manuscript evidence of actual, rather than merely assumed, influence. Bornstein suggests that once the above contexts are restored, a more congenial image of influence, particularly between the modernist poets and their Victorian forerunners, becomes evident. Pound stands as one of Bornstein's key examples of a poet who has a much more comfortable relationship with his literary heritage than Bloom's model would allow. Christopher Beach in "Ezra Pound and Harold Bloom: Influences, Canons, Traditions, and the Making of Modern Poetry," *ELH* 56, no. 2 (1989): 463–83, draws on Bornstein's notion of Pound's challenge to Bloom and offers a detailed examination of Pound's notion of literary influence that shows the narrow nature of Bloom's agon-ridden canon. In his book *Imitating the Italians: Wyatt, Spenser, Synge, Pound, Joyce* (Baltimore: Johns Hopkins University Press, 1991), Reed Way Dasenbrock also argues with Bloom's restrictive notion that literary influence occurs only through conflict and only within a monolingual literary tradition. Again using Pound as an example, Dasenbrock points to the tendency of modernist poets to unanxiously draw on models and engage in useful imitation of works outside their own national/linguistic traditions.

5. Bornstein, *Poetic Remaking*, 139.

6. See Beach on this point, "Pound and Bloom," 469–71.

7. Sandra M. Gilbert and Susan Gubar, *The Madwoman in the Attic: The Woman Writer and the Nineteenth-Century Literary Imagination* (New Haven: Yale University Press, 1979), 48.

8. For a sampling of such works see Patricia Ann Meyer Spacks, *The Female Imagination* (New York: Knopf, 1975); Ellen Moers, *Literary Women* (New York: Doubleday, 1976); Elaine Showalter, *A Literature of Their Own: British Women Novelists from Brontë to Lessing* (Princeton: Princeton University Press, 1977); Margaret Homans, *Women Writers and Poetic Identity: Dorothy Wordsworth, Emily Brontë, and Emily Dickinson* (Princeton: Princeton University Press, 1980); Cheryl Walker, *The Nightingale's Burden: Women Poets and American Culture before 1900* (Bloomington: Indiana University Press, 1982); Wendy Martin, *An American Triptych: Anne Bradstreet, Emily Dickinson, Adrienne Rich* (Chapel Hill: University of North Carolina Press, 1984); Shari Benstock, *Women of the Left Bank: Paris 1900–1914* (Austin: University of Texas Press, 1986); Alicia Ostriker, *Stealing the Language: The Emergence of Women's Poetry in America* (Boston: Beacon Press, 1986); and Sandra Gilbert and Susan Gubar's *No Man's Land*, vol. 1, *The War of the Words* (New Haven: Yale University Press, 1988).

9. Betsy Erkkila, *The Wicked Sisters: Women Poets, Literary History, and Discord* (Oxford: Oxford University Press, 1992). See Erkkila's argument about the conflicts between Bishop and Moore in her chapter "Differences That Kill: Elizabeth Bishop and Marianne Moore," 99–151. Jeredith Merrin, *An Enabling Humility: Marianne Moore, Elizabeth Bishop, and the Uses of Tradition* (New Brunswick: Rutgers University Press, 1990), especially the chapter "Literary Models, Maternity, and Paternity," 107–44.

10. Daniel Mark Fogel, *Covert Relations: James Joyce, Virginia Woolf, and Henry James* (Charlottesville: University Press of Virginia, 1990).

11. Ibid., 164.

12. Ibid., 166.

13. Gilbert and Gubar, *No Man's Land*, 214.

14. Unpublished notes by Marianne Moore, folder VII:10:05, Marianne Moore Collection, Rosenbach Museum and Library, Philadelphia (hereafter referred to as Rosenbach). The material in this folder is mixed and undated, but the content of Moore's notes place them somewhere after 1943. The words enclosed in parentheses indicate the alternative phrasings that Moore considered in making her notes. At the time she wrote this draft, she had not discarded any of the possibilities.

15. Bornstein, *Poetic Remaking*, 6.

16. Ibid., 11.

Chapter 1

1. Donald Hall, "Marianne Moore," in *Writers at Work: The Paris Review Interviews,* second series, ed. George Plimpton (New York: Viking Penguin, 1963), 82. Moore mistakes the date of the Entretiens de Pontigny in her response. The Mount Holyoke conference and her first meeting with Stevens took place in the summer of 1943.

2. Alfred Kreymborg, *Troubadour: An Autobiography* (New York: Boni and Liveright, 1925), 332–33.

3. William Carlos Williams to William Van O'Connor. Comments contained in correspondence between Williams and Stevens, folders WAS 11–23, Wallace Stevens Collection, Henry E. Huntington Library, San Marino, Calif. (hereafter referred to as Huntington).

4. Wallace Stevens, "Sunday Morning," *Poetry* 7 (November 1915): 81–83.

5. Wallace Stevens, "Peter Quince at the Clavier," "The Silver Plough-Boy," *Others* 1, no. 2 (August 1915; reprint, New York: Kraus Reprint Corp., 1967), 31–34.

6. Marianne Moore, "The Accented Syllable," *Egoist* 3 (October 1916): 151–52. Reprinted in Marianne Moore, *The Complete Prose of Marianne Moore,* ed. Patricia Willis (New York: Viking Penguin, 1986), 31–35; hereafter cited as *CPrMM*. All further references are to the reprint edition.

7. Marianne Moore to H. D., 10 November 1916, Rosenbach.

8. Martin Secker, review of *Sinister Street*, vol. 1, by Compton Mackenzie, *English Review*, October 1913, 472–73. Cited in Marianne Moore, unpublished reading diary, 1250/1, 4, Rosenbach.

9. *New York Post*, 1 February 1915. Transcribed in Moore, unpublished reading diary, 1250/1, 110, Rosenbach.

10. See Milton J. Bates's discussion of *Others* and Arensberg in his chapter "Burgher, Fop, and Clown," in *Wallace Stevens: A Mythology of Self* (Berkeley and Los Angeles: University of California Press, 1985), 83–126.

11. Marianne Moore, "Critics and Connoisseurs," *Others* 3, no. 1 (July 1916; reprint New York: Kraus Reprint Corp., 1967), 4–5. Moore revised this poem over the years, and the version that appears in *Others* is slightly different from the one that appears in *Observations* (1924).

12. Marianne Moore, "In the Days of Prismatic Color," *Lantern* 27 (Spring 1919): 35.

13. Marianne Moore, "Those Various Scalpels," *Lantern* 25 (Spring 1917): 50–51.

14. Marianne Moore, "England," *Dial* 68 (April 1920): 422–23. Reprinted in *Others: An Anthology of New Verse,* ed. Alfred Kreymborg (New York: Knopf, 1920).

15. Marianne Moore, unpublished reading diary, 1250/3, 19, Rosenbach.

16. Harriet Monroe, "A Symposium on Marianne Moore," *Poetry* 19 (January 1922): 208–16.

17. Marianne Moore, *Poems,* ed. H.D. and Bryher (London: Egoist Press, 1921).

18. Moore to Bryher, 7 July 1921, Rosenbach.

19. Moore to H. D., 26 July 1921, Rosenbach.

20. Monroe, "Symposium on Marianne Moore," 208.

21. Ibid., 209.

22. Ibid., 210.

23. John Slatin, *The Savage's Romance: The Poetry of Marianne Moore* (University Park: Pennsylvania State University Press, 1986), 127–36. I am indebted to Slatin for his reading of "People's Surroundings" as Moore's survey of contemporary poetry. Slatin sees the poem as a recasting of Moore's earlier unpublished essay "English Literature since 1914" (Rosenbach) in which Moore briefly addresses the work of Pound, Eliot, Williams, and Stevens. As Slatin notes, Moore refers to Pound's "natural promptness" in her essay, and the phrase finds its way into Moore's poem as part of her reference to both his and William Carlos Williams's concrete, minimal verses (127–28). In her essay, Moore also appreciates the "facile troutlike passage of [Eliot's] mind through a multiplicity of foreign objects"—an image that, in Slatin's view, she recasts as the minds that move "like trout" over the great distances of Utah and Texas in "People's Surroundings." "English Literature since 1914" also recalls Moore's pleasure in the "spick torrent" of Stevens's set of poems entitled "Pecksniffiana" (1919). Slatin identifies Moore's tropical habitat in "People's Surroundings" as an extended reference to Stevens's verse, and I agree. Slatin and I, however, disagree on several points. In his overall analysis, Slatin reads "People's Surroundings" as Moore's complete dismissal of Stevens's poetic in favor of Eliot's more histori-

cal and less personal verses—the poems of a "cool sir" with an "explicit sensory apparatus of common sense" (131). But Slatin avoids the issue of Moore's obvious critique of the level-headed cool sirs and their empty environment— images that, even if Slatin is correct in identifying the troutlike individuals with Eliot, make his argument about Moore's preference for Eliot's verse difficult to accept. Slatin also does not address Moore's diary notes, which contain important source materials for "People's Surroundings" that reflect directly on Moore's assessment of Stevens's poetry.

24. Wallace Stevens, "Sur Ma Guzzla Gracile," *Poetry*, 19 (October 1921): 1–9. Stevens reprinted all the poems in the set in *Harmonium* (1923) and again in the expanded *Harmonium* (1931), but he did not preserve the order of the original "Sur Ma Guzzla Gracile." See *The Collected Poems of Wallace Stevens* (New York: Knopf, 1954), 77, 46, 24, 85, 9, 65, 64, 25, 55, 56, 12, 22. All further references to these poems are to *The Collected Poems of Wallace Stevens* (hereafter cited as *CPWS*).

25. Moore, unpublished reading diary, 1250/3, 43, Rosenbach.

26. Marianne Moore, "People's Surroundings," *Dial* 72 (June 1922): 588–90. All subsequent quotations are from the version of the poem cited.

27. Slatin, *The Savage's Romance*, 130–31. Slatin claims that Moore's greatest fear is that she will somehow be seduced into copying the style of Stevens's verse. Bluebeard's touch, Slatin argues, "reveal[s] the extent to which [Moore] has adulterated her own 'creative power' in marrying her 'style' to that of Bluebeard/Stevens. She has been betrayed again into the 'sophistication' (mixture, adulteration) that is rejected in 'In the Days of Prismatic Colour' as unholy and false" (130). Slatin thus types Moore's response to Stevens's verse as an expression of her anxiety of influence. Stevens's tone infiltrates her poetry and, wishing to be original, she instead finds that she has "been undone by her own helplessly mimetic instincts" and lured into copying his style (130). I, however, see Moore's image of Stevens as a self-projection of her anxieties, not about original creativity or style, but about the potentially detached and overly complex nature of her own imagination.

Chapter 2

1. Marianne Moore, unpublished conversation notebook, 1914–21, 1250/24, 36, Rosenbach.

2. Ibid., 33.

3. Ibid., 8.

4. Marianne Moore, unpublished conversation notebook, 1921–1922, 1250/25, 21, Rosenbach.

5. Ibid., 21–22.

6. Ibid., 33.

7. Ibid., 95.

8. Marianne Moore to Yvor Winters, 25 April 1922, Rosenbach.

9. Winters to Moore, 6 June 1921, Rosenbach.

10. Stevens to Monroe, 21 December 1922, in *The Letters of Wallace Stevens,* ed. Holly Stevens (New York: Knopf, 1966), 232 (hereafter cited as *LWS*).

11. Moore, unpublished conversation diary, 1250/25, 66, Rosenbach.

12. Moore to Winters, 30 October 1923, Rosenbach.

13. Moore, unpublished conversation diary, 1250/25, 66, Rosenbach.

14. Marianne Moore, "Well Moused, Lion," *Dial* 76 (January 1924): 84–91. Reprinted in *CPrMM,* 91–98. All further references to this essay are to the reprint edition. Moore conscientiously did her homework when reviewing material with which she was not already familiar. In contrast to her quick work on Stevens, Moore spent an entire summer preparing a review of Mabel Loomis Todd's *Letters of Emily Dickinson,* reading the whole of Dickinson's work. Her review of Dickinson's letters appeared in *Poetry* in January 1933.

15. In *Hints and Disguises,* 27–54, Celeste Goodridge argues that "Well Moused, Lion" reflects Moore's sense of Stevens as a foremost master of disguise. Goodridge claims that Moore's reviews of Stevens's work both celebrate the unpredictable surprises afforded by his many masks and protest his troubling inaccessibility (36). Goodridge associates Moore's dislike of Stevens's wilder imaginative moments with his tendency to hide himself behind endless personae—a quest for anonymity that results, in Moore's view, in uncalled-for cruelty. While I agree with Goodridge that Stevens's propensity toward imaginative change lies at the heart of Moore's essay, I argue that Moore's quarrel with Stevens rests in the "uneasy" nature of many of his imaginative flights—his skeptical inability to accept or put lasting trust in the imagination's more noble visions.

16. Goodridge argues that Moore dislikes Stevens's lines because they reflect his "habitual hesitation to commit himself to a particular position" (*Hints and Disguises,* 40)—his desire to hide his true feelings at all costs. Goodridge does not notice, however, that both Moore's comments about "Thirteen Ways of Looking at a Blackbird" and "The Snow Man" focus on the issue of the poet's ability to create a satisfying fiction.

17. Ibid., 42–43.

18. *Shelley's Poetry and Prose,* ed. Donald Reiman and Sharon B. Powers (New York: Norton, 1977), 505–6. For Moore's transcription of this passage see Marianne Moore, unpublished reading diary, Rosenbach, 1250/4, 36.

19. *Shelley's Poetry and Prose,* 503–4.

20. Marianne Moore, unpublished reading diary, 1250/4, 36, Rosenbach.

21. For a helpful sketch of the stages of Moore's composition of "An Octopus," including biographical material, explication of Moore's allusions, and excerpts from Moore's poetry notebooks, see Patricia Willis's "The Road to Paradise: First Notes on Marianne Moore's 'An Octopus,'" *Twentieth Century Literature* (Fall 1984): 242–72.

22. Ibid., 249.

23. Marianne Moore, "An Octopus," *Dial* 77 (December 1924): 475–81. All subsequent quotations are from the version of the poem cited.

24. Marianne Moore, unpublished poetry notebook, 1251/7, 59, Rosenbach.

25. Harold Bloom, *The Visionary Company: A Reading of English Romantic Poetry* (Ithaca: Cornell University Press, 1971), 294.

26. Willis, "The Road to Paradise," 250–53. Willis is particularly acute in tracing the spatial movement of "An Octopus."

27. *Shelley's Poetry and Prose*, 505. Also see Moore's transcription in her unpublished reading diary, 1250/4, 36, Rosenbach.

Chapter 3

1. Both A. Walton Litz in *Introspective Voyager: The Poetic Development of Wallace Stevens* (Oxford: Oxford University Press, 1972) and George Bornstein in *Transformations of Romanticism in Yeats, Eliot, and Stevens* (Chicago: University of Chicago Press, 1976) suggest that Stevens's poetic silence grew out of his blunt self-assessment of his poetic development in the lines of "The Comedian as the Letter C." Both Litz and Bornstein theorize that Stevens, looking back over his poetic career to date, grew dissatisfied with his current styles and theories and decided to rethink his art. Litz speculates that Stevens, needing the real and the normal, abandoned his art in the 1920s "because his only visitations were from the angel of the imagination" (151). Bornstein focuses on the cyclic nature of the poetic development Stevens sets out in "Comedian" and suggests that Stevens stopped writing because he "did not want merely to inaugurate a new personal cycle by returning to the watered down old romanticism of his youth" (175).

2. Stevens to Hi Simons, 12 January 1940, in *LWS*, 350.

3. Bornstein, *Transformations of Romanticism*, 175.

4. See Stevens to Moore, 3 December 1926 in *LWS*, 248 for Stevens's request. Also see 246, 248, and 249 for Stevens's various polite refusals to Moore's requests for poems.

5. Marianne Moore, "Comment," *Dial* 80 (March 1926): 265–66. Reprinted in *CPrMM*, 160.

6. For a detailed discussion of the effect of America's protective tariffs after the First World War on the world economy see chapter 6, "The Reluctant Giant," in William E. Leuchtenburg, *The Perils of Prosperity 1914–1932* (Chicago: University of Chicago Press, 1958), 104–39.

7. Marianne Moore, "Comment," *Dial* 80 (June 1926): 532–34. Reprinted in *CPrMM*, 167.

8. Ibid., 168.

9. Marianne Moore, "Comment," *Dial* 86 (April 1929): 359–60. Reprinted in *CPrMM*, 218–19.

10. Moore to Burke, 30 November 1932, Rosenbach.

11. Moore to Stevens, 3 January 1933, Huntington.

12. Costello, *Marianne Moore*, 150.

13. Marianne Moore, "The Plumet Basilisk," *Hound and Horn* 7 (October–December 1932): 29–34. All subsequent quotations are from the version of the poem cited.

14. For previous discussions of the connection between Stevens and Moore's "The Plumet Basilisk" see Costello's *Marianne Moore* and Goodridge's *Hints and Disguises*. Costello argues that fluctuation and oscillation are the basilisk's hallmarks and that its indefiniteness saves the creature from forces wishing to reduce or define its essence. The basilisk thus represents a multiplicity that the rational mind cannot order—a magical presence/absence beyond representation that both intrigues and frustrates the viewer. In Costello's view, the ability of Moore's lizard to resist comprehension in an "instability of form" links the basilisk with Moore's sense of Wallace Stevens's verse. Costello further claims that Moore views both basilisk and Stevens wholly favorably in the poem and that Moore's assessment of Stevens's verse as an "incorruptible wall of contributory vagueness" stands as proof of Moore's approval. See Costello's discussion of "The Plumet Basilisk" in her chapter 5, "Fluctuating Charms: Images of Luminosity, Iridescence, and Metamorphosis," 133–58. In her chapter "Moore's Reviews of Stevens," 27–54, Goodridge draws on Costello's discussion of "The Plumet Basilisk" but finds Moore's relationship to Stevens's fluctuating surface a bit more problematic, and I tend to agree. See Goodridge, 33–36.

15. Costello, *Marianne Moore*, 149–50.

16. Marianne Moore, unpublished poetry notebook, 1251/7, 127, Rosenbach.

17. See Costello, *Marianne Moore*, 134, and Goodridge's response to Costello's reading, *Hints and Disguises*, 35–36.

18. Citing Moore's strangely negative diction in regard to the Malay dragon, Costello refers to Moore's creature as one that "cancels out all its potentialities." An "absolute of the spirit," the Malay dragon, Costello notes, lacks dynamic power. See *Marianne Moore*, 141–42.

19. Quoted in Marianne Moore, unpublished reading diary, 1250/5, 29, Rosenbach.

20. Bloom, *The Visionary Company*, 200.

21. Wallace Stevens, "The Noble Rider and the Sound of Words," first given as a lecture at Princeton in April 1941. Reprinted in *The Necessary Angel* (New York: Knopf, 1951), 6 (hereafter cited as *NA*).

22. Marianne Moore, "The Jerboa," *Hound and Horn* 7 (October–December 1932): 108–13. All subsequent quotations are from the version of the poem cited.

23. Moore to Burke, 30 November 1932, Rosenbach.

24. Slatin, *The Savage's Romance*, 206.

25. J. Arthur Thomson, "The Haunts of Life," part 6, "The Mastery of the Air," *Illustrated London News*, 2 April 1921, 442–43.

26. Moore's fascination with the Jurassic bird-reptile dates back to the early years of her correspondence with Bryher and H. D. In 1921, H. D. and Bryher collected Moore's published poems and issued a small volume from the Egoist Press, *Poems*, without Moore's knowledge or consent. Moore responded with a chastising letter to Bryher (7 July 1921, Rosenbach) that indicated her sense of violation: "In *Variation of Plants and Animals Under Domestication*, Darwin speaks of a variety of pigeon that is born naked without any down whatever. I feel like that Darwinian gosling." The thought of a pigeon without down inspired Moore to other thoughts of birds without feathers. Reflecting on an earlier exchange with Bryher in which the novelist claimed that Moore's poetry gave her "a general impression of a world before the fish age where shell clung to a rock," Moore revised her pigeon to accommodate a prehistoric setting. "I am," she writes later in the same letter to Bryher, "a pterodactyl with no rock in which to hide." Forced into print, Moore pictured herself as an ancient monster out of key with her time.

27. Slatin, *The Savage's Romance*, 207. Slatin recognizes the jerboa's crucial weakness, and I am indebted to his reading of the poem.

28. Thomson, "Mastery of the Air," 442.

29. Both Costello and Goodridge, although they note the first appearance of references to Stevens in Moore's worksheets for "The Plumet Basilisk," overlook the later references to Stevens in Moore's notes for "The Frigate Pelican." See Marianne Moore, unpublished poetry notebook, 1251/12, Rosenbach. The pages in this notebook are loose and unnumbered.

30. Ibid., 1251/12.

31. Ibid., 1251/12.

32. Ibid., 1251/12.

33. Marianne Moore, "The Frigate Pelican," *Criterion* 12 (July 1934): 557–60. Moore altered her pelican poem many times throughout her career. The *Criterion* version contains twelve stanzas each of nine lines, a presentation that Moore revised slightly for inclusion in *Selected Poems*. In 1951, however, Moore radically shortened her early version, excising most of stanzas three and four, all of stanzas seven, eight, and nine, most of eleven, and all of twelve. All subsequent quotations are from the 1934 version of the poem cited.

34. Slatin, *The Savage's Romance*, 205.

35. *Shelley's Poetry and Prose*, 500.

36. Ibid., 500–501.

37. Ibid., 501.

38. In *The Poetry of Marianne Moore: A Study in Voice and Value* (Cambridge:

Cambridge University Press, 1987), Margaret Holley reads the separation of the "I" of the frigate pelican from the "we" claimed by the speaker as Moore's denial of the lyrical mode. The "we" who are romantic in a lesser way remain rooted to the ground "gazing upward at unearthly beauty rather than looking down on earth" (82). Where Holley sees Moore's grounded position as a comfortable acceptance of community and a push toward "radical objectivity," I read her position as the self-critique of one unable to generate the imaginative energy to push back against desperate circumstances.

39. In John Slatin's interpretation of "The Frigate Pelican," the community that the frigate generates is not endorsed by the speaker as a possible alternative to the crush of present conditions. In Slatin's view, the birds remain condescending— they look down on the earth in a way that Moore does not deem civil. See *The Savage's Romance*, 207–8. Yet, Moore's harsh picture of the human cost of civility in the present political climate makes the flight of the frigate, in my reading of the poem, seem an indispensable model.

40. Moore to Burke, 30 November 1932, Rosenbach.

Chapter 4

1. Stevens to Ronald Lane Latimer, 10 December 1934, in *LWS*, 272–73.
2. Litz, *Introspective Voyager*, 181–82.
3. Stevens to Ronald Lane Latimer, 12 March 1935, in *LWS*, 276–77.
4. I am indebted to both Litz and Bornstein in my reading of Stevens's approach to a "new romantic." In his chapter, "The New Romanticism of Wallace Stevens," in *Transformations of Romanticism*, 163–230, Bornstein notes Stevens's deep attachment to his romantic precursors and his reshaping of a pejorative romantic through a growing attachment to the "real" in provisional poetry that shuns authoritative statements of transcendence. I agree with Bornstein's assessment that "Stevens distinguished two types of romanticism, rejecting the pejorative and derivative for the positive and vital. He nearly identified romanticism with imagination and used that faculty both to defend poetry in the manner of Shelley and to grapple with reality itself in a new variation of a recurrent romantic struggle. . . . He introduced a radical provisionality into his work while reformulating and elevating notions of violence and cyclicity of imagination. These deflections in aesthetic theory hint at the radical innovations in mental action that pervade his later poetry" (175–76). Litz elaborates on Bornstein's work in his article "Wallace Stevens' Defense of Poetry: *La poesie pure*, the New Romantic, and the Pressure of Reality," in *Romantic and Modern: Revaluations of Literary Tradition*, ed. George Bornstein (Pittsburgh: University of Pittsburgh Press, 1977), 111–32. Citing the "tentative" nature of the poems in *Ideas of Order*, Litz notes the collapse of mountain-minded Hoon's poetic forms in "Sad Strains of a Gay Waltz" and the poet's disgust with old "bric-a-brac," in "Mozart, 1935." Litz

goes on to chart Stevens's search for a new romantic through the writings of Benedetto Croce. As Litz points out, Croce defines for Stevens a split between a pejorative romantic and a romantic as vital force. Litz writes, "As with the two sense of 'pure poetry,' the two senses of the 'romantic' are best understood through Croce. For Croce, Romanticism was an historical movement, but the 'romantic' (like the 'classic') was one of the permanent constituents of the artistic process, an essential element in every work of art. . . . Thus the romantic, for Croce and Stevens, can be pejorative (outmoded figures and feelings) or potent (a permanent tendency of the poetic mind)" (125). Litz states that, throughout the 1930s, Stevens gained confidence in a new romantic made vital by its attachment to reality, growing into a full command of the present (128). My chapter suggests that Stevens's development of the new romantic hinged on his finding a model for his theory in Marianne Moore's poems.

5. Stevens to Ronald Lane Latimer, 12 March 1935, in *LWS*, 277.

6. Stevens to T. C. Wilson, 25 March 1935, in *LWS*, 278–79.

7. Ibid., 279.

8. Stevens to Wilson, 12 July 1935, in *LWS*, 282.

9. Wallace Stevens, "A Poet That Matters," *Life and Letters Today* (December 1935): 61–65. Reprinted in *Opus Posthumous*, ed. Milton J. Bates (New York: Knopf, 1989), 217–22. All subsequent references to this essay are to the reprinted edition in *Opus Posthumous* (hereafter cited as *OP*).

10. Stevens made extensive draft notes for "A Poet That Matters" in the flyleaves of his copy of Moore's volume. See Wallace Stevens's review copy of the American release of Marianne Moore's *Selected Poems* (New York: Macmillan, 1935), Huntington.

11. See Bornstein's discussion of Stevens's "Domination of Black," "The Idea of Order at Key West," "Connoisseur of Chaos," "The Sick Man," and "Landscape with Boat," in *Transformations of Romanticism*, 195–205.

12. Ibid., 198.

13. Marianne Moore, "The Steeple-Jack," part 1 of "Part of a Novel, Part of a Poem, Part of a Play," *Poetry* 40 (June 1932): 119–22. Moore reprinted "The Steeple-Jack" in *Selected Poems* (New York: Macmillan, 1935), 2–3. All further citations are to the version of the poem that appears in *Selected Poems* (hereafter cited as *SPMM*).

14. Michael Benamou, *Wallace Stevens and the Symbolist Imagination* (Princeton: Princeton University Press, 1972), 40.

15. Bornstein, *Transformations of Romanticism*, 179.

16. Stevens took the time to thoroughly annotate and scan several of Moore's poems in his review copy of Moore's volume. See Wallace Stevens's copy of the American release of Marianne Moore's *Selected Poems*, Huntington.

17. In her book *Marianne Moore, Subversive Modernist* (Austin: University of Texas Press, 1986), Taffy Martin argues that "The Steeple-Jack" "reveals a

Marianne Moore fascinated by brilliant precision but drawn as well to a subsurface boiling with contradiction and hidden danger. Chaos triumphs in 'The Steeple-Jack,' and craftsmanship is just as unstable as weather patterns and politicians" (16). Slatin echoes Martin's sense of the menacing instability of the village in the poem. See *The Savage's Romance*, 176–96.

18. Gilbert and Gubar, *No Man's Land*, 149.

19. B. J. Leggett transcribes this passage from the front flyleaf of Stevens's copy of Moore's *Selected Poems* in his article "Wallace Stevens and Marianne Moore: Two Essays and a Private Review," *Wallace Stevens Journal* 10, no. 2 (Fall 1986): 76–83. Leggett argues that Moore's verse exemplifies Stevens's "new romantic" principally "in its intermingling of the imaginative and the genuine, which is to say that in Moore's poetry the imagination has successfully attached itself to a new reality" (78). I argue, instead, that Stevens valued Moore's work for a range of provisionalizing practices.

20. The complete texts of Wallace Stevens's manuscript notebooks, entitled *Adagia I* and *Adagia II*, appear in *OP*, 184–202. See *Adagia I, OP*, 185 for Stevens's reworking of Moore's phrase.

21. Stevens to Ronald Lane Latimer, 31 October 1935, in *LWS*, 288–89.

22. James Longenbach, *Wallace Stevens: The Plain Sense of Things* (Oxford: Oxford University Press, 1991), 150 (hereafter cited as *Plain Sense of Things*). Longenbach notes the connection between Stevens's growing interest in poetic provisionality in the 1930s and his evident distaste for the inflexible political systems of the day that seemed increasingly entrenched. Fearing social and ideological fixity, Stevens began to see a skeptical stance as a workable political tool. "Throughout *Ideas of Order*," Longenbach contends, "the world of Hoon is rejected not simply for the Snow Man's world but for a collective or social vision that protects us from the Snow Man's utterly inhuman existence—'these figures of men'" (154). Stevens's moments of skeptical unmaking lead, not simply to imaginative emptiness, but to contact with his fellows. I agree with Longenbach's assessment of Stevens's poetic shift, and I wish to suggest the importance of Moore's verse to Stevens's formulation of his more social poetic.

23. Bornstein, *Transformations of Romanticism*, 202.

Chapter 5

1. Moore to T. C. Wilson, 5 July 1935, Rosenbach.

2. Moore to Stevens, 11 July 1935, Rosenbach.

3. Geoffrey Grigson, "Answers to an Enquiry," *New Verse* 1 (October 1934): 16.

4. Michael Gold, "Out of the Fascist Unconscious," *New Republic*, 26 July 1933, 295–96.

5. For a helpful discussion of Eliot's role in the debate about social poetry

see David Aaron, *Writers on the Left*, 2d ed. (New York: Columbia University Press, 1992), 231–68.

6. *Criterion* 8 (July 1929): 682–91.

7. Harriet Monroe, "Comment," *Poetry* 44 (July 1934): 212.

8. Ibid., 214.

9. Stanley Burnshaw, "Correspondence: Stanley Burnshaw Protests" *Poetry* 44 (September 1934): 351–54.

10. Eugene Davidson, "Some American Poets," *Yale Review* 24 (June 1935): 848–52.

11. John Finch, "Two Spokesmen for the Man Alone," *Sewanee Review* 44 (January–March 1936): 122–25.

12. Moore to Pound, 31 July 1936, Rosenbach.

13. "Innovations in Poetry To-day: Miss Marianne Moore's Experiments," *Times Literary Supplement*, 18 January 1936, 52.

14. Marianne Moore, unpublished reading diary, folder VII:09:09, Rosenbach.

15. Pound to Moore, 11 July 1934, Rosenbach.

16. Moore to Pound, 4 March 1935, Rosenbach.

17. Moore to William Carlos Williams, 26 January 1934, Rosenbach.

18. Moore to William Carlos Williams, 12 May 1934, Rosenbach.

19. Marianne Moore, "Courage, Right and Wrong," *Nation*, 5 December 1936, 672–74. Reprinted in *CPrMM*. All further references to this essay are to the reprint edition.

20. Moore to William Carlos Williams, 5 January 1934, Rosenbach.

21. Marianne Moore, "Ideas of Order," *Criterion* 15 (January 1936): 307–9, reprinted in *CPrMM*, 329–31; Marianne Moore, "Conjuries That Endure," *Poetry* 49 (February 1937): 268–72, reprinted in *CPrMM*, 347–49. All further references to these essays are to the reprint editions.

22. I am indebted here to Charles Molesworth's connection between Moore's "The Pangolin" and her reviews of Wallace Stevens. In his essay, "Moore's Masterpiece: The Pangolin's Alternating Blaze," in *Marianne Moore: Woman and Poet*, ed. Patricia Willis (Orono, Maine: National Poetry Foundation, 1990), Molesworth argues that Moore's reviews of Stevens's *Ideas of Order* provide a key context for her explorations in "The Pangolin." Molesworth defines the central issue of Moore's *Criterion* review as "the problem of symbolism, or more exactly, how the poet can create a language that will reveal and contain higher truth while not abandoning accurate observation and mimetic consistency" (100–102). While I agree in part with Molesworth's assessment (the poet's attempts to gain access to "higher truth" are central to Moore's reading of Stevens here), I think Molesworth mistakes the thrust of Moore's review when he claims that Moore appreciates Stevens's poetry for revealing "the blessings of the objective world." Molesworth thus claims that Moore reads Stevens primarily as a "realist" who observes the

actual. As I will argue in this chapter, I see Moore reading Stevens in the mid-1930s as a poet of imaginative faith rather than strict observation—one whose vision, in offering a different sense of what is, or could be, "real," provides a key defense against the political and social stresses of the day. Molesworth also does not consider Moore's pangolin in the context of the ongoing arguments over the social role of verse.

23. Marianne Moore, manuscript notes for "The Pangolin," folder I:03:22, Rosenbach.

24. I agree with Molesworth's comment that critics too often assume that Moore's armored creatures "suggest something like hermeticism." Armor, here, as Molesworth notes, allows the poet to venture into the world rather than avoid it. See "Moore's Masterpiece," 118.

25. Marianne Moore, manuscript notes for "The Pangolin," folder I:03:22, Rosenbach.

26. Marianne Moore, "The Pangolin," in *The Pangolin and Other Verse* (London: Brendin Publishing Co., 1936), 17–21. All subsequent quotations are from the version of the poem cited.

27. In June 1935, Moore wrote to William Carlos Williams that she had recited "The Red Wheelbarrow" and the first stanza of "Sailing after Lunch" during a reading of her poetry at Bryn Mawr. See Moore to Williams, 22 June 1935, Rosenbach. When Stevens's *Ideas of Order* came out in August of the same year, Moore marked the poem heavily in her copy, putting heavy bars next to each of the last four stanzas. See Moore's copy of Stevens's *Ideas of Order,* Rosenbach.

28. Holley, *Poetry of Marianne Moore,* 101–2.

29. Babette Deutsch, "The Gaudiness of Poetry," *New York Herald Tribune Book Review,* 15 December 1935, 18.

30. Theodore Roethke, "A Rich and Special Sensibility," *New Republic,* 15 July 1936, 305.

31. Stanley Burnshaw, "Turmoil in the Middle Ground," *New Masses,* 1 October 1935, 41–42.

32. Geoffrey Grigson, "The Stuffed Goldfinch," *New Verse* 19 (February–March, 1936): 18–19.

33. Stevens to Moore, 9 March 1936, Rosenbach.

34. Moore to Stevens, 10 March 1936, Huntington.

35. Stevens to Moore, 3 February 1937, Rosenbach.

36. Stevens to Ronald Lane Latimer, 5 November 1935, in *LWS,* 290, 293.

37. Stevens to Ronald Lane Latimer, 10 December 1935, in *LWS,* 299.

38. Wallace Stevens, *Owl's Clover* (New York: Alcestis Press, 1936). Reprinted in Wallace Stevens, *OP,* 75–101.

39. Longenbach, *Plain Sense of Things,* 166–67.

40. Stevens to Hi Simons, 29 August 1940, in *LWS,* 372.

41. Margaret Dickie, *Lyric Contingencies: Emily Dickinson and Wallace Stevens* (Philadelphia: University of Pennsylvania Press, 1991), 141–42.

42. Helen Vendler, *On Extended Wings: Wallace Stevens' Longer Poems* (Cambridge: Harvard University Press, 1969), 80–81.

43. Longenbach, *Plain Sense of Things*, 186.

44. Stevens first delivered "The Irrational Element of Poetry" at Harvard on 8 December 1936. See Milton J. Bates's transcription of Stevens's talk gleaned from Stevens's typescripts, Huntington, published in *OP*, 229–30. All further references are to Bates's reprint in *OP*.

Chapter 6

1. Marianne Moore, unpublished travel notebook, 1251/19, Rosenbach.

2. Hall, "Marianne Moore," 82–83.

3. Moore's comment about Stevens's "friendliness" appears in her interview with Hall, ibid., 83. Moore's reference to Stevens's "scientific unevasiveness" appears in Marianne Moore, "On Wallace Stevens," *New York Review of Books*, 25 June 1964, 5–6. Reprinted in *CPrMM*, 582.

4. Marianne Moore, unpublished travel notebook, 1251/19, Rosenbach.

5. Marianne Moore, "Feeling and Precision," *Sewanee Review*, 52 (Autumn 1944): 499–507. Reprinted in *CPrMM*, 396.

6. In *Wallace Stevens and the Actual World* (Princeton: Princeton University Press, 1991), Alan Filreis associates what he sees as the escapist impulse of Stevens's aesthetic of "The Noble Rider" with a nationally prevalent isolationist impulse in the years preceding America's entry into the war. In Filreis's view, the Japanese attack on Pearl Harbor propels Stevens into a poetry of contact with, rather than pressure against, the actual world. See Filreis's chapters that address the shift in Stevens's focus, "Playing Checkers under the Maginot Line," 1–28, and "Formalists under Fire," 29–147.

7. Ibid., 28.

8. In his chapter "It Must Be Masculine" (222–36) in *Plain Sense of Things*, Longenbach charts the "violent diminution of feminine power" in Stevens's lyrics of the war years. "During the 1940s," Longenbach suggests, "Stevens struggled harder than ever before to ensure his credentials among the manpoets, the central men, the men of capable imagination—the fellowship of men that do not perish" (227). In her article "'Sister of the Minotaur': Sexism and Stevens," *Wallace Stevens Journal* 12, no. 2 (Fall 1988): 102–17, Jacqueline Vaught Brogan also sees "The Figure of the Youth as a Virile Poet" as evidence of Stevens's desire to suppress the feminine elements of his verse but pronounces Stevens "cured" by the retrieval of his feminine impulse in his 1950 lyric "Final Soliloquy of the Interior Paramour." While Brogan does not offer an explanation for the shift in Stevens's verse, she argues that as of the late 1940s Stevens's poetry becomes

more "humane" in its treatment of female figures. As this chapter will suggest, I see Moore and her verse as central to the changing course of Stevens's poetic before and after the Second World War.

9. Marianne Moore, "Poets Are People," interview broadcast from WNYU, Brooklyn Public Library, January 30, 1945, interviewer: Elaine Lambert Lewis, folder II:08:01, Rosenbach.

10. Marianne Moore, "The Paper Nautilus," in *What Are Years*, 44–45. Moore's poem originally appeared under the title "A Glass-Ribbed Nest" in the *Kenyon Review* 2 (Summer 1940): 287–88. All subsequent quotations are from the version of the poem in *What Are Years*.

11. Stevens to Jose Rodriguez Feo, 13 August 1946, in *LWS*, 533.

12. See Longenbach's discussion of Stevens's difficult quest for a return to personal and poetic normalcy in his chapter "It Must Be Humdrum" in *Plain Sense of Things*, 249–73.

13. Stevens to Garcia Villa, 23 July 1946, in *LWS*, 530.

14. Stevens's "More Poems for Liadoff" first appeared in *Quarterly Review of Literature* 3, no. 2 (Fall 1946): 105–13. The set contained the lyrics "A Woman Sings a Song for a Soldier Come Home," "The Pediment of Appearance," "Burghers of Petty Death," "Human Arrangement," "The Good Man Has No Shape," "The Red Fern," "From the Packet of Anacharsis," "The Dove in the Belly," "Mountains Covered with Cats," "The Prejudice against the Past," "Extraordinary References," and "Attempt to Discover Life." Stevens's set is reprinted with the original ordering maintained in *CPWS*, 360–70.

15. Longenbach, *Plain Sense of Things*, 271–72.

16. In *Wallace Stevens*, Bates notes that by 1944 Stevens's frequent wartime references to the masculine Nietzschean poet/hero were already on the wane, diminishing until Stevens abandoned his "heroic fable," as Bates terms it, in 1945 (254–55, 267). For Stevens, the image of poet as overman did not fit comfortably in a postwar context.

17. Marianne Moore, "A Carriage from Sweden," *Nation*, 11 March 1944, 311. Reprinted in Marianne Moore, *Nevertheless* (New York: Macmillan, 1944), 7–9.

18. Longenbach, *Plain Sense of Things*, 230.

19. For a full discussion of Stevens's passionate pursuit of his heritage see Milton J. Bates, "To Realize the Past: Wallace Stevens's Genealogical Study," *American Literature* 52 (1981): 607–27; Peter Brazeau, *Parts of a World: Wallace Stevens Remembered* (New York: Random, 1983), 265–88; and Thomas Lombardi, "Wallace Stevens and the Haunts of Unimportant Ghosts," *Wallace Stevens Journal* 7, nos. 1–2 (Spring 1983): 46–53.

20. Longenbach, *Plain Sense of Things*, 272. Longenbach argues that "Extraordinary References" suggests a way out of Stevens's bleak postwar poetic angst. "Instead of searching the past for a golden age of peace," he argues,

"Stevens takes comfort in the past's disasters" (272). I agree with Longenbach's assessment that the mother in the poem tells the daughter of her violent heritage, not merely to revel in the past, but to find hope in the present through an object lesson in survival. No matter what the atrocities of the past, the family and the land have recovered and will do so again.

21. H. D. Lewis, "On Poetic Truth," *Philosophy* 21, no. 79 (July 1946): 147–66.

22. Ibid., 147–48.

23. Ibid., 155.

24. Ibid., 154.

25. Ibid., 162.

26. Wallace Stevens, "About One of Marianne Moore's Poems," *Quarterly Review of Literature* 4, no. 2 (Summer 1948): 143–52. Reprinted in *NA*, 94–95.

27. Moore, "He 'Digesteth Harde Yron,'" *Partisan Review*, 8 (July–August 1941): 312.

Chapter 7

1. Marianne Moore, "On Wallace Stevens," *New York Review of Books* (25 June 1964): 5–6. Reprinted in *CPrMM*, 581.

2. In *Marianne Moore: Vision into Verse*, Patricia Willis performs the helpful functions of reprinting Moore's "Pretiolae," which first appeared in *Wake* in 1950, and collecting the source material, both visual and printed, that Moore used to produce the poem. See 66 for Moore's poem and 67–68 for Moore's source materials. All subsequent quotations are from the reprint edition of the poem.

3. Ibid., 67.

4. Moore to Pound, 31 July 1946, Rosenbach.

5. See Moore's excited account of the project in her letter to her brother John Warner Moore, 2 February 1945, Rosenbach. Laurence Stapleton quotes the letter in *Marianne Moore: The Poet's Advance* (Princeton: Princeton University Press, 1978), 159. Also see Stapleton's fine account of the initial stages of Moore's translations, 158–61.

6. Moore to Stevens, 16 March 1947, Huntington.

7. Moore to Pound, 30 July 1949, Rosenbach.

8. Moore to Stevens, 18 September 1948, Huntington.

9. Stevens to Church, 9 April 1947, in *LWS*, 552.

10. Moore to Church, 12 January 1951, Rosenbach.

11. Brazeau, *Parts of a World*, 226.

12. Stevens to Church, 30 November 1951, in *LWS*, 734.

13. Stevens to Church, 27 March 1953, in *LWS*, 772.

14. Moore to Church, 12 January 1952, Rosenbach.

15. Stevens to Moore, 16 January 1952, Rosenbach.

16. Moore to Stevens, 20 January 1952, Huntington.

17. Stevens to Norman Holmes Pearson, 24 January 1952, in *LWS*, 737.

18. Stevens to Church, 9 April 1951, in *LWS*, 715.

19. Moore to Stevens, 7 March 1951, Rosenbach.

20. Stevens to Weinstock, 12 November 1951, Huntington.

21. Du Sautoy to Moore, 22 June 1951, Rosenbach.

22. Stevens to Weinstock, 5 November 1951, in *LWS*, 732–33.

23. See Stevens's letter to Weinstock, 29 November 1951, in *LWS*, 732–33. Moore typed "Final Soliloquy" and sent the poem on to du Sautoy immediately after she met with Stevens on 26 November. See the copy of Moore's letter to du Sautoy dated 26 November 1951, Rosenbach, a copy of which she also sent to Stevens.

24. Marianne Moore, "The World Imagined . . . Since We Are Poor," *Poetry New York* 4 (1951): 7–9. Reprinted in *CPrMM*, 428.

25. Harold Bloom, *Wallace Stevens: The Poems of Our Climate* (Ithaca: Cornell University Press, 1976), 302–4.

26. Stevens to Sister M. Bernetta Quinn, 29 May 1952, in *LWS*, 753.

27. Marianne Moore, "A Bold Virtuoso," first delivered by Moore at Bryn Mawr in 1952 and reprinted in *CPrMM*, 444.

28. Stevens to Church, 9 April 1951, in *LWS*, 715.

29. Wallace Stevens, "How Now, O, Brightener . . ." *Shenandoah* 3, no. 1 (Spring 1952): 21. Reprinted in *OP*, 124.

30. Moore's postcard is filed in a folder of enclosures, WAS 40, Huntington. The folder contains a copy of Moore's translation of La Fontaine's "The Crow and the Fox" that she sent to Stevens in October 1951 and the postcard that she included in her *Collected Poems*.

31. Marianne Moore, "Well Moused, Lion," *Dial* 76 (January 1924): 84–91. Reprinted in *CPrMM*, 91–98. Marianne Moore, "There Is a War that Never Ends," *Kenyon Review* 5 (Winter 1943): 144–47. Reprinted in *CPrMM*, 379–83. Moore quotes much of Stevens's poem "Poetry Is a Destructive Force" in "There Is a War" and uses the image of the lion again in "Feeling and Precision," *CPrMM*, 396.

32. Church to Moore, 20 April 1951, Rosenbach.

33. Moore to Stevens, 31 January 1952, Rosenbach.

34. Folder WAS 40, Huntington.

35. Stevens to Moore, 30 November 1951, Rosenbach.

36. Moore kept a record of her enclosures to Stevens in the pages of her daily diaries. She sent "The Crow and the Fox" to Stevens in October of 1951, "The Dragon" to Stevens as part of a Christmas greeting 25 December 1952, and—as she termed it—"my wolf" to Stevens in a letter of 16 March 1951. Samuel French Morse also recalls an uncharacteristic moment of literary gossip on Stevens's part for Brazeau's *Parts of a World* that confirms Stevens's involve-

ment with Moore's fables. Morse remembers: "He [Stevens] talked once [for example] of Marianne Moore's endless revisions of the fables of La Fontaine; she used to send him revisions" (153).

37. Stevens to Moore, 26 December 1951, Rosenbach.

38. Moore to Stevens, 16 March 1951, Huntington.

39. Ibid.

40. Moore to Church, 8 January 1952, Rosenbach.

41. Stevens to Church, 21 March 1952, in *LWS*, 743.

42. Filreis, *Stevens and Actual World*, 227, 240–41.

43. Church to Stevens, 1 June 1952, Huntington.

44. Stapleton, *Marianne Moore*, 162.

45. Moore to Church, 12 June 1952, Rosenbach.

46. Moore to Church, 23 March 1953, Rosenbach.

47. Stevens to Church, 26 June 1952, in *LWS*, 756.

48. Church to Moore, 23 March 1953, Rosenbach.

49. Moore to Church, 25 March 1953, Rosenbach.

50. Moore to Stevens, 26 March 1953, Huntington.

51. Stevens to Moore, 27 March 1953, in *LWS*, 771.

52. Stevens to Church, 8 June 1953, in *LWS*, 780–81.

53. Moore to Church, 18 June 1953, Rosenbach.

54. Moore, "The Web One Weaves of Italy," *Times Literary Supplement*, 17 September 1954, xlviii. Reprinted without revision in *The Complete Poems of Marianne Moore* (New York: Viking Penguin, 1967), 164. Hereafter cited as *CPMM*.

55. Holley, *Poetry of Marianne Moore*, 142.

56. La Fontaine, "The Monkey and the Leopard," in *The Fables of La Fontaine*, trans. Marianne Moore (New York: Viking Press, 1954), 211.

Bibliography

Aaron, David. *Writers on the Left.* 2d ed. New York: Columbia University Press, 1992.

Bates, Milton J. "To Realize the Past: Wallace Stevens's Genealogical Study." *American Literature* 52 (1981): 607–27.

———. *Wallace Stevens: A Mythology of Self.* Berkeley and Los Angeles: University of California Press, 1985.

Beach, Christopher. "Ezra Pound and Harold Bloom: Influences, Canons, Traditions, and the Making of Modern Poetry," *ELH* 56, no. 2 (1989): 463–83.

Benamou, Michael. *Wallace Stevens and the Symbolist Imagination.* Princeton: Princeton University Press, 1972.

Benét, William Rose, ed. *Fifty Poets: An American Auto-Anthology.* New York: Duffield and Green, 1933.

Benstock, Shari. *Women of the Left Bank: Paris, 1900–1914.* Austin: University of Texas Press, 1986.

Bloom, Harold. *The Anxiety of Influence: A Theory of Poetry.* New York: Oxford University Press, 1973.

———. *A Map of Misreading.* New York: Oxford University Press, 1975.

———, ed. *Marianne Moore: Modern Critical Views.* New York: Chelsea House, 1987.

———, ed. *Romanticism and Consciousness: Essays in Criticism.* New York: Norton, 1970.

———. *The Visionary Company: A Reading of English Romantic Poetry.* Ithaca: Cornell University Press, 1971.

———. *Wallace Stevens: The Poems of Our Climate.* Ithaca: Cornell University Press, 1977.

Bornstein, George. *Poetic Remaking: The Art of Browning, Yeats, and Pound.* University Park: Pennsylvania State University Press, 1988.

———, ed. *Romantic and Modern: Revaluations of Literary Tradition.* Pittsburgh: University of Pittsburgh Press, 1977.

————. *Transformations of Romanticism in Yeats, Eliot, and Stevens*. Chicago: University of Chicago Press, 1976.

Borroff, Marie. *Language and the Poet*. Chicago: University of Chicago Press, 1979.

————. "Questions of Design in William Carlos Williams and Marianne Moore." *William Carlos Williams Review* 14 (Spring 1988): 104–15.

Brazeau, Peter. *Parts of a World: Wallace Stevens Remembered*. New York: Random House, 1983.

Brogan, Jacqueline Vaught. "'Sister of the Minotaur': Sexism and Stevens." *Wallace Stevens Journal* 12, no. 2 (Fall 1988): 102–17.

Bryer, Jackson R., ed. *Sixteen Modern American Authors*. Vol. 2, *A Survey of Research and Criticism since 1972*. Durham, N.C.: Duke University Press, 1989.

Burnshaw, Stanley. "Correspondence: Stanley Burnshaw Protests." *Poetry* 44 (September 1934): 351–54.

————. "Turmoil in the Middle Ground." *New Masses*, 1 October 1935, 41–42.

Carroll, Joseph. *Wallace Stevens' Supreme Fiction: A New Romanticism*. Baton Rouge: Louisiana State University Press, 1987.

Costello, Bonnie. "The Feminine Language of Marianne Moore." In *Women and Language in Literature and Society*, ed. Sally McConnell-Ginet, Ruth Borker, and Nelly Furman. New York: Praeger, 1980.

————. *Marianne Moore: Imaginary Possessions*. Cambridge: Harvard University Press, 1981.

————. "Marianne Moore's Debt and Tribute to Wallace Stevens." *Concerning Poetry* 15, no. 1 (Spring 1982): 27–33.

Dasenbrock, Reed Way. *Imitating the Italians: Wyatt, Spenser, Synge, Pound, Joyce*. Baltimore: Johns Hopkins University Press, 1991.

Davidson, Eugene. "Some American Poets." *Yale Review* 24 (June 1935): 848–52.

Deutsch, Babette. "The Gaudiness of Poetry." *New York Herald Tribune Book Review*, 15 December 1935, 18.

Dickie, Margaret. *Lyric Contingencies: Emily Dickinson and Wallace Stevens*. Philadelphia: University of Pennsylvania Press, 1991.

Diehl, Joanne Feit. *Women Poets and the American Sublime*. Bloomington: Indiana University Press, 1990.

Doyle, Charles, ed. *Wallace Stevens: The Critical Heritage*. London: Routledge and Kegan Paul, 1985.

Eliot, T. S. *Selected Essays*. London: Harcourt Brace Jovanovich, 1932.

————. *The Use of Poetry and the Use of Criticism*. London: Faber and Faber, 1933.

Erkkila, Betsy. *The Wicked Sisters: Women Poets, Literary History, and Discord*. Oxford: Oxford University Press, 1992.

Filreis, Alan. *Wallace Stevens and the Actual World*. Princeton: Princeton University Press, 1991.

Finch, John. "Two Spokesmen for the Man Alone." *Sewanee Review* 44 (January–March 1936): 122–25.

Fogel, Daniel Mark. *Covert Relations: James Joyce, Virginia Woolf, and Henry James.* Charlottesville: University of Virginia Press, 1990.

Gilbert, Sandra M., and Susan Gubar. *The Madwoman in the Attic.* New Haven: Yale University Press, 1979.

———. *No Man's Land: The Place of the Woman Writer in the Twentieth Century.* Vol. 1, *The War of the Words.* New Haven: Yale University Press, 1988.

Gold, Michael. "Out of the Fascist Unconscious." *New Republic,* 26 July 1933, 295–96.

Goodridge, Celeste. *Hints and Disguises: Marianne Moore and Her Contemporaries.* Iowa City: University of Iowa Press, 1989.

Grigson, Geoffrey. "Answers to an Enquiry." *New Verse* 1 (October 1934): 16.

———. "The Stuffed Goldfinch." *New Verse* 19 (February–March 1936): 18–19.

Hadas, Pamela White. *Marianne Moore: Poet of Affection.* Syracuse: Syracuse University Press, 1977.

Hall, Donald. "Marianne Moore." In *Writers at Work: The Paris Review Interviews.* Second series, ed. George Plimpton. New York: Viking Penguin, 1963.

———. *Marianne Moore: The Cage and the Animal.* New York: Western Publishing Co., 1970.

Holley, Margaret. *The Poetry of Marianne Moore: A Study in Voice and Value.* Cambridge: Cambridge University Press, 1987.

Homans, Margaret. *Women Writers and Poetic Identity: Dorothy Wordsworth, Emily Brontë, and Emily Dickinson.* Princeton: Princeton University Press, 1980.

"Innovations in Poetry To-day: Miss Marianne Moore's Experiments." *Times Literary Supplement,* 18 January 1936, 52.

Joost, Nicholas. *Scofield Thayer and the "Dial."* Carbondale: Southern Illinois University Press, 1964.

Kappel, Andrew J., ed. *Twentieth Century Literature* 30 (Summer–Fall 1984). Special issue on Marianne Moore.

Kreymborg, Alfred. *Troubadour: An Autobiography.* New York: Bone & Live right, 1925.

Leggett, B. J. "Wallace Stevens and Marianne Moore: Two Essays and a Private Review." *Wallace Stevens Journal* 10, no. 2 (Fall 1986): 76–83.

———. *Wallace Stevens and Poetic Theory: Conceiving the Supreme Fiction.* Chapel Hill: University of North Carolina Press, 1987.

Leuchtenburg, William E. *The Perils of Prosperity, 1914–1932.* Chicago: University of Chicago Press, 1958.

Levenson, Michael. *A Genealogy of Modernism: A Study of English Literary Doctrine 1908–1922.* Cambridge: Cambridge University Press, 1984.

Lewis, H. D. "On Poetic Truth." *Philosophy* 21, no. 79 (July 1946): 147–66.

Litz, A. Walton. *Introspective Voyager: The Poetic Development of Wallace Stevens.* Oxford: Oxford University Press, 1972.

———. "Wallace Stevens's Defense of Poetry: *La poesie pure,* the New Romantic, and the Pressure of Reality." In *Romantic and Modern: Revaluations of Literary Tradition,* ed. George Bornstein. Pittsburgh: University of Pittsburgh Press, 1977.

Lombardi, Thomas. "Wallace Stevens and the Haunts of Unimportant Ghosts." *Wallace Stevens Journal* 7, nos. 1–2 (Spring 1983): 46–53.

Longenbach, James. "The 'Fellowship of Men That Perish': Wallace Stevens and the First World War." *Wallace Stevens Journal* 13, no. 2 (Fall 1989): 85–108.

———. *Wallace Stevens: The Plain Sense of Things.* Oxford: Oxford University Press, 1991.

Martin, Taffy. *Marianne Moore: Subversive Modernist.* Austin: University of Texas Press, 1986.

Martin, Wendy. *An American Triptych: Anne Bradstreet, Emily Dickinson, Adrienne Rich.* Chapel Hill: University of North Carolina Press, 1984.

MacLeod, Glen G. *Wallace Stevens and Company: The Harmonium Years 1913–1923.* Ann Arbor: UMI Press, 1983.

Merrin, Jeredith. *An Enabling Humility: Marianne Moore, Elizabeth Bishop, and the Uses of Tradition.* New Brunswick: Rutgers University Press, 1990.

Moers, Ellen. *Literary Women.* New York: Doubleday, 1976.

Molesworth, Charles. "Moore's Masterpiece: The Pangolin's Alternating Blaze." In *Marianne Moore: Woman and Poet,* ed. Patricia Willis. Orono, Maine: National Poetry Foundation, 1990.

Monroe, Harriet. "A Symposium on Marianne Moore." *Poetry* 19 (January 1922): 208–16.

Moore, Marianne. *Collected Poems.* New York: Macmillan, 1951.

———. *The Complete Poems of Marianne Moore.* New York: Viking, 1967.

———. *The Complete Prose of Marianne Moore.* Ed. Patricia Willis. New York: Viking, 1986.

———, trans. *The Fables of La Fontaine.* New York: Viking, 1954.

———. *Like a Bulwark.* New York: Viking, 1956.

———. Marianne Moore Collection. Papers. Rosenbach Museum and Library, Philadelphia, Pennsylvania.

———. *Nevertheless.* New York: Macmillan, 1944.

———. *Observations.* New York: Dial Press, 1924.

———. *The Pangolin and Other Verse.* London: Brendin Publishing Co., 1936.

———. *Poems.* Ed. H.D. and Winifred Bryher. London: Egoist Press, 1921.

———. *Predilections.* New York: Viking, 1955.

———. *Selected Poems.* New York: Macmillan, 1935.

———. *What Are Years.* New York: Macmillan, 1941.

Morse, Samuel French. *Wallace Stevens: Poetry as Life.* New York: Pegasus, 1970.

Ostriker, Alicia. *Stealing the Language: The Emergence of Women's Poetry in America*. Boston: Beacon, 1986.

Parisi, Joseph, ed. *Marianne Moore: The Art of a Modernist*. Ann Arbor: UMI Research Press, 1990.

Richardson, Joan. *Wallace Stevens: The Early Years, 1879–1923*. New York: William Morrow, 1986.

———. *Wallace Stevens: The Later Years, 1923–1955*. New York: William Morrow, 1988.

Riddel, Joseph N. "The Climate of Our Poems." *Wallace Stevens Journal* 7, nos. 3–4 (Fall 1983): 59–75.

Roethke, Theodore. "A Rich and Special Sensibility." *New Republic*, 15 July 1936, 305.

Schulman, Grace. *Marianne Moore: The Poetry of Engagement*. Urbana: University of Illinois Press, 1986.

Sheehy, Eugene P., and Kenneth A. Lohf, comps. *The Achievement of Marianne Moore: A Bibliography, 1907–1957*. New York: New York Public Library, 1958.

Shelley, Percy B. *Shelley's Poetry and Prose*. Ed. Donald Reiman and Sharon B. Powers. New York: Norton, 1977.

Showalter, Elaine. *A Literature of Their Own: British Women Novelists from Brontë to Lessing*. Princeton: Princeton University Press, 1977.

Slatin, John. *The Savage's Romance: The Poetry of Marianne Moore*. University Park: Pennsylvania State University Press, 1986.

———. "Scarecrows and Curios." *Marianne Moore Newsletter* 1, no. 2 (1977): 13–15.

Spacks, Patricia A. M. *The Female Imagination*. New York: Knopf, 1975.

Stapleton, Laurence. *Marianne Moore: The Poet's Advance*. Princeton: Princeton University Press, 1978.

Stevens, Wallace. *The Collected Poems of Wallace Stevens*. New York: Knopf, 1954.

———. *Letters of Wallace Stevens*. Ed. Holly Stevens. New York: Knopf, 1966.

———. *The Necessary Angel*. New York: Knopf, 1951.

———. *Opus Posthumous*. Ed. Milton Bates. New York: Knopf, 1989.

———. *Selected Poems*. London: Faber and Faber, 1953.

———. *Sur Plusieurs Beaux Sujects: Wallace Stevens' Commonplace Book*. Ed. Milton Bates. Stanford: Stanford University Press, 1989.

———. *Wallace Stevens Collection*. Papers. Henry E. Huntington Library, San Marino, California.

Thomson, Arthur J. "The Haunts of Life." Part 6, "The Mastery of the Air." *Illustrated London News*, 2 April 1921, 442–43.

Tomlinson, Charles, ed. *Marianne Moore: A Collection of Critical Essays*. Englewood Cliffs, N.J.: Prentice-Hall, 1969.

Vendler, Helen. *On Extended Wings: Wallace Stevens' Longer Poems*. Cambridge: Harvard University Press, 1969.

Walker, Cheryl. *The Nightingale's Burden: Women Poets and American Culture before 1900*. Bloomington: Indiana University Press, 1982.

Willis, Patricia, ed. *Marianne Moore Newsletter* 1–7 (1977–83).

———. *Marianne Moore: Vision into Verse*. Philadelphia: Rosenbach Museum and Library, 1987.

———. "The Road to Paradise: First Notes on Marianne Moore's 'An Octopus.'" *Twentieth Century Literature* (Fall 1984): 242–72.

Index

Aeolian harp, 79
Alcestis, 101, 136, 139
Alcestis Press, 101, 135
Aldington, Richard, 15, 37
Anvil, 129
Arensberg, Walter, 15–16, 21
Auden, W. H., 191

Bates, Milton, 21
Beach, Christopher, 4
Beardsley, Aubrey, 22, 31
Benamou, Michael, 112
Bishop, Elizabeth, 6
Blast, 129
Bloom, Harold, 2–9, 35, 52, 79, 99,
    115, 200–201; *The Anxiety of Influ-
    ence,* 2–4
Bluebeard: Moore's depiction of Ste-
    vens as, 28–36, 40, 43, 49–50, 55,
    85
Bollingen Prize in Poetry, 196, 204
Bornstein, George, 4, 8–9, 63–64,
    110–12, 124
Bragdon, Claude, 65–66, 75, 86
Brazeau, Peter, 195
Brooklyn Public Library, 162
Bryher, (Winifred Ellerman), 23–24,
    37–38, 41, 89
Bryn Mawr College, 201, 214

Burke, Kenneth, 66–67, 72, 84, 97
Burnshaw, Stanley, 118, 129–30, 144,
    146

Carlyle, Thomas, 19
Church, Barbara, 157, 194–96, 199,
    202, 204, 208–18
Church, Henry, 13, 157–59, 194–95
Coleridge, Samuel Taylor, 79, 159;
    Biographia Literaria, 75
Costello, Bonnie, 2, 69–72
Conversation diaries (Moore), 37–42
Crispin, 43, 47, 63, 68, 70, 81, 92–93,
    99
Criterion, 68, 129, 135–36, 144, 146
cummings, e. e., 15, 145

Dalston, D. F., 17
Dasenbrock, Reed Way, 4
Davidson, Eugene, 131
Depression. *See* Great Depression
Deutsch, Babette, 144
Dial, 25, 37, 42, 63–66, 75, 78, 127,
    145
Dickie, Margaret, 149
Dictatorship, 84–85, 97. *See also* Fas-
    cism; Mussolini
Doolittle, Hilda (H.D.), 15, 19, 23,
    37–38, 41, 89

247